THE ALTAR BOYS

WARNING

The Altar Boys deals with issues of clerical sexual abuse
and its cover up, and self-harm and suicide, which some
readers may find disturbing.

If you find any of the content triggering, or need to talk to someone,
confidential 24-hour support is available. Call:

Lifeline – 13 11 14

Kid's Help Line – 1800 551 800

THE ALTAR BOYS

SUZANNE SMITH

To Louise,

Thank you for
your interest a
support

ABC
BOOKS

Best wishes

Suzanne Smith

The ABC 'Wave' device is a trademark of the Australian Broadcasting Corporation and is used under licence by HarperCollins*Publishers* Australia.

HarperCollins*Publishers*
Australia • Brazil • Canada • France • Germany • Holland • Hungary
India • Italy • Japan • Mexico • New Zealand • Poland • Spain • Sweden
Switzerland • United Kingdom • United States of America

First published in Australia in 2020
by HarperCollins*Publishers* Australia Pty Limited
Level 13, 201 Elizabeth Street, Sydney NSW 2000
ABN 36 009 913 517
harpercollins.com.au

Copyright © Suzanne Smith 2020

The right of Suzanne Smith to be identified as the author of this work has been asserted by her in accordance with the *Copyright Amendment (Moral Rights) Act 2000*.

A catalogue record for this book is available from the National Library of Australia.

ISBN 978 0 7333 4017 8 (paperback)
ISBN 978 1 4607 1149 1 (ebook)

Cover design by HarperCollins Design Studio
Front cover image courtesy of the Nash family: Carmel, Geoffrey and Andrew Nash, 1967
Back cover image by Jonathan Carroll / *Newcastle Herald*: Sacred Heart Cathedral, Hamilton
Typeset in Bembo Std by Kirby Jones
Printed and bound in Australia by McPherson's Printing Group
The papers used by HarperCollins in the manufacture of this book are a natural, recyclable product made from wood grown in sustainable plantation forests. The fibre source and manufacturing processes meet recognised international environmental standards, and carry certification.

For Steven, and the ones who did not make it.

CONTENTS

Organisational Structure of the Catholic Church*

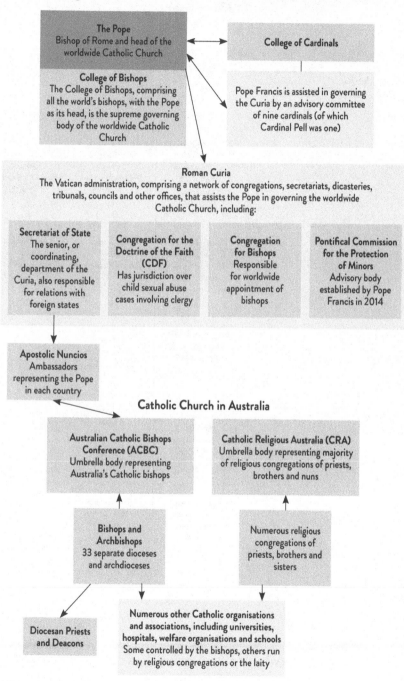

The Pope
Bishop of Rome and head of the worldwide Catholic Church

College of Cardinals

College of Bishops
The College of Bishops, comprising all the world's bishops, with the Pope as its head, is the supreme governing body of the worldwide Catholic Church

Pope Francis is assisted in governing the Curia by an advisory committee of nine cardinals (of which Cardinal Pell was one)

Roman Curia
The Vatican administration, comprising a network of congregations, secretariats, dicasteries, tribunals, councils and other offices, that assists the Pope in governing the worldwide Catholic Church, including:

Secretariat of State
The senior, or coordinating, department of the Curia, also responsible for relations with foreign states

Congregation for the Doctrine of the Faith (CDF)
Has jurisdiction over child sexual abuse cases involving clergy

Congregation for Bishops
Responsible for worldwide appointment of bishops

Pontifical Commission for the Protection of Minors
Advisory body established by Pope Francis in 2014

Apostolic Nuncios
Ambassadors representing the Pope in each country

Catholic Church in Australia

Australian Catholic Bishops Conference (ACBC)
Umbrella body representing Australia's Catholic bishops

Catholic Religious Australia (CRA)
Umbrella body representing majority of religious congregations of priests, brothers and nuns

Bishops and Archbishops
33 separate dioceses and archdioceses

Numerous religious congregations of priests, brothers and sisters

Diocesan Priests and Deacons

Numerous other Catholic organisations and associations, including universities, hospitals, welfare organisations and schools
Some controlled by the bishops, others run by religious congregations or the laity

* The author acknowledges this is just a small part of the organisational structure of the Catholic Church. This graphic is designed to add comprehension to the roles, titles, organisations and committees mentioned in the book.

Organisational Structure of the Maitland–Newcastle Diocese 1931–present

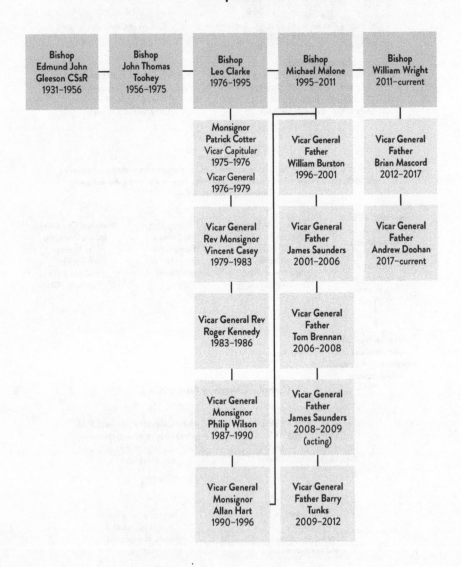

Bishop
Edmund John
Gleeson CSsR
1931–1956

Bishop
John Thomas
Toohey
1956–1975

Bishop
Leo Clarke
1976–1995

Bishop
Michael Malone
1995–2011

Bishop
William Wright
2011–current

Monsignor
Patrick Cotter
Vicar Capitular
1975–1976
Vicar General
1976–1979

Vicar General
Father
William Burston
1996–2001

Vicar General
Father
Brian Mascord
2012–2017

Vicar General
Rev Monsignor
Vincent Casey
1979–1983

Vicar General
Father
James Saunders
2001–2006

Vicar General
Father
Andrew Doohan
2017–current

Vicar General Rev
Roger Kennedy
1983–1986

Vicar General
Father
Tom Brennan
2006–2008

Vicar General
Monsignor
Philip Wilson
1987–1990

Vicar General
Father
James Saunders
2008–2009
(acting)

Vicar General
Monsignor
Allan Hart
1990–1996

Vicar General
Father Barry
Tunks
2009–2012

Key People and Organisations

Administrator (priest in charge): Temporary appointment of a
priest pending the arrival of the parish priest. The parish priest had
tenure protected by canon law.

Alward, David and Peter: Brothers of Steven Alward.

Alward, Steven: Journalist, writer, author, former head of
international news and Radio National at the Australian
Broadcasting Corporation. Brother of David, Peter and Libby.

Apostolic Nuncio: Vatican diplomatic representative in Canberra
- Franco Brambilla: February 1986 to November 1998
- Ambrose De Paoli: December 2004 to October 2007
- Adolfo Tito Yllana: February 2015 to present (current)

Australian Catholic Bishops Conference: The national assembly
of all bishops in Australia. It meets regularly to address issues of
national importance to the Church.

Bambach, Anthony (Tony): Former schoolteacher of the Maitland-
Newcastle Diocese who committed child sex offences.

Benedict XVI, Pope: Retired Pope who served as head of the
Catholic Church from 2005 until his resignation in 2013.
Full name: Joseph Aloisius Ratzinger.

Brennan, Father Tom: Former principal of St Pius X High School,
former vicar-general to Bishop Malone. Convicted of concealment
charges. Child sex offender.

Brock, Father Peter: Former executive officer of the National
Commission for Clergy Life and Ministry. Charged with multiple
child sex offences. Trial aborted. In 2012, he was the National
Project Officer for the Australian Catholic Bishops Conference.
He died in September 2014.

Burston, Father Bill: Psychologist with a Masters of Psychology
degree from University College, Dublin. Assistant parish priest at

the Sacred Heart Cathedral in Hamilton in 1974. Former director of Centacare in Newcastle. Vicar-general, 1996 to 2001. Assistant vicar-general, 2001 to 2005. Removed from ministry in 2015 following the findings of the Hunter Special Commission of Inquiry into the Maitland-Newcastle Diocese.

Butler, Brother Thomas 'Patrick': Former teacher at Marist Brothers Hamilton. The Marist Brothers have apologised for his sexual assaults on former students.

Byrne, Brendan (not his real name): The second victim of Father Fletcher to come forward to police.

Byrne, Elizabeth (not her real name): Sister of Brendan Byrne.

Cable, Brother Francis 'Romuald': Former teacher at Marist Brothers Hamilton. Convicted child sex offender.

Cahill, Maurie Father: Former parish priest in Hamilton, Newcastle, and former chaplain at Marist Brothers Hamilton school.

Callinan, Will: Former principal of Branxton (St Brigid's) and Greta (St Mary's) Catholic primary schools during the time of Father Fletcher. No relation to Jim Callinan.

Cassian, Brother: Marist Brother and teacher at Marist Brothers Hamilton in the late 1960s and 1970s. He was renowned for being a harsh disciplinarian and used extreme physical violence against the boys. His nickname was 'Bashin Cassian'.

Catholic Church Insurance Limited (CCI): Underwrites the property, workers' compensation and liability risks of entities of the Catholic Church in Australia.

Catholic Commission for Employment Relations: An advisory body for Catholic employers, such as schools, also providing advice, support and training on employment relations and the management of people.

Catholic Schools Office: The Maitland-Newcastle Diocese office that dealt with issues involving the diocesan schools and educational organisations.

Centacare: Catholic Church welfare agency that delivers a range of services to families and individuals in need.

Chancellor of a Catholic Archdiocese: This person keeps the official archives of the diocese, as a notary can also certify documents, and generally manages the files of a diocese. They can also manage personnel and finances. Father Brian Lucas held this position at the Archdiocese of Sydney.

Chiu, Hilbert: Senior counsel for the Royal Commission into Institutional Responses to Child Sexual Abuse. Barrister.

Clarke, Bishop Leo: Former bishop of the Maitland-Newcastle Diocese from 1976 to 1995.

Congregation for Bishops in the Vatican: The department of the Roman Curia that oversees the selection of most new bishops. All proposals require papal approval.

Congregation for the Doctrine of the Faith (CDF – Vatican Committee): One of nine congregations in the Roman Curia (the Court of Rome), it is the body responsible for Catholic doctrine. The CDF has ultimate authority over priests and clergy, whether they are laicised, defrocked or moved from parish to parish.

Coolahan, Monsignor Frank: Director and assistant director of Catholic Education in the diocese from 1974 to 1990.

Cotter, Monsignor Patrick: Came to the Maitland-Newcastle Diocese in 1938 from Ireland. Second-in-command to Bishop Toohey and then Bishop Clarke. He was vicar capitular (stands in position of bishop) from 24 September 1975 to 3 June 1976 when there was a short vacancy before Clarke arrived.

Council of Priests: A group of priests who represent the presbyterium and who are the bishop's senate. The Council of Priests' role is to assist the bishop, in accordance with the law, in the governance of the diocese.

Creigh, Peter: Survivor of Father James Fletcher. Crown witness in the court case against Archbishop Philip Wilson regarding his charges of misprision of felony.

Davis, Libby: Steven Alward's sister.

Davoren, John: Former director of NSW Professional Standards Office of the Catholic Church.

Denham, Father John: Former priest of the Maitland-Newcastle Diocese. Former teacher at St Pius X High School.

Diocesan Child Protection and Professional Conduct Unit (DCPPCU): The coordinated diocesan response to child protection in 2005 in the Maitland–Newcastle Diocese. A unit of experienced social workers, investigators and support staff headed by Helen Keevers.

Director of Catholic Education: Head of Catholic Schools (apart from Marist Brothers schools) and adviser to the bishop in the diocese. The bishop had ultimate control over all schools in the diocese including those run by institutes such as the Marist Brothers.

Encompass Australasia: Specialist psychological service for people in helping ministries and professions who may be struggling with psychological issues; preferred provider of psychological assessment and treatment services for clergy of Catholic Church of Australia.

Faber, Detective Sergeant Kristi: Currently the head of police Strike Force Georgiana. Senior investigator with the NSW Police.

Feenan, Daniel: Victim of Father Fletcher. Brother of Luke, Dominic and Bernard.

Feenan, John: Former business manager of the Maitland–Newcastle Diocese, and father of Daniel Feenan.

Feenan, Patricia: Mother of Daniel Feenan, former wife of John Feenan.

Fletcher, Father James: Former priest of the Maitland–Newcastle Diocese. Convicted of nine counts of child sexual assault.

Fox, Detective Chief Inspector Peter: Formerly Maitland police officer, then a detective sergeant, who investigated Father Fletcher.

Francis, Pope: Current head of the Catholic Church and sovereign of the Vatican City State. Full name: Jorge Mario Bergoglio.

Gogarty, Peter: Victim of Father James Fletcher. Lawyer and academic.

Grant, Troy: Former senior constable who investigated Father Vince Ryan. Entered state Parliament (NSW) as the member for Dubbo and was appointed police minister and deputy premier of New South Wales.

Hall, Ted: Teacher at St Pius X High School in the 1970s. Convicted of 21 child sex offences against eight students. He is serving a 20-year sentence. He has launched an appeal that is due to be heard in late 2020 or early 2021.

Harrigan, Father Des: Close friend of convicted child sex offender Father Fletcher. Executor of Fletcher's estate.

Hart, Monsignor Allan: Chairperson of the Council of Priests, responsible for administration of the Maitland Clergy Fund. Former Vicar-general and priest at Shortland parish.

Helferty, Father Patrick: Former deputy principal of St Pius X High School. Former parish priest in Taree.

Hill, Brother Michael: Marist Brother and former provincial (head) of the Marist Brothers from 1995 to 2001. Vice provincial from 1993 to 1995. From 1996 to 2007, he was a member of the Bishops Conference and Catholic Religious Australia, and the National Committee for Professional Standards. Hill was involved in the drafting of the *Towards Healing* policy of the Catholic Church.

Jackson Inquiry: Internal Catholic Church inquiry by David Jackson QC, commissioned by Cardinal Pell and Archbishop Wilson in 2005 into Bishop Malone's handling of complaints against Father Brock, Father Fletcher and other matters. An internal report was finished in July 2005 and it was never released to the public.

Keevers, Helen: Former manager of Zimmerman House, the Diocesan Child Protection and Professional Conduct Unit (DCPPCU).

Leon, Brother (Noel Mackay): Marist Brother and teacher at Marist Brothers Hamilton in the 1950s. Catalyst for Bob O'Toole to begin the Clergy Abused Network (CAN) in the Hunter Region.

Lucas, Father Brian: Former general secretary of the Australian Catholics Bishops Conference and chancellor of the Archdiocese of Sydney. Currently national director of Catholic missions.

Maitland Clergy Fund: A special fund administered by the Diocese to fund necessary disbursements for priests such as living expenses, the purchase of vehicles, and study and travel costs. Once a year, parishes held a special Clergy Fund collection at the mass.

Malone, Bishop Michael: Bishop of the Maitland-Newcastle Diocese from 1996 to 2011. Retired.

Marsden, John: Solicitor and former president of the Law Society of New South Wales who represented Father Denham at his first trial from 1996 to 1998.

Master of Ceremonies: He organised and oversaw the liturgical functions in the cathedral whenever the bishop was present.

McAlinden, Father Denis: Catholic priest who arrived from Ireland in 1949. Committed child sex offences over four decades.

McCarthy, Joanne: Former investigative reporter with the *Newcastle Herald* and multi-award winning journalist.

McDonald, Michael: Executive director of the Catholic Commission for Employment Relations (CCER) from 1996 to 2008. From 1999 to 2005 he was a member of the Professional Standards Resource Group of the Catholic Church.

Ministries of the Sacred Heart: Religious order that provided support for Father Denham.

Nash, Andrew: Former student at Marist Brothers Hamilton. Son of Audrey and Bert Nash.

Nash, Audrey: Mother of Andrew, Geoffrey, Carmel, Patricia and Bernadette. Wife of Bert. Worked for Monsignor Cotter and Father Ryan.

National Committee for Professional Standards: Committee established by the Australian Catholic Bishops Conference to advise on professional conduct issues including child protection issues, complaints against clergy and religious and integrity in ministry. Replaced in 2019 with the Australian Catholic Centre for Professional Standards.

Nestor, Brother (John Aloysius Littler): The principal of Marist Brothers Maitland from 1972 to 1977. He was previously the dormitory master at St Joseph's College in Hunters Hill, Sydney, and before that at the St Vincent's Boys home in Westmead, Sydney. Child sex offender.

O'Brien, Brother John: Former teacher and football coach at Marist Brothers Hamilton and St Joseph's College in Hunters Hill. Former principal of Marist Brothers Kogarah.

O'Hearn, Father David: Former parish priest. Convicted of multiple child sex offences.

O'Sullivan, Brother Darcy 'Dominic': Former teacher at Marist Brothers Hamilton. Convicted of indecently assaulting twelve boys at two schools over a thirteen-year period.

O'Toole, Bob: Founder and head of the Clergy Abused Network (CAN) in the Hunter Region. Survivor.

Pell, Cardinal George: Archbishop of Melbourne (1996 to 2001) then Sydney (2001 to 2013) and also a cardinal (2003 to 2018). Promoted to the Vatican to the post of prefect of the Secretariat for the Economy from 2014 to 2018. Victoria Police charged Cardinal Pell with a series of sexual assault offences on 29 June 2017. Convicted of child sex offences in Victoria on 11 December 2018. Upheld by the Victorian Court of Criminal Appeal but overturned by the High Court in April 2020. On 7 May 2020, the Royal Commission released the unredacted report into the diocese of Ballarat. It found Cardinal Pell was aware of children being sexually abused in the Archdiocese of Ballarat by the paedophile Gerald Risdale, and it was implausible that other senior Church figures had not told Pell the abuse was occurring.

Picken, Ron Father: Parish priest at Wingham, near Taree in NSW, from 1978 to 1983. Close friend of Father John Denham. He died on 22 April 2015.

Professional Standards Resource Group: Internal Catholic Church national group that advised the bishops about allegations of professional misconduct by clergy and religious.

Provincial of the Marist Brothers: The provincial of the Sydney or Melbourne province has direct authority over the Marist Brothers in that province. Marist Brothers schools are answerable to the bishop in each diocese, but the Provincial Council has overall responsibilities for schools, institutions and ministries.

Ryan, Father Vince: Priest convicted of multiple child sexual abuse offences.

Saunders, Father Jim: Former vicar-general of the Maitland-Newcastle Diocese, 2001 to 2005. He died in 2015.

Second Vatican Council: Also known as Vatican II. Pope John XXIII liberalised many Church policies and gave bishops much greater influence and power. Lay people were allowed to play a greater role in Church ceremonies.

Sykes, Brother Geoffrey 'Coman': Senior Marist Brother who was elected to the Sydney Provincial Council of the Marist Brothers, including 1973 to 1978. He was a principal and senior teacher at several Marist Brothers schools and the St Vincent's Boys Home in Westmead, Sydney. Influential member and leader of the Marist Brothers retreat teams.

Toohey, Bishop John: Bishop of the Maitland-Newcastle Diocese, 1956 to 1975.

Towards Healing: Catholic Church policy response to the issue of sexual abuse by clergy. Australian policy from 1996.

Tunks, Father Barry: Parish priest at Taree from 1973 to 1982. Charged on 5 April 2017 with historical child sex offences concerning a twelve-year-old boy in the late 1970s. Former vicar-general of the Maitland-Newcastle Diocese from 2009 to 2012. Charges were dropped on 10 December 2018.

Turton, Brother Alexis: Marist Brother and former principal of Marist Brothers Hamilton. Provincial of the Marist Brothers from 1989 to 1995. Vice provincial from 1983 to 1989.

Wade, Brother William 'Christopher': Former principal of Marist Brothers Hamilton and Canberra. Convicted child sex offender.

Wakely, John: Former principal and teacher in six Catholic schools in the Maitland-Newcastle Diocese. Former school captain of Marist Brothers Hamilton. Cousin of Mark Wakely.

Wakely, Mark: Former student at Marist Brothers Hamilton. Writer, author, journalist. Partner of Steven Alward for thirty-eight years.

Walsh, Father Glen: Priest of the Maitland-Newcastle Diocese. Witness for the Crown in the prosecution of Archbishop Philip Wilson.

Walsh, John: Brother of Father Glen Walsh.

Wilson, Archbishop Philip: Former archbishop of Adelaide and former president of the Catholic Bishops Conference. In 2015, Wilson was charged with concealing a serious offence regarding child sexual abuse. He was found guilty by a jury in 2018 but was acquitted on appeal later that year.

Woodward, Sister Evelyn: Sister of the Saint Joseph order and qualified psychologist.

Wright, Bishop Bill: Current bishop of the Maitland-Newcastle Diocese. Appointed in 2011.

Old sins cast long shadows.

English proverb

Preface

I NEVER EXPECTED TO WRITE A BOOK ABOUT THE CLERICAL ABUSE scandal[1] in the Maitland-Newcastle Catholic Diocese, although I spent about eight years covering the issue for the Australian Broadcasting Corporation. In 2012, one of my stories for *Lateline*, the ABC TV current affairs show, helped to trigger the Royal Commission into Institutional Responses to Child Sexual Abuse, one of the most comprehensive public inquiries in the world.

I was part of a group of journalists from several media outlets who focused on the national clerical abuse issue over the past twelve years or so. One of the most tenacious, the *Newcastle Herald*'s Joanne McCarthy, was an incredible force in exposing criminal networks in the Catholic Church, and other churches and institutions as well. She has made this her life's work, and the world is the better for it.

I decided to once again return to reporting this scandal on 17 January 2018, when my friend and former ABC colleague Steven Alward took his own life.

Steven had been my constant support during those tough eight years, and his suicide was a complete shock to everyone who knew him. He had grown up in Newcastle and was engaged to be married in March 2018, to his partner of thirty-eight years, Mark Wakely.

Steven had recently asked me to investigate the death of Father Glen Walsh.

In November 2017, the news of Glen's passing had shocked many of his family members and friends – including Steven, who had kept in touch over the decades with his childhood friend and clearly admired him.

A day after Glen's death was announced in the media, I'd received a Facebook message from Steven:

Hi Suzie. Not sure if you heard but a priest who was due to give evidence against the Archbishop of Adelaide about a paedophile priest in Newcastle [Fletcher] killed himself on Monday. His name was Father Glen Walsh and he was a very close friend of mine when I was in primary school. He lived in my street. He tried to report Fletcher but he was treated appallingly by the Church in Newcastle (mainly Alan [sic] Hart) … The collateral damage of this hideous story goes on and on. Hope all is well with you. Love s.

Steven was referring to Monsignor Allan Hart, his and Glen's assistant parish priest way back when they were kids, as someone who had bullied Glen.

I replied, 'Yes, I know. It's terrible … How are you? Can we meet for a coffee?'

'I'm going OK,' Steven responded, 'but I was really sad to hear about this. A coffee would be nice sometime. I am just waiting to hear when Glen's funeral is. So, once I hear, I will rearrange my week and get back to you. Thanks for posting the story. Glen and I knew each other from about the age of two.'

We spoke about catching up in January; at that time, Steven was going to tell me the story about Glen and Hart.

Life got away from us. I went overseas in December 2017, then Christmas came and went. As I was preparing to contact Steven in January 2018 about our catch-up, the terrible news came through.

Steven had died before he could give me any more information. But I had made a pact with him, and I felt the need to keep my promise. And so here is what could be described as his very last commission as an editor.

In May 2018, another of my close contacts in Newcastle died. Helen Keevers had been head of the child protection unit for the Maitland-Newcastle Diocese from 2005 to 2009. In 2008, I'd filmed a *Lateline* story with Helen and the bishop of the diocese, Michael Malone; it was about the Pope's upcoming visit to Australia and whether he should apologise to the survivors of child abuse perpetrated by Catholic clergy and religious.[2] I met a vivacious, smart woman who was determined to reform the Church from the inside.

After we'd become close, Helen had asked me to help her write a book about her time as an outsider, an atheist, inside the Church at the centre of a major child sex abuse scandal. I'd agreed to help, just as a support person. Then Helen suffered a ruptured aorta in her heart on a Friday night; she was dead by that Sunday. She had sent me a draft chapter alongside her submission to the Royal Commission, and some of that material has become part of this book.

Two of my friends had died. The professional became personal.

My decision to keep these promises to Helen and Steven has led me here. For the most part I've written this book from the point of view of the victims and their families, those lost and those left behind – the collateral damage from this huge conspiracy against children in the Maitland-Newcastle Diocese, a conspiracy connected to many other schools and dioceses across New South Wales, and beyond.

At least sixty men who attended three Catholic schools in the Maitland-Newcastle Diocese have died either from suicide or as a result of risky behaviour. The local police say there are many more than sixty. The majority of these men took their own lives, and they are all believed to have been victims of clergy and religious in their diocese. And they're far from alone – there have been similar deaths all over the nation. Decades after they were abused by clergy and religious, hundreds of Australian men have died in their forties, fifties and sixties, and possibly thousands. It is a tragedy of epic proportions that demands its own coronial taskforce and/or commission of inquiry.

I've focused on the Catholic Diocese of Maitland–Newcastle (known as the Diocese of Maitland until 1995), because Glen worked as a priest there, and because Steven and Glen went to Catholic schools, as did Andrew Nash, another victim whose story features in this book. During my time as a journalist I have reported on the epidemic of clerical abuse in the Anglican Diocese of Newcastle, and I'm not claiming that the abuse committed by Catholics in the region was worse than that committed by Anglicans. There are concerns that some Anglican and Catholic clergy and religious may have offended together, and investigations into this matter are ongoing.

I want to make it very clear that the Catholic schools now operating in the Maitland–Newcastle Diocese are nothing like they were back when Andrew, Steven and Glen were students. I've heard many great things about the teachers at these schools and the programs available to students. There are many wonderful Catholics who work tirelessly for the betterment of children, and they are the heart and soul of many communities and towns across Australia.

But I also want to emphasise that what *did* happen back then needs to be recorded and reflected upon so it never happens again, and we need to make sure that everyone who perpetrated and covered up these crimes is brought to justice. In fact, many contributors to this book are practising Catholics who want to see concrete and lasting change in their Church. I was raised Catholic, my mother was Catholic, and my father converted to Catholicism in his later years, after being an atheist for most of his life.

This is not a bleak tale, but a story of resilience, courage and humanity in the face of dark criminality.

Suzanne Smith
July 2020

Prologue

FOR THOUSANDS OF YEARS BEFORE THE BRITISH INVADED IN 1788, the Hunter Region of New South Wales was inhabited by Indigenous peoples: the Awabakal, Worimi, Gamilleroi, Wanarua, Gweagul, Darkinjung and Biripi. Some lived along the banks of the Hunter River, the lifeblood of what would become the city of Newcastle.

In the early days of the settlement, elders from the Awabakal tribe had direct communication with the British missionaries, settlers and military personnel, generously allowing them to record their stories.[1] Their nightly campfires, once a treasured meeting place for stories and song, would soon be replaced with the billowing smoke from industrial furnaces. The colonists would attempt to transform the land into a replica of Mother England, complete with all its class-based brutality.

Life in the early days of the Sydney colony was unimaginably harsh, and convicts frequently fled to its outer reaches to escape violence and oppression. One group, including the infamous couple Mary and William Bryant, absconded from Sydney Cove in 1791 with one of Her Majesty's Ships and sailed north past Port Stephens, an idyllic bay of white sands and blue water. As the ship floated up the Hunter River at night, the convicts saw the flickering of campfires in the bush like stars in a night sky.

Immediately the colonial government, under Governor John Hunter, despatched Lieutenant John Shortland to catch the runaways. It wasn't long before Shortland noticed the prevalence of coal seams along the Hunter River. The convicts were never apprehended, but Shortland had unwittingly hit the jackpot.

The government decided to build a second penal colony for recidivist convicts in that area. Early convict writings speak of the harsh brutality of the operations, where men worked underground for six days a week; Sundays were reserved for worship and whippings. The free labour helped make coal from the Hunter Region one of the colony's first commodity exports to Mother England. These were the inhumane seeds from which a feudal underclass was born.

The settlement was officially named Newcastle in 1804. Throughout the first half of the nineteenth century, Catholic immigrants began arriving from the coalfields of Northern England, Wales and Scotland, and then from Ireland, all hungry to work in the collieries. Eventually, from 1915 to 1999, their descendants, along with fresh groups of immigrants, would work at the mammoth BHP steelworks that came to define the city.

And with the influx of settlers came the churches.

In 1898, eleven Marist Brothers were the first of their institute to arrive in Newcastle, via an overnight steamer from Sydney. The Marist Brothers had been founded in 1817 by the French Saint Marcellin Champagnat, who championed education for the poor. 'I cannot see a child without wanting to tell them how much God loves them,' is one of his treasured quotes. This flourishing, resource-rich region held the promise of a smorgasbord for finding 'vocations' or new recruits into the Brothers, as well as a burgeoning population in which they could establish their schools.

They weren't the only ones. The Presbyterians and Baptists and other protestant religions were also establishing their turf but, as every Catholic knew, the greatest rival to beat was the Anglican Church. The region quickly became stratified on class and religious lines: the Anglicans and Protestants administered to the middle and upper classes while the Catholics tended to the working classes. The churches competed aggressively for the hearts, minds and souls of a growing community.

Life in these religious enclaves was interdependent and deeply driven by a sense of identity, separation, and the pride of belonging. Schools and community centres were being built, and the Catholic Church enjoyed a level of support, involvement and attendance unimaginable today. The devoted parishioners didn't know that their Church was harbouring, protecting and even nurturing some of the worst paedophiles Australia has ever known.

* * *

Many of the suburbs of Newcastle are named after their sister cities in England, such as New Lambton, Charlestown and Mayfield, all packed in tightly a few kilometres from the crashing waves of a stunning sweep of coastline. The city is surrounded by tremendous natural beauty, ringed by hectares of bushland, and close to lakes and beaches where parents can give their kids a classic Australian childhood – loads of freedom and fresh air.

The nineteenth-century settlers had built miners' cottages, hewn from local forests, above the old collieries. By the 1950s, most families lived in fibro-siding war service houses with manicured front lawns. Catholics belonged to a parish, which was a geographical area within a diocese that included a parish priest, often assisted by assistant priests or curates. Each Catholic parish had a church and its presbytery – the residence for the priest and assistant priest, primary schools and some also had a convent for nuns working at the schools.

Catholic families prayed, worked and played together. They lived and breathed the rules and rituals of their religion. To outsiders, the culture could seem impenetrable, confusing, and often bizarre. But to these mostly working-class families, it was everything. Believing in God and following the teachings of Jesus provided the possibility of a life that could transcend poverty and despair. Being part of the Church community offered hope and gave comfort in hard times, and if adherents followed the rules – which were many, varied and strict – they were certain their prayers would be answered. The mindset of fearful obedience in order to attain salvation was ingrained from a very young age.

Many of these families adhered to the old sectarian divide from their European homelands: Catholic versus Protestant. British authorities had brought an anti-Catholic bias to the original colony of Newcastle, and antipathy between the two sides flourished until the 1970s, leading many Catholics to develop a strong solidarity with and loyalty to their Church.

The Catholic schools could propel their students into the professional classes. Many Catholic parents worked two jobs, scraping together what money they had to send their children to these institutions; they were hoping, praying, that their offspring would leave the working classes by entering into tertiary studies. The kids could see how much it meant to their parents, and the boys in particular carried the burden of knowing it would be up to them to deliver their families out of poverty. They dared not complain or question the life choices being made for them.

Three main high schools looked after the growing male Catholic population in the diocese: a Marist Brothers school in the Newcastle suburb of Hamilton (known then as Marist Brothers Hamilton), St Pius X in the nearby suburb of Adamstown, and a Marist Brothers school about half an hour's drive away in the city of Maitland (known then as Marist Brothers Maitland). St Pius X was co-educational in Years Eleven and Twelve. Two of these schools were run by the Marist Brothers, the other, St Pius X, was managed by the diocese. Nevertheless, the bishop had ultimate power over all the schools in his diocese. He also appointed the Director of Catholic Education, who was the key adviser to the bishop on all aspects of Catholic school education. The Marist Brothers would appoint their own teachers but the bishop could always overrule these appointments. The bishop, like in Roman times, was all powerful: he was judge, jury and legislature.

Back then, every parish priest was in charge of all the primary schools in his parish. These men wielded the power to hire and fire teachers, (in consultation with the Catholic Schools Office), and the staff knew this.

The Church was a very powerful men's club and essentially a law unto itself. It used its own internal canon law, ecclesiastical regulations authorised by the Popes, to deal with clerical sexual abuse, sexual harassment of students and other crimes such as theft and fraud. Before the 1990s, the State did not apply appropriate checks and balances to the Church. Internal letters between the Maitland-Newcastle Diocese and the Vatican in that era reveal a complete lack of understanding among clergy and religious about the consequences of sexual abuse and the terrible harm it wrought well into adulthood. Add to this a widespread ignorance about civil laws until they were reformed in the 1990s and 2000s, and you have the makings of a terrible calamity. Although NSW law was clear on the age of consent for sexual relations – sixteen for girls and eighteen for boys – some Church leaders ignored civil laws whenever it suited them, especially when it came to offending priests. The Church's own policies were often honoured in the breach, especially the canon law on celibacy that forbade priests and brothers from any sexual behaviour, including masturbation. The Church had historically viewed clerical child sex abuse as a moral failure rather than a crime; the focus was on trying to help the priest in question to overcome what was seen as his problem.

For centuries, the Vatican had seen itself as an independent empire unaccountable to any civil or secular authorities. In 1974, Pope Paul VI renamed 'The Secret of the Holy Office'[2] 'The Pontifical Secret', which decreed that any allegation or investigation of sexual abuse against a cleric or religious was to be kept secret. Any bishop or clergy that defied this decree and went to the local state authorities could be ex-communicated.

Most Australians, including the police and most Catholics, didn't know about The Pontifical Secret. Bishops and other senior clergy and religious in Newcastle made their decisions based on this edict in order to protect the reputation of the Church, and to cement a growing separation from secular law as they fostered a culture of secrecy.

The affected families were left to fend for themselves. Partly because of their religious devotion, parents only saw the warning signs after it was too late. Many children endured violence and abuse in silence, with devastating consequences.

PART
ONE

CHAPTER 1

The Night That Never Ends

Tuesday, 8 October 1974

IT SEEMED LIKE ANY OTHER WEEKDAY FOR THE NASH HOUSEHOLD. Audrey had picked up her youngest son, Andrew, and two of his sisters, Bernadette and Carmel, from their respective schools. Geoffrey, her eldest, had come home from St Pius X College in the late afternoon and gone to his bedroom to begin an evening of study; he was preparing for the Higher School Certificate in his final year. Patricia was away from the house in Sydney. Their father, Bert, worked as a seaman on the big iron-ore ships that traversed the oceans around Australia to as far away as Japan; that day, he was off the coast of Wollongong with a long and arduous trip ahead of him.

This typical working-class Catholic family lived in a crowded but cosy miner's cottage in the inner-city suburb of Hamilton, close to the railway line and right near Newcastle's main Catholic cathedral, Sacred Heart, with its imposing red-brick edifice, which had been built in the late 1920s with funds from the local Catholic community. Each family had to raise 'a shilling a brick', so one by one bricks were purchased with the sweat of the congregation. Along with hundreds of others, Audrey's father, who earned a low wage as a coalminer in the nearby Hunter Valley, worked extra hours to help build the church.

Bert had met Audrey at a dance in 1953, when his ship docked in Newcastle. They'd married soon after and gone on to have their five children: Patricia, Geoffrey, Andrew, Carmel and Bernadette. All the Nash kids studied hard at school; they understood the sacrifices their parents had made for them. The Catholic Church, and the local priests and nuns were a constant in their lives. There wasn't much money, but there was a lot of love.

The seven Nashes were a tight-knit crew, and the kids often played together on the patch of green grass beneath the Hills hoist in the backyard. But that day, the youngest boy, Andrew, was unusually quiet. He seemed out of sorts. Preoccupied. Not his usual bubbly self.

The thirteen-year-old had nearly finished his second year of high school at Marist Brothers Hamilton, known as one of the best Catholic schools for boys in the area. He had a quick wit and loved to play tricks on his siblings and friends. He also loved to sing. As a member of the school choir he enjoyed performing resurrection hymns such as 'Yours Be the Glory, Risen Conquering Son'. He was an altar boy[1] at special masses and had volunteered to serve at the Mothers' Mass held every year in the school chapel. He believed in God and revelled in Church rituals. He loved being an altar boy and prayed often. He was quiet and unassuming. On more than one occasion, Audrey's parish priest, Father Maurice Cahill, had told her that Andrew would make a fine priest. He was a golden child.

Andrew had a part-time job at a local pharmacy delivering medicine to elderly people in his suburb. He developed close relationships with many of his customers, who looked forward to his regular visits.

He loved sport and was in the rugby team. He attended swimming lessons at the local ocean baths, and he was enrolled in the Duke of Edinburgh's International Award. The scheme included courses such as 'lifesaving, civil defence, hobbies, physical efficiency and expeditions'.[2] It was run by his class master, Brother Francis 'Romuald' Cable, who would take the boys bushwalking at nearby Sugarloaf Mountain. They also took trips to the Myall

Lakes, where they spent their days canoeing and swimming, and camping on the sandy beaches at night. In the playground, Romuald would supervise the boys doing push-ups, shuttle runs, broad jumps and stamina runs, the winner being the boy with the quickest time.

Andrew liked to challenge himself. He rarely caused any trouble for his parents or teachers.

That Tuesday evening, Audrey called the kids in for dinner, eaten as always with noisy appreciation for her traditional cooking. Meat and three veg. Andrew seemed a bit withdrawn; she put it down to tiredness after a hectic day at school. Nothing to worry about.

After dinner, Andrew had a bath and asked Audrey to iron his sport clothes for the next day. He then went to his bedroom to do his homework. It was their usual weekday evening routine.

A short time later, Bernadette went to Andrew's bedroom near the front door to borrow an eraser. When she nudged the door, an unusual weight was in the way, so she called to her mother to come and help her. What was Andrew doing in there? Audrey walked out from the kitchen and put both hands on the door, using all her strength to push it open.

Andrew's lifeless body was hanging from the back of the door.

Bernadette's screams filled the house. The family ran to her aid, and Geoffrey tried to hold Andrew up in a desperate bid to save him. The cacophony of screaming and wailing from Audrey, Carmel and Bernadette was bloodcurdling.

Andrew, pale and still, was lying on the carpet in his striped pyjamas. Only minutes before, he'd been eating his dinner. Meat and three veg.

Audrey, panicked and in deep shock, ran out onto the street, hoping to flag down a taxi. The family had no telephone – they couldn't afford one. As she sprinted along the roadside, she prayed for help. *Please, God, please send a taxi for Andrew.*

A taxi eventually came, and Audrey begged the driver to get an ambulance and to call Father Cahill. She wanted a priest to administer the last rites, a Catholic sacrament, to her dying son so he would go to heaven. The cab driver radioed ahead, and soon the ambulance sirens could be heard howling from several streets away.

* * *

The paramedics arrived first and entered Andrew's bedroom. The men hovered over the boy, checked his pulse and put their faces close to his, searching for even the faintest breath. They told Audrey there was nothing they could do, then they packed up and left the house.

Two hours after Andrew's body had been found, the assistant parish priest, Father Bill Burston, arrived and administered the Catholic rites for people who had already died. Burston was a registered psychologist with a Masters of Psychology degree from University College in Dublin. He was also the Director of the Catholic Family Welfare Bureau (later known as Centacare). He was new to the parish, and Audrey hadn't met him before. He told her that Cahill was away.

Shortly afterwards, two more priests arrived: Father Tom Brennan, the headmaster of St Pius X, Geoffrey's high school; and his deputy principal, Father Patrick 'Pat' Helferty.

Then three Marist Brothers from Andrew's school were on the doorstep: the principal, Brother William 'Christopher' Wade; Brother Romuald Cable, Andrew's class master; and Andrew's footy coach, Brother John O'Brien.

Audrey was surprised to see them all; she'd only asked for her parish priest. *How did the Marist Brothers find out so quickly?* she wondered.

The priests and Brothers huddled in a circle in the cramped living room, away from the family, and spoke quietly to each other. In front of them was a display of all the Nash family photos, nearly covering the entire wall. Happy family shots. The men did not look up; they only looked at each other.

Audrey was still in shock, and she gathered her thoughts as best she could. Her mind turned to Andrew's quiet demeanour when she'd picked him up that afternoon.

She faced Romuald. 'Did anything happen at school?'

He broke away from the circle of men, but he ignored Audrey's question. He looked up at her while not meeting her eyes. 'Did Andrew leave a note?' he asked.

'No,' she told him.

'Did he say anything?' Romuald enquired.

'No.' Audrey shook her head. Her sobs filled the house.

The men spoke a few words of condolence before leaving the house, one by one.

Andrew's body was still lying on his bedroom floor, his siblings around him weeping in shock and grief. Audrey was left alone in her lounge room, her beloved son dead and no answer as to why. Her thoughts turned to her husband, Bert, who was out at sea, oblivious to the fact his youngest son was dead. Anguish burned inside Audrey. How to tell him?

After she managed to contact the ship, Bert was called to the captain's quarters and told the devastating news. The ship docked at Wollongong to allow him to rush home to his family. He hailed a taxi and travelled nearly three hundred kilometres north to Newcastle, a three-hour trip.

Audrey didn't sleep that night; the pain was like a boulder crushing her chest.

Bert arrived the day after Andrew's death to a house drowning in tears. He comforted Audrey as best he could, but he couldn't fathom his son's actions. The guilt seared his brain – he told himself he hadn't been there for his son. His heartache was so great, he couldn't face going to the morgue for the official identification.

Instead, Geoffrey went. Apart from the morgue attendant, he was by himself with his brother's dead body in the cold, airless room.

The attendant pulled back the sheet.

'Yes, that's him,' Geoffrey said.

The image of his brother's corpse was burned into Geoffrey's memory for life.

* * *

The peal of the morning bell echoed across the asphalt playground at Marist Brothers Hamilton. Hundreds of teenage boys were milling around laughing and talking as they waited for the school assembly. They formed scrappy lines, jostling and punching each other, telling silly jokes. Shirts were being adjusted and tucked in as Marist Brothers patrolled the perimeter, ordering the boys to fix their ties and tie their shoes.

The school motto was *Viriliter age* or 'act manfully'. It was staffed mainly by Brothers who each wore a long black-and-white soutane, a type of cassock, with a cord around the waist that represented the three vows they had taken: poverty, chastity and obedience.

Glen Walsh waited patiently in the Year Seven class line. He had followed his older brother, John, to the school, and had three younger sisters. The Walshes lived in the suburb of Shortland, named after the British lieutenant who had spotted the region's coal seams; it was an enclave of devout Catholic families, a quick bus ride from the school.

Glen looked up to watch the headmaster, Brother Christopher Wade, step to the edge of the second-floor balcony. He had a commanding presence above the boys as he gazed down into the school quadrangle, a sterile landscape without any trees or shrubbery. It could have been an army barracks, and Wade often called his students 'the troops', particularly during these assemblies.

The boys were expecting the usual boring announcements and reminders. They had no idea what was coming.

Wade waited until they were quiet. 'Boys, I am very sad to inform you that one of our students, Andrew Nash, has died in an accident.'

A deep hush fell over the assembly. Glen was stunned. He searched for his brother, John, in the crowd.

The Walshes knew the Nashes through their Catholic connections: their sons were in the school choir together, and John was in Andrew's year. Andrew and Glen were both altar boys who loved God and were devoted to their faith. They were gentle kids who were very obedient, doing everything they could to please their families and teachers.

Wade told the assembled students that details of a requiem mass for Andrew would be posted in the parish bulletin.

A few more items were then announced over the microphone, but the boys hardly registered their content. The principal's voice sounded like a muffled record player.

Their schoolmate had died at the age of thirteen.

* * *

Brother Romuald didn't comfort Andrew's classmates after his death, while rumours swirled around the school about how he had died.

Father Burston, the assistant parish priest who was also a psychologist, told a group of altar boys it had been a 'prank gone wrong' involving Andrew's sister, Bernadette. Meanwhile, Marist Brothers at the school told students that Geoffrey Nash had shut a door on Andrew and accidently got his tie caught, strangling him.

Then another rumour spread like wildfire: Andrew had died while he and Geoffrey were playing on the Hills hoist in their backyard and Andrew's tie got caught in the wires.

The rumours spread from the school around the parish, sending shockwaves through the community. In this very Catholic society, the word 'suicide' could not even be uttered – the act was considered a mortal sin that would condemn a soul to hell forever. Andrew would have been taught that if someone took their own life they could not go to heaven or be buried in the Catholic section of a cemetery. In this environment, the disgrace and shame experienced by the family of someone who died from suicide would have been profound. This partly explains why in this case, no one openly countenanced the possibility of suicide – Andrew's death could only have been an accident.

At the requiem mass in the Sacred Heart Cathedral the following Sunday, hundreds gathered to pay their last respects to Andrew. They passed under the beautiful white Carrara marble statue of Jesus, arms outstretched in welcome, that stood above the main entrance. The elderly people to whom Andrew had delivered medicine were all present despite their frailty. He was much loved.

This was where Andrew had been baptised as a newborn and made his first Holy Communion at the age of eight. It was the place he often served in the long red robe and white overgarment of an altar boy.

Father Cahill, Andrew's parish priest and his school chaplain, celebrated the mass and, after the gospel, gave a homily or sermon to the crowd. 'Andrew took up the way of Christ enthusiastically,' he said, 'through the splendid example of his parents' faith. It was mainly in this role of server that the people of Hamilton came to know and love him. We priests loved him dearly.' Cahill went on:

I wondered often if perhaps he would stand one day at the altar, as a priest. But it was not to be. Nor was he to go through adolescence, that gateway to a wider, fuller life, though not necessarily a happier one. It seems such a tragedy in purely human terms, but if we could see things as God does, it would be different. And God took him as he is, at his best. He was at a wondrous height of innocence and beauty and holiness. Who knows what might have been? God has taken him into His care, as he was, so spiritually good and beautiful. But isn't that the aim in life for us all?

What did Andrew Nash achieve in his fourteen short years? He gave us who knew him well a glimpse of the beauty of a life unclouded by sin. He created joy, he spread happiness … he confirmed the truth that the Kingdom of Heaven is for little children and those like them …[3]

Andrew Nash was thirteen years old when he died. Cahill had got it wrong. An article about this homily appeared a few weeks later in a school magazine. The author wrote, 'Andrew's death on 8 October came as a great shock to everyone, one of those sad and puzzling occurrences that we all meet during our lifetimes, and that cannot be explained at all, if not in terms of faith.'

Why would God take a thirteen-year-old?

The police described it as death by misadventure. The coroner released an open finding.

The family was left to grieve. No one from the parish, not even Cahill, came to the house to provide pastoral care. And the Nashes knew in their hearts that Andrew's death had not been an accident.

* * *

Confusion and despair gnawed away at Audrey. She would often cast her mind back to the weeks leading up to Andrew's death, looking for clues. One incident stood out.

It had been an afternoon in April. Andrew hadn't come home from school on time. When it got to six o'clock and the sky was getting dark, Audrey became worried.

Finally Andrew walked in, but he was subdued and quiet. Usually he'd come in full of smiles and happy shouts.

'Where have you been?' Audrey asked him. 'What were you doing?'

Andrew didn't meet his mother's eyes. 'I've been to Bar Beach,' he said.

Audrey wondered how Andrew had got to the beach from school – had he made the forty-minute trek? But in the face of her son's evasive answers, Audrey eventually dismissed her uneasiness and said no more about it. She was just relieved he was safely home.

The next day, Andrew, normally compliant and well behaved, was reluctant to go to school. Audrey was having none of it – she could see he wasn't ill. But he behaved the same way the next morning, and then it started to become a habit. Andrew would repeatedly say he wasn't well enough to attend school; Audrey was adamant that he had to go. He responded by becoming more withdrawn as the year went on. Now he was gone.

Audrey and Bert couldn't explain why their son had done something so drastic, so final. But life had to go on; they still had four children to care for. Bert took up drinking and spent much of his time in bed with depression, becoming a shadow of his former self.[4] In contrast, Audrey threw herself into the Church, attending almost every day; it was her lifeline. The prayers, the rituals, the teachings that Andrew was in heaven with God – they all comforted her. Her devotion to Christ and her beloved Church was the key to her survival.

Many times family members walked into Andrew's room and paused for a moment, looking for some connection to their brother and son. His old-fashioned single bed made of iron, with its boyish blue-grey bedspread, was still pushed against the wall; his clothes were still inside the rickety cupboard; a few treasures – a book, a knife, a cross – sat on the dresser.

It took a long time for the family to realise Andrew was never coming back.

CHAPTER 2

Early Beginnings

IN THE MARIST BROTHERS HAMILTON YEARBOOK FOR 1974, Andrew Nash's Year Eight class photo has the inscription 'RIP' printed next to his name. On 20 January 1975, the grief-stricken Nash family endured his fourteenth birthday.

Meanwhile, Andrew's schoolmates and their families had been enjoying the summer holidays with trips to the beach, barbecues, and hot days playing cricket with the neighbourhood kids.

Families like the Walshes.

Glen Walsh had grown up in the tight-knit Catholic community of Shortland. The non-Catholic families, or 'publics' as they were known, occupied the outer reaches of the neighbourhood; there was an invisible boundary the kids knew not to cross.

Glen was the second of five kids – John, Glen, Maree, and twins Trish and Kate – and his parents, John and Louise, ran a very disciplined ship. John worked on the Newcastle wharves as a customs officer ensuring tariffs were paid on goods coming in. Back then a lot of crooks were trying to import materials without paying the duty, and Glen's dad often worked with the federal police during gun seizures.

The Walshes lived on Malta Street in one of the countless fibro-siding houses. At the top of the street was their local

Catholic church, the primary school and a convent for the nuns who worked at the school.

Shortland was a good place to grow up in, and most of the living was done in the street. Kids would clamber over the fences to get into each other's backyards. On Saturdays there were pianola afternoons with people crowding around the instrument; everyone would bring a couple of bottles of beer and sing tunes like 'Teddy Bears' Picnic'. These singalongs would last into the evening, becoming lounge-room parties with Frank Sinatra and Dean Martin blaring from the record player.

Mothers were the backbone of the community. They would often do many hours of volunteer admin for the parish or manual labour required by the nuns and priests. They would conscript their children into cleaning the nuns' convent at the top of the hill. Cakes would be baked for neighbours, and collections would be organised for families in need.

Families in Malta Street took turns inviting some of the neighbours over to recite the rosary, in honour of Mary, the mother of Jesus. It was one of those rituals many Catholic families participated in back in the 1960s and '70s. Everyone gathered around a statue of the Blessed Virgin, clutching their rosary beads and reciting the decades of the rosary. 'Hail Mary, full of Grace, the Lord is with thee. Blessed art thou amongst women and blessed is the fruit of thy womb, Jesus. Holy Mary Mother of God, pray for our sinners now and at the hour of our death, Amen!' The rosary was a repetitive prayer made up of fifteen decades – the repetition of ten Hail Marys. The kids were bored, but for the adults it was meant to be a group meditation on the mysteries of Christianity. After each family took its turn with the statue of the Blessed Virgin, they would put it in a special box and deliver it to the next house.

Away from prying eyes, domestic violence poisoned the lives of some families in the community. There was a general sense of this just being the way of things, when husbands came home worn out from work and couldn't get any peace. Many women put up with it, burying themselves in the Church, which provided a haven from their home lives. Priests became their confidants and friends, as their husbands were off at work much of the time.

Hostility also tainted the lives of local schoolkids. Before starting at Marist Brothers Hamilton, Glen had attended Our Lady of Victories, the primary school at the top of his street. It was a pretty tough place; there were some aggressive boys and a lot of punch-ups. Glen's brother, John, would sometimes come home with a fat lip from a scuffle. There was also a lot of bullying, despite the efforts of a certain disciplinarian nun who didn't spare the strap and was known among the boys as 'that tough old bitch'.

All the local Catholic kids attended Our Lady of Victories, including the Alward kids from across the street. Steven Alward was in the same year as John, a year ahead of Glen.

Steven was one of Joan and Brian's four kids; the others were David, Peter and Libby. Brian, like his father before him, worked at the huge BHP steel mill, the mainstay of industry in Newcastle. Brian had shifts as a heater in the bloom mill, where the steel rods were made. He'd started there at fifteen, and it was arduous and tough work. The noise and heat in the hangar where fires raged to make the ingots was overwhelming. It could also be dangerous: industrial accidents were common, and according to poorly kept records at least two people died each year.[1] The children knew to be quiet during the day while Brian slept, recovering from the long hours of shift work. There wasn't much time for recreation with their dad, apart from when he got the chance to teach the eldest boys, David and Peter, how to box.

Joan worked in the post office at Islington, another predominantly Catholic suburb, but she was really renowned for her baking. In the small, cluttered kitchen she would bake ten cakes in a sitting, giving eight of each batch to visitors when they left the house. She taught Steven, her youngest, to make her famous boiled fruitcake. Joan also provided free labour to the Church, looking after priests and nuns, taking minutes at parish council meetings. To her, it was a duty and an honour.

Brian and Joan didn't show their kids a lot of affection until much later in life. This was pretty normal behaviour; the kids knew they were loved by parents who worked long hours to make ends meet. Libby got more cuddles than the boys.

The Alwards' extended family were also very close to the Church.

Steven's Aunty Mary, his dad's only sister, was a devout Catholic and one of his favourite people. Whenever a relative passed away, she would be called upon to prepare the body for the wake. She'd put rolled-up towels under the chin to avoid leakage, and keep the eyes closed by placing pennies on the lids. She was well liked by many priests, who would often visit her for a cup of tea.[2]

Steven's maternal grandma, Ella Hopley, was the housekeeper for the senior priests at the Sacred Heart Cathedral in Hamilton. This matriarch cooked lunch for the immediate family every Saturday until she died. She lived in an idyllic place at Warners Bay on Lake Macquarie. Her house was makeshift, with bits added on here and there, and louvred windows at the front. There was a corrugated-iron shed at the back that many family members used when they needed a place to stay.

The Alwards spent dreamy summers on the lake, mucking about in boats and canoes. The days were long and hot, and there were barbecues down by the water's edge. The Walshes joined the Alwards there on a couple of occasions.

Around Christmas time, the Alward clan – about forty people – would gather in Grandma Ella's backyard and sit under a huge willow tree with drums and guitars, singing well into the night.

The children would play together all day, then lie in their makeshift beds on the front veranda, listening to the songs and laughter, and watch, through the louvred windows, the light fade over the lake.

* * *

Despite the rough and tumble at Our Lady of Victories, Steven and Glen liked school. They always did their homework and were model students. In their spare time, they played in a little neighbourhood gang with Glen's brother, John, Steven's sister,

Libby, and her friend Narelle from up the road. They got up to good-hearted fun, such as making up skits and putting on a show for everyone on Malta Street. Sometimes they got up to mischief, cashing in bottles for coins at the corner shop to buy a small packet of Viscount cigarettes for eighteen cents and a box of matches for two; another five bought a bag of hot chips. They would run off, laughing, to enjoy their spoils in the park.

Glen may have appeared gentle on the outside, but on the inside he could be tough. Once, in a street fight, he managed to lasso a guy with a garden hose. However, he also had a well-developed moral code: if John did anything wrong, Glen would dob him in to their parents.

Glen's temperament came to the attention of the nuns and priests. When he was in Year Six, a nun gave his mum a book on religious studies for him to read. The Church was on the lookout for religious recruits or 'vocations' from the pupils – not only was this God's mission, but the number of nuns, priests and Brothers was starting to dwindle.

Priests and brothers were held in the highest esteem. When a priest or brother came to dinner at your house, he'd be welcomed like a prince. The best plates and cutlery came out, and the women would slave in the kitchen to cook something special. The priest would get the lamb chops, while the kids got the sausages. The children watched the way their parents behaved during these visits – it was as if God had entered their homes. These were men to be in awe of, to listen to, and to obey.

One of these men was Father Allan Hart, a groovy young assistant priest in his twenties. He drove around in a yellow Sandman panel van, and often took altar boys to the beach in it. Hart was part of a group of young priests who arrived around the same time as the second Vatican Council, also known as Vatican II. Pope John XXIII liberalised many Church policies and gave bishops much greater influence and power. Laypeople were allowed to play a greater role in Church ceremonies and mass was now said predominantly in English, whereas before this time it was often in Latin. Hart became almost part of the Alward family, and old Father Smythe, the senior priest, would tell the kids that the young Father Hart would be bishop one day.

Glen and Steven were altar boys for these two priests, and it was an honour – for them and their families – to be chosen for this rite of passage. Every Sunday at mass, Steven and Glen could be seen up the front in their white and red robes. Girls could become 'angels', which involved doing chores at the church every Saturday morning; they were forbidden to serve at the altar.

As the summer holidays ended after Year Six, high school beckoned. In 1973, Steven went to St Pius X, while Glen went a year later to Marist Brothers Hamilton.

* * *

The mission of the Marist Brothers was to make 'Jesus known and loved through the education of young people, especially those most neglected.'[3] Many of the Brothers appointed to schools like Glen's had gone through their training as teenagers in the Marist Brothers Novitiate, a boarding school for young recruits. Some had started even earlier in the Juniorate, a high school in Mittagong, a small town an hour's drive south of Sydney, for Marist Brothers hopefuls. It was a grand place, built in 1906, with handsome brick cloisters and wide verandas, surrounded by extensive farmland. At the Juniorate, the young men and boys, some as young as twelve, would be dropped off with their suitcases into a furtive environment with a culture of 'don't ask, don't tell'.

The trainee brothers slept in cavernous dormitories with steel bedsteads lined up in rows, the only decoration a statue of the Blessed Virgin in a wall niche.

After being woken at 5.30 a.m. to say prayers and attend mass, they'd spend their days doing manual labour, cleaning or working in the fields or the laundry or the bakery. They participated in 'The Great Silence', when it was forbidden to talk for long hours; schooled in the inappropriateness of certain songs and books; and lectured on the holiness of celibacy. They were discouraged by their teachers from developing intimate relationships, so they snatched whatever affection they could get in secret, starting a pattern that would continue throughout their lives as Marist Brothers.

They would adopt new names, often those of saints – a sign of their absolute belonging and allegiance to the Brothers.

A priest has a higher status and more responsibility than a brother. Priests go through an ordination ceremony, where their hands are consecrated by a bishop. They are allowed to say mass and hear confessions. Catholics are supposed to attend mass every Sunday; this involves the Liturgy of the Eucharist, a ceremony in which bread and wine – according to Catholic beliefs – is transubstantiated into the body and blood of Jesus Christ. Catholics also go to confession, formally known as the Sacrament of Reconciliation or Penance, from the age of seven. Back in the 1960s and '70s, the priest would be hidden behind a screen or inside a booth, while the person seeking absolution would get down on a hard wooden kneeler and wait for him to slide a panel across; the person would then recount their sins in order to receive forgiveness. Many kids made up the sins – you couldn't go into the confessional and say nothing.

Those boys in the diocese who wanted to be priests were placed six hours drive south at St Columba's College Seminary in Springwood, in the Blue Mountains west of Sydney. Some who were barely out of primary school and others who had finished school were thrown together in a sandstone castle of sorts, surrounded by bush, and isolated from familial warmth and contact. Many found solace in the beauty of the gum forests as they were trained to endure long silences, to partake in many hours of prayer, study and sport, to submit to rules, to conform, to remain obedient and celibate. This was the years of 'formation' before they were sent to St Patrick's College Seminary in Manly, in Sydney's northern suburbs, to complete their training.

The mothers of these boys would sew their name tags to their clothes, which would include a brand-new soutane that had been prescribed in canon law in 1604 and worn by priests since the Reformation. Later, at the seminary, the boys would wear a hand-crocheted lace surplice or liturgical shirt.[4]

For both trainee priests and brothers, parental contact was minimal, and they were isolated from all of their loved ones and old friends. They were allowed family visits a few weekends a year, and they could return home for the July and Christmas holidays. On Sunday afternoons, they wrote letters to friends and family, knowing these could be censored.

Most of the boys came from lower socioeconomic Catholic families, and their parents were pious and devoted to the Church.

These boys grew to adulthood in this place; their ideas about almost everything were formed and moulded there. It appears some of them were badly affected by the deprivation, leading to outbursts of rage and violence. They were then despatched to schools across Australia with very little scrutiny from the State.

* * *

Many of the Marist Brothers at the Hamilton high school fostered a culture of fear and terror. The school's disciplinarian Irish culture had been imported many decades before, and in the early part of the twentieth century it wasn't unusual to witness violence between students and teachers. Brothers would fight bare fisted with students in order to settle scores and to show who was the superior being, and students would frequently be caned for minor rule-breaking such as uniform breaches.

Often parents wouldn't object because they thought these strict boundaries were good for the boys – after all, they'd been brought up the same way. Their deep respect for the Church caused them to never question the authority of the Brothers. Their sons, dressed in second-hand blazers, inherited that respect and were full of fear and awe for the Brothers.

In the 1970s, the violence of one Brother stood out from the rest. Brother Cassian seemed consumed by an unabated rage for the world and any student he didn't like. He hated the Beatles, saying they'd lead people to the devil. Once, he was seen dragging a boy from his desk and throwing him onto the floor with such force, his friends thought he might have been killed. On another occasion, the Brother smashed a boy's head against the blackboard to make a point.

Other Brothers who wielded great authority were Brother Christopher (the principal), Brother Dominic, Brother Patrick and Brother Romuald. The last three were particularly feared by the boys.

John Walsh fretted about his younger sibling attending Marist Brothers Hamilton, given its punitive and violent culture. Glen truly had a gentle countenance, and John understood that the men he knew as Brothers Dominic, Patrick and Romuald – birth names Darcy O'Sullivan, Thomas Butler and Francis Cable respectively – seemed to target a particular type of boy. Sensitive boys who came from devout families. He warned Glen to keep his distance.

CHAPTER 3

Viriliter Age – Act Manfully

THE MARIST BROTHERS WHO TAUGHT AT THE HAMILTON HIGH school lived on site, right next to the classrooms. The students could look up to the windows of their teachers' bedrooms from the street at the front entrance.

Brother Romuald was a tall, imposing man with dark hair and a dominating physical presence. He had arrived at the school in 1971 after stints at various Catholic institutions, having graduated from the Marist Brothers Novitiate in Mittagong in 1952. Romuald was the Year Eight class master and in charge of sport. He had a reputation for caning the boys in a vicious manner; before striking them, he would call them names like 'the Anti-Christ'![1] Many of the boys, and his fellow Brothers, were scared of him.

At the beginning of the year, Brother Romuald would ask every boy to fill out a survey for sex education purposes. It was known to include such intimate questions as 'Do you have pubic hair yet?' and 'Have you had a wet dream yet?' He once singled out some boys and asked them to accompany him to the bike shed, next to the playground toilets, where he questioned them about their survey responses. 'You've marked in your survey that you've never had an orgasm. Well, I find that very hard to believe.' And so it went on. The boys were mortified and ashamed.

Romuald seemed to leave the physically tougher, sportier kids alone. He tended to pick on boys from the most Catholic families, perhaps figuring that the more devout the parents, the less likely they would be to question his behaviour. He also seemed to target boys whose fathers had drinking problems; these kids were already vulnerable, often trying to resolve their parents' bitter fights.

Brother Romuald would take the boys for swimming lessons at the local sea baths, including at Bar Beach. He was notorious for exposing himself to the boys in the change rooms. After one incident where he exposed his erection to the boys, he later told a student, 'What happened at the pool change rooms was nothing to worry about. It's nothing you need to tell your parents about. What I did was a sex education situation because I know that some of the boys don't have a father.'

All the boys assembled in the baths that day had fathers. It was a pathetic excuse, and the boys knew it.

John Walsh warned his young brother about the various Brothers and which situations to avoid at all costs. He was relieved when his concerns about Brother Romuald targeting Glen never eventuated: the Year Eight class master was suddenly transferred out of the school two months after Andrew Nash died; he was sent to a rougher school in Sydney's western suburbs, Marist Brothers Dundas, and retired from the Brothers in 1978. But John still worried about the remaining teachers.

Brother Cassian's sex ed classes were legendary. One day he showed his Year Seven class a slide show that began with diagrams of genitalia, then transitioned to pictures of frogs having sexual intercourse, then to a photograph of a violent car crash, smears of blood clearly visible on the car doors. 'I know what all you boys want to see,' he said to the class, before flicking to the next slide. It was an image of a naked African girl suffering from starvation; her stomach was swollen, and her labia seemed hugely out of proportion. Some boys, as young as twelve, were frightened. Afterwards one of them said, 'I think he wants to turn us off having sex altogether.'

Brother Dominic was also well known among the schoolboys for all the wrong reasons. Many knew to avoid going to sickbay because Brother Dominic would go with them – and the story was he'd groped one boy under the blanket while he lay there waiting for his mother to pick him up. Others said that Brother Dominic would come up behind boys in class and put his right hand down their pants, rubbing their naval region and pubic area. The talk in the playground was that Brother Patrick did the same.

These young students were always on their guard. The behaviour was labelled 'gay'. The boys thought they were 'poofters'.

* * *

At the other Marist Brothers school in the diocese, Marist Brothers Maitland, a new principal had arrived. Brother Nestor (his real name was John Aloysius Littler) was principal from 1972 to 1977. He'd been working as the dormitory master at the prestigious Marist Brothers school St Joseph's in Hunters Hill, Sydney, and before that at the St Vincent's Boys home in Westmead, Sydney. Children from the boys' home would sometimes spend some of their holidays at camps at the Marist Brothers school in Maitland.

* * *

By the early 1970s, the Marist Brothers had become seriously concerned about the dwindling numbers of young men joining their ranks. The senior leadership had come up with a plan: older boys would go on retreats every year, and the Brothers would use these occasions to observe and get to know their students better. Many students went to the Brothers' stately estate in Mittagong, which was renamed the Retreat Centre in 1972.

The retreats were conducted under the watchful eye of the team leaders, two influential and senior Marist Brothers: Brother Geoffrey 'Coman' Sykes and Brother Mark 'Baptist' Gillogly. They came up with an effective selection process for the retreats, one that involved identifying the 'better boys'.[2] It was Sykes's belief that if they could get a 'group of their better boys to Mittagong for a leadership course … for a few days during the school time, then after some good liturgies and a faith experience, they might be ready to talk about vocations to the priesthood or a religious life'.[3]

Many of the brothers involved in this recruitment strategy were senior leaders on the Marist Brothers Provincial Council. The Marist Brothers were divided into two provinces – the Sydney and Melbourne provinces. The Sydney Province covered New South Wales, Queensland and the ACT. The Melbourne Province covered Victoria, the Northern Territory, South Australia and Western Australia.

Brother Coman had been involved in a growing movement, the Christian Living Camps, since the 1960s. The formation of the Youth Retreat Teams within the Marist Brothers was his brainchild. From 1974, brothers and lay teachers were asked to find the 'better boys' in each of their schools.[4]

Each retreat ran from Monday to Thursday, and about forty-five senior boys, those in the last two years of high school, would attend from one school. The first day would begin with a substantial lunch, then students could play games of cricket, football, tennis and soccer, or they could relax and explore the place. After that, there were six sessions with titles such as 'Self-Discovery, Jesus, prayer and faith'.[5] The boys and their mentors would gather together and talk well into the evening. They went to mass most days, which was accompanied by loud singing, guitars and drums.

In 1975, another senior Marist Brother joined the Retreat Teams. Brother Michael Hill worked closely with Brother Coman and by the end of 1975, all students at Marist Brothers schools in Sydney, Maitland, Newcastle and Canberra had participated in the program.

In 1976, the principal of Marist Brothers Hamilton, Brother Christopher, was transferred out of the school, to be replaced by Brother Alexis Turton, who was a keen supporter of the Retreat Teams recruitment strategy.

In 1977, when Glen was in Year Ten, he was spotted as a 'better boy'. He'd survived at the school by being a model student, volunteering for the choir, and excelling at religious studies. Brother Alexis, his headmaster, raised the possibility of him becoming a Marist Brother. In 1978, Glen's Year 11 form attended a retreat at Eraring with Brother Coman, Brother Michael Hill, Brother Patrick and Father Allan Hart. The boys were between 16 and 17 years old.[6]

In 1979, Brother Coman handed over the Retreat Team leadership to Glen's principal, Brother Alexis Turton. Brother Alexis took over the job as a 'Vocations Recruiter' and leader of the Youth Retreat Team based at the Novitiate in Winston Hills, Sydney.[7]

As Glen finished Year Twelve, the Brothers encouraged him to enter the Postulancy in Winston Hills while attending the Catholic Teachers College in Castle Hill, a nearby suburb. He would become a Marist Brother with a teaching qualification. The Postulancy was the intermediary step between the Juniorate and the Novitiate.

The Novitiate was an 18–24 month apprenticeship where the trainee formally entered the Institute of the Marist Brothers and learned to be a Brother.

Glen thought he might like to become a nurse or an overseas missionary, but in the end, the Marist Brothers' offer seemed too good to pass up. He was also keen to please his parents, who were very supportive of the idea.

Glen packed up a suitcase of clothes and books, and headed to Winston Hills. The following year, he would live as a postulant in the house of formation with twenty-two other young men.[8]

* * *

Back in 1974, Glen's neighbourhood friend Steven Alward had been in Year Eight at St Pius X High School. All Steven's brothers had gone to Marist Brothers Hamilton, but they'd copped many a harsh beating at that school. They particularly disliked Brother Cassian, who the boys called 'Bashin' Cassian'. Steven was smaller and gentler than them, and he looked young for his age, so, not wanting him to be picked on, Joan and Brian Alward had chosen the other school.

St Pius X was built on a hill in the working class suburb of Adamstown. Bishop John Toohey, who controlled the whole Maitland-Newcastle Diocese, had acquired the old Lustre Hosiery Factory in 1960 and converted the building into the school. It was a large, cavernous space partitioned into multiple classrooms and an assembly hall. At the northern end, past all the classrooms, were the priests' quarters, a sick bay and a chapel. The priests lived on site, as the Marist Brothers did at the Hamilton school – although even back then it was unusual for the religious and clergy to live at the schools.

A thousand boys in a small, overcrowded space made for an atmosphere of simmering violence, especially in the junior school, from Years Seven to Ten. In Years Eleven and Twelve, there was a separate school on the campus for girls called St Anne's but there was some interaction with the boys, so the atmosphere became more pleasant. For some students there was violence at home, in the streets and at school. They had three main ways to survive: get good with your fists, get good with your mouth (make a joke, embarrass your attacker, deflect, lie) or become invisible.[9]

Schoolyard fights broke out at regular intervals. A circle of students would form around the melee, and sometimes the outside circle would drench the brawlers in spit. Eventually, a teacher or a priest would turn up, and the kids would make a big show of being seen to be breaking up the fight.

The Alwards' belief there was far less corporal punishment at St Pius X than at Marist Brothers Hamilton was unfounded. Steven escaped much of it because he was a model student, but other boys weren't so lucky. The students faced an old-fashioned disciplinarian culture in which caning was an everyday occurrence. Some priests and lay teachers were feared because of their skill with the stick, while others were sneered at because they could scarcely make a mark. Among the students it became a matter of perverse pride to be whipped by the best and not flinch or, God forbid, cry.[10]

The surfers, nerds, footy types and druggies were lumped together in a swamp of testosterone. Some were academically gifted and aspired to be suburban solicitors, engineers or schoolteachers; for almost all of them, this would be the highest credential they would try to attain – this was a working-class Catholic school, not Geelong Grammar.[11]

While the Catholic boys of Newcastle were trapped in the stifling atmosphere of their high schools, the world around them was experiencing the 1970s social and cultural revolutions. They were taught about the Vietnam War through a Catholic lens: it was a necessary war to fight the scourge of communism, the greatest evil, reds under the bed, and all that. The schools were anti-abortion, anti-feminism, anti-atheism – lots of antis, very few pros. They were taught the world was a very dark place.

Newcastle at that time was an unapologetically working-class town. The majority of people played hard and drank hard, and it was extremely macho, with the culture at the BHP steelworks permeating the city. Most jobs were about manual sweat and labour; those in the creative arts were in the minority.[12] Steven, a boy who loved the English language and the arts, had entered high school desperate for the intellectual nourishment he wasn't getting at home. He always did his homework, and he was a voracious reader. He loved to study.

The Catholic schools in the Maitland-Newcastle Diocese during the 1970s were under the control of a powerful cleric: the Director of Catholic Education was a priest by the name of Father Frank Coolahan. He was the bishop's chief adviser and he could hire and fire teachers and principals at will. He took a special interest in St Pius X.

The headmaster, Father Tom Brennan, seemed a dapper chap. A slim, good-looking man, he spoke with a slightly posh accent. When he was teaching religion classes, he would wear a long white cassock with style, but at other times he wore a black suit. Around the parish he was likened to the Hollywood star Paul Newman. Some students watched the mothers who worked in the office, doing the school fees and general admin, openly flirt with him. They would offer to do chores or run errands for him, and a few of them seemed to dress up for him; he paid them back with oodles of charm.

Other significant teachers at Steven's school were Father Pat Helferty, the deputy principal, also known as 'Fat Pat' for his portly appearance. He was liked and hated in equal measure by the students.

Ted Hall was a maths, geography and history teacher, not a priest or Brother, who arrived in 1976 after serving a significant time in the army. The former sergeant would shake his students' hands with particular force, then ask them, 'Are you a man or a mouse?' He often called his students 'poofters' or 'dogs'.[13] It seems likely he was far from Steven's favourite teacher.

A year earlier, a teacher had arrived who seemed able to help Steven gain deeper learning about the arts and the world at large. This teacher was a priest by the name of Father John Sidney Denham.

Denham embodied all the traits of a bumptious, slightly camp academic. He talked as though he was a superior intellectual with a penchant for classical music, highbrow literature and fine wines. He would sit at the front of his classes and stare at the boys while stroking his beard. He would tell the boys smutty jokes.

During a religion class, Denham sketched a giant penis on the blackboard before turning to see the boys' reactions. He then drew a circle at the top, signifying the hole at the top. Some boys sniggered. The implicit message from Denham was that if you can't see the humour in this, you're not one of us – you aren't part of our club.

Denham could be witty, and he would cut people to pieces with his retorts. He would fawn over certain boys and make them feel special. Others were singled out and demeaned; he would bully them in front of the whole class. No one wanted to become the butt of Denham's jokes, as their classmates would start picking on them as well. And being caned by Denham was genuinely terrifying; it left bruises and welts on the boys' hands that would last for weeks. But Denham seemed to treat it as a kind of game. The punishment never fit the crime, and the boys thought Denham enjoyed it.

Denham was born in the inner-city Sydney suburb of Surry Hills during World War II. It was a rough place then, its residents living on the edge. His father returned from serving in the war, traumatised and depressed, and left Denham's mother for a much younger woman, a great scandal at the time. His parents then divorced when he was eight. Denham excelled at his studies. At the age of twenty-three he entered the priesthood against the wishes of his mother, grandmother and aunt.[14] He entered St Columba's College Seminary in Springwood and began his religious life as a deacon (assistant priest) in the Maitland-Newcastle Diocese in 1972, first at the Mayfield parish and then, after his ordination, in Singleton a year later. Two years after that, he arrived at St Pius X where he was head of discipline and taught history, religion and German.

For the boys he admired, like Steven, he was the most attentive and encouraging teacher at the school. He sometimes took these favoured students on excursions to places like Luna Park, a funfair with rides on Sydney Harbour. On one occasion another religion teacher, Father Philip Wilson, accompanied them; one boy said Denham's breath often smelt of alcohol.

Denham was privy to private information about the struggles families were going through. He would often seek out boys he knew were having a hard time at home, befriending them and regularly speaking to them about their issues. Some of them came to see this priest as a counsellor and friend, as well as another tier of authority under their parents. Soon Denham would regularly attend the boy's home for dinner, becoming an important fixture in the child's life. A second father figure to some.

Unlike many of Denham's favoured boys, Steven had a strong and loving family life. His devout parents were proud of their son, and they felt honoured that the priests at his school paid him special attention because he showed promise. From an early age Steven had loved the classics, Latin and Ancient Greek, and Denham would have long conversations with the boy to help him to deepen his knowledge. Soon, Steven's best subject at school was Latin. His parents didn't see that Denham could be attentive and helpful towards boys in a way that seemed overly accommodating – as if he expected something from them in return.

* * *

In Steven's third year of high school, a major event happened in the lives of all Catholics in the Maitland-Newcastle Diocese. A new bishop-in-waiting, known as the coadjutor bishop, was appointed to the diocese in 1975, following the death of the incumbent, John Toohey. On 2 June 1976, Leo Morris Clarke became bishop. To mark the occasion, hundreds of Catholic school students lined the highway to greet him, waving and cheering. Their parents were dressed in their best clothes. When he alighted from his car, he was mobbed by groups of primary school-aged students who excitedly tried to shake his hand. It was as if royalty had arrived and his loyal subjects were there to greet him.

Born in 1923, Clarke had attended the Corpus Christi Seminary in Werribee, Victoria,[15] in 1942, and then studied under then archbishop of Melbourne, Daniel Mannix. In 1974, he'd become the vicar-general, or second-in-command, under the new archbishop, Frank Little, at a time when clerical child sex offending was rife in Ballarat and other Victorian parishes.

Clarke would now be in charge of all the Catholic schools in the diocese. He was advised by his Director of Catholic Education, whom he appointed and could fire. Every local Catholic child would meet the bishop either at their confirmation ceremony,[16] which typically occurred in Year Four, or at special masses or assemblies. Clarke was often at St Pius X for such occasions.

In 1978, Father Wilson was made the diocesan director of religious education. In this role, he was in charge of the religious programs in all the diocesan schools, working alongside the Director of Catholic Education. He lived in the priests' quarters at St Pius X for nine months between 1978 and '79. A boy from humble beginnings at Cessnock, near Maitland, Father Wilson was an assistant parish priest at East Maitland in 1976, the same year Clarke was appointed.

Clarke and Wilson were Denham's mentors and superiors.

* * *

Denham often travelled to his favourite places in the diocese. He would visit fellow priests in remote parishes – in particular, those to the north in Wingham and Taree, rich dairy-farming communities. He wasn't alone in this: many city-dwellers liked to escape from the daily grind on holidays up north, especially in the heavily wooded hills where marijuana plantations were plentiful, and whatever you got up to could be shielded from prying eyes.

One of Denham's closest friends at the Wingham parish was Father Ron Picken. Picken sometimes felt lonely and isolated. Denham would come up for the weekend, about a two-hour drive from Newcastle, with a couple of students in tow. Picken would have local boys stay over as well.

Picken's family had a holiday house on the coast at Fingal Bay, about one hour north of Newcastle. One holiday, Picken brought four local boys to the bay and let them do as they pleased; they even hitchhiked around the place on their own. Their parents never knew.

Steven would occasionally go to another property in the local area around Taree with Denham and another priest. Other teenage boys would visit there as well. At the time, Steven told his family scant details about these visits, only that there was a big swimming pool, and it was fun. His sister, Libby, was quite jealous, and his parents were happy for him to go – after all, he'd been invited by a senior teacher and a priest to boot. His mentor at school. His academic adviser who thought he was a brilliant student with a great career ahead of him.

Father Denham knew another priest in Taree during this time – Father Barry Tunks – who was the parish priest in Taree from 1973 to 1982. They were in the seminary together.

When Steven graduated from St Pius X, Joan and Brian Alward wrote to the principal, Father Tom Brennan, thanking him for Steven's schooling. On 7 November 1978, he replied, 'It has been a pleasure and a privilege to share Steven with you. He has been a fine student and deserves success. I have always found him pleasant, friendly and courteous – a real credit to his family.'

CHAPTER 4

The Aftermath

FOR ANDREW NASH'S FAMILY, LIFE WENT ON. HIS DEATH WAS never far from their thoughts, like a dark shadow hanging over them.

Audrey spent most days at the offices next to the Sacred Heart Cathedral in Hamilton. She was always involved in school fundraising events, and she helped with working bees and organised barbecues and picnics. She was also the treasurer of the Saint Vincent de Paul Society, and every Sunday collected donations left by the congregation in a special box at the cathedral.

In 1976, in recognition of her tireless work for the Church, Audrey was offered a job looking after one of the senior priests, Monsignor Patrick Cotter.[1] Cotter had presided over Audrey's marriage to Bert; he was tall and imperious with a thick Irish accent. Born in 1914 in County Cork, Ireland, he was ordained a priest at the age of twenty-three and then came to the Maitland-Newcastle Diocese in 1938. It was thought he came from a rich family in Ireland and he did nothing to dispel this rumour. He had bought a private house with another Irish priest in Wangi Wangi, on Lake Macquarie, using his family's money – even though owning property went against his religious vows of poverty, chastity and obedience.

At first, Audrey worked for him one day a week so the regular housekeeper could have a day off. Each week Audrey accepted a payment of $10 in cash, though the average female salary was twice that amount. It was off the books. She prepared meals, cleaned, and ironed the altar cloth and vestment garments for the resident priests.

Not long after Audrey started working for Cotter, another priest arrived to be his assistant priest. Father Vince Ryan had grown up in the Hunter, but had spent several years in Rome and had been ordained there. Now he had all the trappings of a European intellectual, with a knowledge of wines and an appreciation of art and classical music. He developed a close friendship with Audrey.

One of Ryan's tasks was to supervise Friday Night Clubs, a youth initiative for boys from the local primary school, and he grew close with many of the boys who attended. Girls weren't invited.

Audrey noticed that he'd begun to take altar boys up to his bedroom in the presbytery. Two or three boys would go up at a time. She thought it was rather cheeky of them to be in the presbytery at all, and she noticed that they would refer to the priest as 'Vince', which didn't seem appropriate to her.

After the children had been upstairs with Ryan for some time, Cotter would ask Audrey to go up and knock on the bedroom door to tell the boys to go home. One day the door opened slightly when she knocked, and she saw one of the boys without a shirt on.

It was the first time Audrey witnessed this type of behaviour from a cleric. She thought it was odd, but then comforted herself that Ryan was a priest and there must be nothing to worry about.

* * *

Steven graduated from St Pius X in 1978 with excellent marks in English. December and January meant long days at the beach, catching up with friends at the pub, and waiting for university and job offers.

The editor of the *Newcastle Herald* was so impressed with Steven's marks that he offered him a cadetship. This was a big honour for Steven, as everyone in his circle read the *Herald*; it was the heart and soul of the Hunter, reflecting the region's working-class mining heritage. The masthead, when Steven started there, carried a sketch of a colliery pit-top.

It was all very exciting for the new cadet, with journalism on the cusp of the digital age. On one side of the newsroom were brand-new computers, or visual display units. On the other, twenty to thirty reporters were clacking away on typewriters, and the sound resonated around the room along with the flicking of their cigarette lighters.

At the end of Steven's first year at the *Herald*, December 1979, he met a fellow reporter, Mark Wakely, a former student of Marist Brothers Hamilton. About five years older than Steven, Mark had finished an honours degree in English literature at the University of Newcastle. Amid the hum of the typewriters and cigarette lighters, their relationship blossomed.

Mark and Steven had each had romances with women before they met, but after their first encounter they knew theirs would be a long relationship. Mark loved Steven's gentle countenance and his kindness, and he fell deeply in love. Steven felt the same way.

Steven's epiphany about his sexuality had an enormous impact on him.

The first person he told was his old schoolteacher and priest, Father Denham. Steven felt that the liberal-thinking priest, who was still teaching at St Pius X, was someone he could trust with this information. Denham had shown great interest in Steven during his high school years, and they were still close friends. Steven told Mark that he felt that coming out to the priest would be easy; he would be accepted and there would be no ridicule. While growing up in Newcastle, Steven had turned to Denham for intellectual stimulation, as they had a mutual love of the classics. Now he turned to him for support of a much more emotional kind.

But when Steven told his mother about his relationship with Mark, she was horrified and asked her youngest son to move out of the family home. She apologised soon after, however, and welcomed Mark into their clan. Still, the news had been a shock to her. Meanwhile, Denham had remained his ally through all of it.

Steven's life was in good shape. He had a boyfriend, a good job, money and plans to travel overseas. He was promoted to become the youngest ever state political reporter for the *Newcastle Herald* and got to spend time in Sydney where he could indulge his tastes in art, fashion and music. His by-line was on all the important stories in the *Herald*, while his flair for writing and editorial nous were getting noticed. The future looked very bright indeed.

* * *

After Glen moved to Winston Hills in early 1980, he began his training as a Marist Brother along with his diploma at the Catholic Teachers College in Castle Hill, about seven kilometres away.[2]

Glen had turned eighteen years old the previous November and most of the young men were aged between eighteen and twenty. The postulants lived on the ground floor, while most of the professed older Brothers lived on the floor above.

Glen's week consisted of several days at the college, and the rest of his time taken up with prayer, celebrations of various liturgies and visits by external speakers. Overall, the atmosphere in the house was happy, like that of any student environment but with a religious focus.

For the first two months, Glen was terribly homesick and unsettled. He missed his family and friends in Newcastle, and worried that he'd fail his studies even though he had a sound academic record from high school. At least there were a couple of familiar faces: Brother Alexis Turton,[3] Glen's former principal from 1977 to 1979, the man who had recommended he become a Marist Brother; and Michael Hill, another senior Brother. Hill was the facilitator of spiritual retreats for Year Twelve boys from Marist Brothers schools in New South Wales and had resided in Winston Hills from 1976.[4]

Another Brother in residence was Hill and Turton's close colleague Coman Sykes, one of the masterminds behind the 'better boys' recruitment strategy. Brother Coman lived on the lower floor with the new recruits and was responsible for the postulants' spiritual formation. He was always around the students, attending all meals with them and rarely having a day off. He seemed caring and dutiful while maintaining a sense of authority – he had a lot of power and could recommend a postulant be removed from the Marist Brothers. He was also able to reward students for good service.[5]

By the time Glen arrived in Winston Hills, 52-year-old Sykes had spent many years in senior positions at various Marist Brothers schools and institutions, and was well liked and respected in the community. In 1968, he had been promoted to the Marist Brothers Provincial Council, where he remained until 1994, and he exerted great influence over all aspects of the institution. There was even a wing of a building at Marist Brothers North Shore High School named in his honour after he was the principal there from 1964 to 1968.

Sykes was renowned for his support of Rugby League, the main football code in New South Wales. With encouragement and zeal he coached many boys in the sport, and quite a few went on to be well-paid stars. He was very close to the most famous League commentators on commercial television.

Brother Coman showed a particular interest in Glen, who became something of a 'favourite'. When the postulants were given their duties, Glen always got what he wanted, which was to work in the sacristy. He started to settle in to the rhythm of life in Winston Hills with his fellow twenty-two postulants, gradually finding his place while others weren't so lucky.

Around winter time in 1980, Glen was attending lectures in Castle Hill when he fell ill and collapsed. Later the same day, he woke to find himself in his bedroom in Winston Hills, with no idea as to how he got there. During the course of that day he fainted several more times, and eventually Sykes took him to hospital, only for him to be released shortly thereafter with no specific diagnosis.

Brother Coman Sykes suggested that Glen recuperate at a house owned by the Marist Brothers in Leura, west of Sydney in the

Blue Mountains. The two-storey house, surrounded by bushland, was often used by Brothers who needed rest and relaxation. Glen and Sykes were the only ones staying that weekend. They spent the days taking gentle walks, and the fresh mountain air seemed to help.

During one of the nights that weekend, Glen woke with a start to find Sykes on top of him, kissing him hard on the lips. Glen was frightened and didn't know what to do. He knew that Brother Coman was very senior in the Marist Brothers, a holy man who was thirty-four years older than him. Brother Coman had a lot of power over him: he could terminate his studies, bringing shame on Glen's family. In the end, Glen succumbed to the kiss.

Back at the Winston Hills house, postulants were regularly called to Brother Coman's room at nights and on weekends for guidance and direction. Soon after the Leura trip, Brother Coman summoned Glen to his room and attempted to kiss him again. Glen pulled away and tried to resist, but Coman pulled down his own trousers and exposed his erect penis to Glen, before forcing the young student to hold it and masturbate him until he ejaculated. At the same time, he ran his hands over Glen's body and attempted to masturbate him.

This pattern of behaviour became an almost daily occurrence, generally taking place at night. Out of fear, Glen submitted to Coman's approaches and did not report them to anyone.

Several months later, Glen suffered another health collapse and was admitted to hospital. A male nurse asked him whether he was being sexually assaulted and he said no. Glen told his friends, this time, that doctors diagnosed petit mal epilepsy.

At the end of the year, all the postulants painted buildings at the Mittagong Retreat Centre as part of their chores and service to the Marist Brothers. Brother Coman continued to assault Glen most nights while they were there. Glen was counting the days until the Christmas break, when he could go home to his parents in Newcastle. But once he was there, he didn't tell them about the abuse. By then he'd been assaulted by Brother Coman at least a hundred times.

Glen spent the summer holidays at the beach with his sisters and brother. But the days passed too quickly, and soon he returned to the Novitiate training centre.

He was becoming increasingly anxious about the treatment he had received so he asked to be moved to the Marist Brothers monastery in Auburn, a suburb in western Sydney. His wish was granted – however, he still had to attend Winston Hills for spiritual formation. Whenever the opportunity arose, Brother Coman Sykes continued to sexually assault him.

The abuse didn't stop until May 1981, when Glen decided to leave the order. The last straw came when he was propositioned by a novice while staying at another Marist Brothers house, in Mollymook on the South Coast. He'd had enough of being a target.

On his return to Sydney, Glen had three interviews with Brother Colin 'Kieran' Geaney, one of the most senior leaders of the Marist Brothers. He never told him about the abuse. But now he knew what it was like to be a victim – the never-ending feelings of shame and anger – and it would change his life forever.

CHAPTER 5

The Ties That Bind

IN 1983, STEVEN TOOK LEAVE FROM HIS JOB AT THE *NEWCASTLE Herald* and followed Mark to London, where they spent much of the year travelling and working in the UK and Europe.

In London, they found punks and misfits, music and drugs, and a vibe of anger and disruption. This place was a far cry from the Catholic-Irish culture of their home town and they loved it.

In 1984, they returned to Australia and Steven landed a job in foreign language news at SBS Radio and Television, while Mark worked at Associated Press, before they both transferred to the Australian Broadcasting Corporation. By 1987, they were working in the radio news department.

The office was up near Kings Cross, or The Cross as it was known, on William Street. This inner-city suburb was a collection of bars, strip joints, brothels and 24-hour food places. Like central London, where Mark and Steven had spent some time, it was a bit seedy and exciting; Steven had to dodge the drunks, sex workers and general carousers up the road to get into the office in the wee hours of the morning. It was dark when he arrived except for the lights of passing cars and the red glow of the massive Coke sign on top of the hill.

The radio news shift started at 4 a.m. Steven was one of the senior editors, or subs as they were known, and he'd be at his desk fixing the sometimes illegible copy. By 2 p.m. the usual suspects would walk to any number of local watering holes and stay for several hours.

It was the era of the Sydney dance party scene. A group of newsroom partygoers, including Steven and Mark, would dress up in spangly outfits and dance until early morning, meeting each other at so-called recovery bars in the city.

Steven was sometimes the only youngish guy in a team of cranky curmudgeons. He dressed impeccably at work, and was calm and serious most of the time until he let his guard down and was very funny. His extremely irreverent humour was often delivered in a deadpan sarcastic voice. He worked hard, was a great writer and had a lot of pride in his work. Editorial judgement was hardwired in him; he had an innate news sense that was usually right.

Steven and Mark were a dapper pair. They were living in Surry Hills, another inner suburb, which was once very poor but had developed into a gay ghetto because of its proximity to the hub of Oxford Street. The couple enjoyed regular gatherings on the footpath outside the Albury Hotel on warm Sunday evenings. Inside there were drag shows in Polly's Bar, named after a drag queen who ran the place.

It was during his time living in Surry Hills that Steven reconnected with his former teacher and mentor Father Denham, when the priest moved to the suburb. Until then they'd kept in touch periodically through family and student connections.

Back in 1980, Denham had been transferred out of St Pius X and gone to the Charlestown parish, about a twenty-minute drive from Newcastle. A year later, he was moved again, this time to the regional town of Taree, a couple of hours drive north, where he'd stayed until 1986. The former deputy principal of St Pius X Father Helferty had followed Denham to the outlying parish in 1982, and a priest named Father Jimmy Hughes had joined them there for a time.

Taree was mainly a farming community, with a smattering of hippies in the mountains behind the town, and tin holiday shacks in the bush.

In Taree, Denham joined Father Barry Tunks, whom Denham already knew from the seminary. As soon as he arrived, Denham ruffled a few feathers especially when he developed a close relationship with the eighteen-year-old son of a prominent business owner. Townspeople complained directly to Bishop Leo Clarke, claiming Denham was 'parading' his boyfriend around town against the teachings of the Church. Some locals claimed Denham had regular visitors to the presbytery at night. Father James Hughes, who was staying at the presbytery, let it be known to several parishioners that he'd received a phone call at two o'clock in the morning from a young man looking for Denham; apparently Father Hughes had told the person at the end of the phone, 'If you come anywhere near here, I'll kick you in the balls.'

Denham's activities were presenting a problem for the Church. There were reports he'd been giving the altar boys the altar wine and some had become drunk. So, in 1986, he was moved again and appointed chaplain at Waverley College, a prestigious Christian Brothers boys' school in eastern Sydney. The male Irish teaching order was founded in the nineteenth century to provide education to poor children and they founded many schools and orphanages across Australia, several were in Ballarat in Victoria. In the Waverley College *Year Book* of 1986, Denham wrote about his contact with 1300 students and how the 'priest-chaplain role is one of friendship building and faith-salesmanship'. He wrote, 'Friendship building implies contact with students on this level. It is a natural development once trust is established and offers a heavy responsibility to those involved.'[1]

Father Denham chose to live in Surry Hills, not far from Steven and Mark's place.

Steven and Denham would sometimes go down the road to a local pub, where they might meet up with another former student, this one from Waverley College. Denham taught religion and history at the school, and this student, who was in his late teens, enjoyed the priest's intellect and his encouragement just as Steven had back at St Pius X.

In fact, Denham had a circle of ex-students who looked up to him. He taught them about classical music and told them to read the *New York Review of Books*. Many of these keen-minded young men were from working-class backgrounds, and Denham had introduced them to a wider world of books and music and history.

Mark, however, didn't like Denham. He found the priest's presence unsettling and perplexing. And if Denham heard Mark's voice at the end of the phone line, he wouldn't acknowledge him; instead he'd gruffly ask for Steven in a curt, proprietorial manner, as if he had a special relationship with Steven, one from which Mark was excluded.

Mark sensed there was something unsavoury about Denham, but he wasn't sure why or what it could be.

* * *

Glen remained a devout Catholic. He'd completed his teaching studies in Castle Hill in 1982, then taught for three years at Our Lady of Fatima Catholic Primary School in Caringbah, a suburb in southern Sydney. As part of his job he had access to the latest teaching methods and ideas about education, including new policies on child protection and wellbeing. But while the work was satisfying, he was keen to challenge himself further, and to go to places where he was really needed. Ever since he was in high school, he'd wanted to work in the developing world as a nurse, teacher or missionary. By the late 1980s, he finally got his chance when he was appointed principal of Our Lady of the Sacred Heart Primary School in Kavieng, on the remote Papua New Guinean island of New Ireland, or Latangai. It was a place of immense beauty, featuring high mountains that rose up from the coast with clouds at their peaks, and never-ending coastlines with white and black sand beaches.

After a short stint at the school, Glen applied to teach at the Saint Peter Chanel Minor Seminary in Kokopo, in the Province of East New Britain, about thirty kilometres south of the capital, Rabaul. It was run by the Missionaries of the Sacred Heart, who'd been operating in PNG since the nineteenth century, and its purpose was to help older boys and young men, most from traditional villages, finish their schooling to Year Twelve so they could reach the educational standard required for them to study at the major seminary in Port Moresby.

Glen taught the students English and history, and was in charge of first aid. Along with a nun, he directed the annual passion play – a dramatic re-enactment of the Passion of Christ – for the Year Eleven students. Glen wasn't sporty but loved playing basketball with the other seminarians, some of whom sensed he was a bit fragile at times but also a committed and dedicated teacher.

Every Saturday night, students and priests would gather at the shrine of the Blessed Virgin and say a decade of the rosary. Glen was always there – in fact, he took part in as many Catholic rituals as he could. His bedroom was adorned with religious paraphernalia such as rosary beads and pictures of saints. Later, a fellow teacher who was also a psychologist wondered if Glen was trying to purify himself – from what, he didn't know.

In 1988, about eighteen months into his placement, Glen developed the worst type of malaria, the cerebral kind. It can cause the brain to swell, leading to seizures. For many days and nights, Glen felt as if his blood was boiling; he was incandescent with heat, the sweat pouring off his body. At first he was treated at the nearby Vunapope Hospital, which was also run by the Sacred Heart missionaries, but his health deteriorated. At night, as fevers racked his body, he told one of his closest friends that he dreamed of being crucified.

Glen became so sick he was evacuated in early May to Port Moresby and then on to Australia. He nearly died. Reluctantly, he resigned from his PNG teaching position.

His time away had sparked a deep interest in returning to a religious vocation. On one occasion in Kavieng, the villagers had sent a delegation to the local bishop, asking him to send Glen away to study for the priesthood. Many years later, Glen wrote about this time when he was applying for more missionary work in India; he said that while he was flattered by the locals' quest to make him a priest, he'd decided not to follow that path because he 'ran away from God on this occasion'.[2]

Glen returned to his family in Newcastle where he received more treatment for his malaria. Once he was back on his feet, he took up a position as a teacher at St Therese's Catholic Primary School in the Newcastle suburb of New Lambton. Later, he would also be engaged in a teaching role at St Brigid's Catholic Primary School in Branxton, a small town an hour north-west of Newcastle.

Bishop Clarke would regularly visit both schools for confirmation ceremonies, and he would spend those days talking to parishioners and teachers. After one such visit, Glen wrote, 'At the supper after the Confirmation, the bishop approached me and said that during the course of the day, many teachers, parents and parishioners had spoken of me in relation to the priesthood. He then asked me directly, "Glen have you ever thought of becoming a priest?"'[3]

After six years of teaching, at the age of twenty-seven, Glen decided to follow this advice. Many years later, he wrote, 'Christ commenced his whisper – his call to priesthood. After resisting for just over two years, after three profound "calling" experiences, I [did] surrender and paid a visit to the … Bishop Leo Clarke DD, Bishop of Maitland who "had been waiting for me to visit".[4]

* * *

Glen spent 1989 at the diocesan house of formation in Maitland. This was a year of spiritual study, teaching and contemplation before he entered St Patrick's College Seminary in Manly, Sydney. During this time, he met with the local community and the priests who served in the cathedral and surrounding parishes. It was an opportunity for him to discuss deep issues of theology and spirituality with the senior priests, and it also gave him insight into what being a parish priest was like. He came into closer contact with several priests whom he'd previously met as a high school student and then as a teacher, including Bishop Clarke and Father

Philip Wilson, who had played an important role managing all the religious education for the diocesan Catholic schools. Glen met other senior priests, including Father James Fletcher.

Clarke lived in the Bishop's House next to the Pro-Cathedral, a sandstone church built in 1846, with pinnacles and battlements, typical of churches built in colonial times. It became the main cathedral of the Maitland-Newcastle Diocese in 1866. It was the seat of power until the bishop moved to Hamilton in Newcastle in 1995. At this time, Clarke lived there, and at other times, Wilson and Fletcher lived there too, sometimes simultaneously. The three men were well known in the diocese for being thick as thieves. Both Fletcher and Wilson had been in senior posts since 1978, working very closely with Clarke.[5]

Wilson, later Monsignor Wilson, was Clarke's loyal deputy throughout his time as bishop. In 1987, Wilson had been promoted from director of religious education to vicar-general: second-in-command, with the authority of the bishop whenever he was absent. Clarke would direct Wilson to deal with clerical child and adult sexual abuse cases, including taking statements from victims. In the late 1980s, Wilson provided reports to the bishop analysing the effectiveness of child protection strategies and abuse-reporting systems in the diocese. In 1990, he was sent to the United States to study canon law in Washington, DC.

* * *

During his year in Maitland, Glen met a large Catholic family, the Byrnes (not their real surname), who were very close to the Church and to Wilson and Fletcher.

There were several Byrne sons, all of whom had been or were altar boys. Normally they were assigned to a particular parish priest, such as Fletcher, but they could be called upon by other clergy when needed. The Byrne boys had all served under Fletcher at various times until they reached their middle teenage years; the younger ones would also wash his car, and sometimes Wilson's car, for a few cents. They called him 'Uncle Jim'.

One of the brothers had left school at the age of sixteen. Brendan (not his real name) had started an apprenticeship and was sometimes having a hard time at work. Glen got to know him quite well. They would meet for a coffee in the town, and Glen would offer him words of support. Glen also became close to his sister, Elizabeth (not her real name).

* * *

As part of his year of formation, Glen spent some weekends at St Patrick's College Seminary in Manly, a beachside suburb of Sydney, in preparation for the next stage of his training. St Columba's College Seminary in Springwood had closed down in 1977 due to declining numbers, so young men from the Hunter district would be sent to Manly. In 1990, Glen began his formal studies there.

The seminary was where the NSW Church moulded young men, some much younger than Glen, into obedient priests.[6] Its monastic-style community lived inside a nineteenth-century mansion with beautiful neo-Gothic architecture, in secluded grounds overlooking picturesque Manly Beach. The magnificent buildings had once been filled with hundreds of seminarians. In the early 1960s two hundred students had attended classes there,[7] but by Glen's time the number had dwindled to fewer than sixty. This gave the place a sense of loneliness, with darkened corridors and empty rows of wooden desks.

Glen, like his fellow seminarians, had a small room with a narrow bed, a tiny desk, a bookcase, a chest of drawers, a washbasin and a hard chair. Life was organised in a tight routine: morning prayers, mass, breakfast in the refectory, then classes, the rosary, and so on.

The Catholic Church was continuing to react and respond to the Second Vatican Council (known as Vatican II), which had occurred in the early 1960s. Progressive elements were vying for ascendancy in the Church. Once a month, the St Patrick's seminarians would attend a class of spiritual reflection, which involved sharing in trust exercises and making clay figures to reveal their inner lives in group counselling sessions. But sex was still never talked about publicly, only in theoretical terms in psychology and theology lectures.

In 1987, Tony Abbott wrote about the time he'd spent in St Patrick's earlier in the decade, saying he 'wouldn't wish it on his worst enemy'. He quoted a 1984 report by the then president of the seminary, which said, 'the over-introverted and celibate life of the seminary risked producing loyal and devoted members of the clerical club, at the expense of truly human development'.[8]

Glen told his brother, John, that he found his years there very difficult. While the lectures focused on the religious aspects of celibacy, the behaviour of many students was the exact opposite. Glen said he'd reported his concerns to his superiors, Father Bill Wright, who was vice-rector at the seminary, and Bishop Clarke.[9]

* * *

In 1994, during his final year at the seminary, Glen spent some of his holidays with another family from the Maitland area, the Feenans. John and Patricia Feenan and their four boys were a typical Catholic family with Irish roots. John was the business manager for the diocese. He liked a wine and a laugh, and he and his boys loved their cricket. Pat was very involved in the Church and would volunteer to cook meals for the priests. She was a little dynamo, with a wicked sense of humour and a cheeky laugh.

Every year, the Feenans spent the last two weeks of January in Nelson Bay, a beautiful coastal region north of Newcastle. They would invite some friends who often brought Glen, the trainee priest, and their afternoons would be filled with beach cricket, swimming and surfing in the sandy bays, alive with dolphins and schools of fish.

The Feenans would rib Glen about a tattoo on his foot, and he would laugh and enjoy this family's jokes and stories. It was an idyllic time, and there were no warnings that dark clouds would soon gather over Glen's life.

* * *

By 1995, the Vatican decided to close St Patrick's College Seminary in Manly and move it to Strathfield, in the inner west of Sydney. But Glen was no longer there.

Years later, he wrote about his experiences as a seminarian: 'I found my years in the seminary most challenging, as there appeared almost immediately a chasm between my love of the Church and her teachings and the seminary "formation". While my vocation remained strong, this chasm remained throughout my 5 years at Manly until finally, the bishop Clarke judged it to be unworthy to prepare his students for priesthood and I was sent overseas to complete my studies. In Florence (learning Italian), Israel (walking in the steps of Jesus) and in Rome (completing my thesis) my love of Christ and the desire to serve His Church as a priest strengthened – in fact, it flourished.'[10]

This year of travel and study in Europe was magical for Glen. In Munich, he found a chalice he dearly wanted to buy. A chalice is a wine goblet, often plated in gold or brass, used in the Liturgy of the Eucharist; from the chalice, the priest drinks wine that in Catholic teachings becomes the blood of Jesus Christ. Glen called home to his mum, Louise, and told her he wanted this to be the chalice he used on the altar once he was ordained. Louise transferred the equivalent of A$1500 to Glen, and he went on to use this chalice during his very first mass as a priest and for many masses after that.

In Rome and the Vatican, Glen enjoyed the art, the history and the grandeur of the churches. He took photos of St Peter's Basilica, one of the holiest places in the Vatican, which sat atop a maze of catacombs that included the tomb of St Peter, the head disciple of Jesus Christ. Glen felt very at home here; he thought of himself as a disciple in one of the holiest places on earth.

After Rome, Glen travelled on to Jerusalem, where he encountered difficulties at border crossings, receiving angry tirades from young Israeli soldiers. His parents later described him as never being afraid to face any danger head on. His faith was strong.

At the end of 1995, Glen was awarded the Church qualification of a Bachelor of Sacred Theology. A year would pass before his ordination as a priest in the Maitland–Newcastle Diocese. He thought his life path was set in stone: he would devote all his being to his beloved Church, his God and his parishioners. But nothing was what it seemed.

CHAPTER 6

'The De-sexto Business'

– Monsignor Patrick Cotter

IN 1992, NEARLY TWENTY YEARS AFTER ANDREW'S DEATH, THE Nashes had something special to celebrate: Carmel had met the love of her life and returned to Newcastle to get married. She asked her mother's good friend Father Vince Ryan to officiate at the service.

The wedding went off without a hitch. Audrey and Bert, Geoffrey, Patricia and Bernadette enjoyed the party and were overjoyed for Carmel, but there was always an empty space.

Afterwards, Audrey and Carmel were perplexed and upset when Ryan suddenly disappeared. He'd told them he would come to the reception – to Catholics, it was important for the priest to be there.

The following week, Audrey was still fretting about Ryan's no-show. What could have dragged him away? She decided to write him a letter.

In his reply, he explained that he'd been looking after a boy from one of his former parishes who had been rushed to hospital after a terrible car accident. Ryan said this sixteen-year-old was a 'friend' of his. He told Audrey the boy didn't have a father, only a mother and two sisters, and that he felt responsible for the young man.

Ryan didn't tell Audrey all the distressing details of what had happened that night. The hospital staff had found Ryan in the boy's hospital bed, crying uncontrollably. They couldn't move him. He lay next to the boy, trying to hug and comfort him, even while the staff were trying to administer treatments. Eventually, the Catholic chaplain at the hospital was called to remove Ryan from the boy's bed. None of the doctors or nurses reported the strange behaviour to the police or child protection services – after all, Ryan was a priest.

The boy had taken Ryan's car for a long drive and, on a quiet stretch of road, something had happened. The priest's car had smashed into a tree, leaving the boy in a coma, and the car a mangled wreck on the side of the road.

* * *

In 1992, a major problem reared its head for Bishop Clarke: a paedophile priest from the Maitland-Newcastle Diocese was charged in Western Australia.

Over the years, Bishops Gleeson, Toohey and Clarke had all dealt with this offending priest, moving him from parish to parish. He was a prolific offender with a penchant for girls as young as five, although he had also abused some boys. There were hundreds of victims.

His name was Father Denis McAlinden. By the early 1950s, there had been complaints he was touching young girls; a few years later, the complaints had included sexual assault allegations. He had a violent temper and would sometimes punch children around the head if they upset him. In the 1960s he'd been moved between four parishes, and in 1969 the Church had transferred him to a diocese in Papua New Guinea where he'd stayed for four years. He had returned to the Maitland-Newcastle Diocese in 1973, on relief duties.

Two deputations of parents came to see the diocesan director of Catholic Education, Father Frank Coolahan, who wielded a lot of power in the diocese. Between 1974 to 1990, he was in charge of fifty primary schools and close to ten high schools. Although he was answerable to the bishop, Coolahan had the ultimate responsibility for thousands of students and controlled the movement of priests, Brothers and lay teachers; in those days, teachers didn't apply for a job and then get it – they were told where to go.

Coolahan told Monsignor Patrick Cotter, who was vicar-general at the Sacred Heart Cathedral, that the first deputation had raised McAlinden's physical abuse of students while the second one raised his sexual abuse of young girls. Coolahan added that the second delegation included a parent who was a solicitor.

On 17 May 1976, Cotter wrote to Clarke: 'The de-sexto business. Fr Mac has an inclination to interfere (touching only) with young girls aged perhaps 7 to 12 or so ... I had a long session with Fr Mac ... slowly slowly he admitted some indiscretion ... a condition that has been with him for many years. He feels no such inclination towards the mature females but the little ones only.'[1] This was in the year Cotter began to employ Audrey Nash.

McAlinden served as the parish priest in the town of Merriwa, about a two-hour drive north-west of Newcastle, between 1984 and 1988. During this time, a local principal complained directly to Clarke about the priest's behaviour, which included fondling an eight-year-old girl, and Clarke deputised his secretary, Father Wilson, to deal with the complaints. Father Wilson confirmed the allegation with the girl's mother and wrote a report for Bishop Clarke. He did not report it to the police but advised the mother she could do so.

On 1 February 1988, Clarke wrote to a bishop in Papua New Guinea, looking for another diocese that would agree to take McAlinden off his hands: 'In view of the allegations, in [McAlinden's] own opinion, it would be unwise for him to continue to work in this diocese. It would be a charity for some Bishop to take him on, knowing the problems that have arisen.'

In 1988, Clarke found a temporary solution: McAlinden was bundled off to the Bunbury diocese in Western Australia. By

1992, he was the parish priest at St Bernard's in the remote WA town of Kojonup.

On 4 March 1992, he was charged with three incidents of indecent dealing with a child. The local press and the ABC covered the story in Western Australia. McAlinden managed to escape a conviction, but Clarke knew it was only a matter of time – they'd been lucky the story hadn't reached the eastern states.

In 1993, Clarke banned McAlinden from working in his diocese, but the paedophile priest still moved freely around others both in Australia and the Philippines. He had access to hundreds of primary school-aged children wherever he went, and Clarke kept paying him a stipend; he was listed as 'on leave' from the Maitland–Newcastle Diocese.

In May 1993, a story about a paedophile priest from the Ballarat Diocese in Victoria was covered by every media outlet in Australia and many across the world. It was one of the first of these cases that shocked Australia. Father Gerald Ridsdale was summoned to the Melbourne Magistrates' Court charged with 30 incidents of indecent assault involving nine boys aged between twelve and sixteen. He pleaded guilty. Channel Nine's cameras caught him walking to the court with his support person – an auxiliary bishop of Melbourne, George Pell.

Much of the public interest in this case had come from a small group of researchers and survivors called Broken Rites Australia. Before the internet age, Broken Rites would send out a paper newsletter about six times a year to its subscribers. It was based in Melbourne, but it represented survivors all across the country. It was made up of academics and other people with an interest in clerical abuse and it soon became a force to be reckoned with. In 1993, they set up a telephone hotline for Ridsdale's victims, which caused him to be charged with further offences.

Back in Maitland, in 1993, Brother Nestor (the principal of Marist Brothers Maitland from 1971 to 1977) was charged with three counts of indecently assaulting a boy in 1962 at the St Vincent's Boys Home in Westmead, Sydney. Nestor pleaded guilty and was given a five-year good behaviour bond. Nestor fled Australia to the US and police brought him back in 1996 to face more charges, brought by former boys at the home.

* * *

In May 1994, the NSW government announced the Wood Royal Commission (named for the commissioner Justice James Roland Wood) into allegations of corruption within the NSW Police Force. By December that year, the Royal Commission was extended to examine whether state police had protected paedophiles. Its investigators looked at the majority of institutions in society, including churches, and they found paedophilia was widespread.

The Church leadership, at archbishop and bishop level, knew about all the complaints from their parishioners that had been dealt with internally, behind closed doors. They knew the Church was at risk of exposure – there were five decades of potential child sex abuse crimes committed by clergy and religious in New South Wales, and the Royal Commission recommendations were likely to contain far-reaching law reform on the issue of this type of abuse.

Time was running out for Bishop Clarke in the Maitland-Newcastle Diocese. He signalled his intention to retire. A replacement would need to be found among the many ambitious clerics vying for the position.

Father Wilson, Clarke's longstanding adviser, wasn't chosen for the role despite his many years of service in the administration of the diocese and the fact that he had risen to the rank of vicar-general, one below the bishop.

This puzzled many people throughout the diocese.

Another cleric in the running was Monsignor Allan Hart, Clarke's then vicar-general. Glen and Steven had served as his altar boys back when he was just one of their local priests. An ambitious cleric, he was very upset when he was passed over for the position.

Instead, a relatively inexperienced priest from a Gosford parish, an hour's drive south of Newcastle, was picked out for this very prestigious position.

No one was more surprised than Father Michael Malone. He hadn't even thought he would be considered. But in November 1994, Malone received a letter from Archbishop Franco Brambilla, the Apostolic Nuncio in Canberra (the Pope's ambassador, or diplomatic representative, in Australia), appointing him the coadjutor bishop of Maitland.

Malone had a sleepless night. In the morning, while preparing for the regular morning mass, he read Psalm 42 to calm his nerves. 'Lord, send forth your light and your truth, let these be my guide.' The priest decided these words would form his motto as bishop: 'Light and Truth'.

* * *

In December 1994, Malone arrived in Newcastle dressed in a T-shirt and shorts, and driving his own removalist truck. This was a shock to some locals, who were used to the more aloof and formal manner of Clarke, while many others welcomed the modern, approachable style of the new bishop. He'd come from a working-class family in Gosford, where he'd grown up by the beach without too many airs and graces.

When it came time for Bishop Leo Clarke to leave the diocese, he invited Malone into his office and motioned him to sit opposite. Clarke then slid a large pectoral cross[2] across the desk and said, 'This is yours.' He then pointed to a rather large briefcase in the corner of the office. Both men looked over at it. Malone asked if it contained any skeletons he should know about, and Clarke didn't answer. In Malone's words, the former bishop 'was out of there like a rocket'.[3] Malone intuited the briefcase contained secret files on priests.

In the preceding years, Clarke's Council of Priests, the powerful body elected by all the priests to advise the bishop, had included Father Peter Brock, Father Pat Helferty, Father Tom

Brennan, Father Allan Hart, Father Philip Wilson, Father Vince Ryan and Father David O'Hearn. They and the other consultors had become the guardians of the Church's secret processes and procedures.

One of Clarke's last acts was to try to laicise Father McAlinden (terminate his clerical status); Clarke followed canon law procedure by notifying the Vatican and requesting the Pope's permission to terminate his ministry. Clarke wrote to McAlinden about this on 19 October 1995 and said 'your good name will be protected by the confidential nature of the process'. Plans were made by Clarke and Hart to buy the paedophile a one-way ticket out of the jurisdiction, as more victims in Western Australia and New South Wales were now threatening to go to the police.

Malone entered this world as an outsider. He was a progressive thinker who didn't stand on ceremony and wasn't liked by some of the senior leadership. But he liked to be liked. He was affable and told amusing anecdotes. He had a healthy ego. However, the staff in the diocesan offices had served under Clarke for some years and remained loyal to him; they had their secrets. The priests and Brothers attached to the Maitland-Newcastle Diocese had been trained and moulded together in seminaries and novitiates. They'd spent many years in these cloistered establishments, and their relationships had continued after they were posted to parishes in the diocese. They were bonded in the brotherhood of the Church. Malone too had his favourites.

Malone's apprenticeship as coadjutor bishop lasted about nine months under Clarke, who by November 1995 had retired to the coast.

It was at this time that Glen Walsh met with Bishop Malone and told him about the sexual abuse he had suffered at the hands of Brother Coman Sykes. Under canon law, priests were not allowed to keep secrets from their bishop. Glen would be ordained a priest the following year. He'd been close to Bishop Clarke and was now developing a new relationship with his replacement.

But Malone would soon have major challenges that would focus all his attention.

There was a specific reason Clarke had retired so quickly in October 1995, one month before Malone was made bishop. Disturbing rumours had spread among the clergy and religious in the diocese that the NSW Police Force was about to charge a very senior priest with multiple child sexual assault offences.

The priest was quietly withdrawn from all parish appointments. The faithful lay parishioners were told nothing.

His name was Father Vince Ryan.

PART
TWO

CHAPTER 7

Operation Sentol

ON 16 OCTOBER 1995, THE *NEWCASTLE HERALD* BROKE THE story: an unnamed priest in the diocese had been arrested on child sexual assault charges.

Father Vince Ryan's actual arrest took place five days before at Our Lady of the Rosary Parish in Taree, on the outskirts of the diocese. He had been moved there in 1995 to avoid too much scrutiny, but this strategy had failed – his offences were too many and too horrific.

At the Taree police station on 11 October 1995, Father Vince Ryan told police he couldn't answer any questions until he had spoken to Father Brian Lucas from the archdiocese of Sydney.

Ryan, born in 1938, had been raised in Maitland. Before entering the seminary at the age of nineteen, he'd told a priest in confession that he had desires for young boys. The priest had assured him that 'if he said his prayers God would look after him'.[1]

Less than forty years later, in May 1996, after an extensive police investigation, Ryan pleaded guilty to multiple charges against seven victims: mostly primary school-aged altar boys at the time of the offences.

One month later, on 1 June 1996, Father Glen Walsh was ordained. The Sacred Heart Cathedral in Hamilton – the tall brick building that, two decades earlier, had hosted Andrew

Nash's requiem mass – was full of well-wishers, including Glen's family members. His parents were so proud of him, and all the senior priests attended with Bishop Malone as they welcomed Glen into their brotherhood.

Glen also addressed an assembly at his old school, Marist Brothers Hamilton, which was now known as St Francis Xavier's College. In the past, headmasters had granted the students a half-day off every time a priest was ordained, but now each new clergyman was welcomed back to give a speech and say mass. The school took a photo of Glen at the ceremony; standing behind him is Father Wilson, smiling with happiness – a new priest was rare in those days.

It was a bit of good news as the diocese was swallowed up in the dark stench of Ryan's offending.

In the wake of this scandal, Glen would be sent to the parish of Taree, a place reeling from the news of Ryan's offending. At this time, most people in the diocese believed Ryan was a one-off, a bad apple. That was what the Church officials told everyone.

As a victim himself, Glen hoped this was true.

* * *

Nine months earlier, senior constable Troy Grant had been sitting at his desk in the Newcastle Police Station when an intake officer told him that a young man wanted to see him.

In 1992, at the age of sixteen, this young man had been in a terrible car accident while driving Father Ryan's car. He'd spent four months recovering in hospital.

What he told Grant, on that spring day in October 1995, would be seared into the constable's memory for the rest of his life. Ryan had abused this boy between the ages of twelve and sixteen, committing more than two hundred acts of sexual assault on him. The abuse had occurred from 1989 to 1994 when Ryan was the parish priest in Cessnock, a rural town about an hour west of Newcastle. The assaults only stopped when the boy was in hospital.

Nothing could have prepared Grant for his long investigation into the first paedophile priest to be charged in the Maitland-Newcastle Diocese. Victims would come forward from all of Ryan's parishes, including Hamilton, Cessnock and Merewether.

* * *

In 1995, twenty-one years after complaints were first made about Ryan, Troy Grant was sent from Cessnock to join the Major Crime Squad North (Child Protection Team) based in Newcastle. His superior, Detective Sergeant Rhonda Mulligan, gave him an assignment in a manila folder that contained the names of two victims of Ryan. After receiving the complaint and meeting the men – who were both twenty-five years old, the same age as Grant – he set about gaining their trust and confidence. It was a hard road for all three men. The victims' statements outlined atrocities against themselves as children that they recounted as grown men to a near complete stranger.

After Grant had completed the interviews, he asked for a meeting with Mulligan and his Commander, Detective Chief Superintendent John Ure. Grant told them, 'I think this is a big brief. I'm only here for six months, I'm only a newbie – do you want to give it to a more senior investigator?' The two older officers refused and said with a little smile, 'Just yell if you need any help.'

Operation Sentol was born. Grant investigated Ryan and members of the Church hierarchy above him, including Monsignor Cotter. The senior constable had up to ten or more investigations going on at the one time, and the most daunting was Ryan's. Back then there was no internet surveillance, so investigations involved a lot of hard work on the road, knocking on doors. Grant knew he had to make sure everything was procedurally right, legally right and as thorough as possible.

The two victims had identified others in certain acts of abuse committed by Ryan, and Grant had to try to locate these men. Whenever he found one, he had to ask the most terrible question,

'Were you a victim of child sexual assault?' Often he would ask his colleagues on the force, 'How do you word that?'

Sadly, one victim had suicided.

The Church hierarchy, until then, had thought the police knew their place when it came to Church business. There was an unsaid pact that officers wouldn't pry too much into Church affairs. When similar complaints had been made to police, these matters had been handled in secret; the Church had moved the offending priest out of the jurisdiction. But now stories of clerical paedophile clusters were hitting the media, and Grant and his superiors were treating the Church hierarchy as suspects. The veil of secrecy was slowly being lifted.

Grant insisted that members of the senior hierarchy be interviewed by police, something unprecedented in the diocese. The walls were closing in.

In October 1995, Grant issued simultaneous warrants on Ryan's home and several Church properties, raiding the secret archives and gathering hundreds of documents on the case. Ryan's home yielded a bounty of material including his diary. Another great score was his registration papers, which helped to verify the statement of a victim who said Ryan had assaulted him in the back seat of his car, a brown Kingswood. There was also a list of altar boys, all victims, with a cross drawn next to each of their names. It was like a trophy of Ryan's conquests. Grant knew the scrappy bit of white paper was one of the best things an investigator could find: corroborating evidence.

In mid-October, when Ryan was arrested and charged in Taree, his friend Father Bill Burston – the priest and psychologist who had attended Audrey Nash's house the night Andrew died – was there to support him; they had studied in Rome together.

Ryan was moved from parish to parish. As a new complaint came in, he would be transferred until he was appointed to the very outer reaches of the diocese. In Taree.

From 1973 to 1975, Ryan was moved to St Joseph's Primary School in Merewether, an inner-city school in Newcastle. He taught religion and was in charge of the altar boys and committed multiple acts of masturbation, oral sex and anal rape on boys aged between the ages of ten and twelve.

After pleading guilty to all the Merewether and Cessnock offences, Father Vince Ryan was sent to Junee Correctional Centre, about nine hours drive south of Newcastle, near the Snowy Mountains.

It wouldn't be the last time Ryan would see Grant, because as the headlines hit the newspapers, more victims decided to come forward.

Notably, the next lot of cases came from the time Vince Ryan had been a priest at the Sacred Heart headquarters in Hamilton, from 1979 to 1983. Between them, these boys were abused at least 150 times between the ages of eight and ten. The priest would take pictures of the boys naked with his instamatic camera and keep the trophies in a photo album. Even after two of the boys were teenagers and the abuse stopped, Ryan would keep in touch with birthday cards, letters and visits.

One day, Ryan had decided to take some of the boys to a nudist beach in Newcastle, where one child nearly drowned and had to be rescued by a nude surfer. The parents wouldn't find out until many years later.

* * *

In 1974, the same year Pope Paul VI issued his decree known as 'The Pontifical Secret', Monsignor Patrick Cotter received a formal complaint about Ryan.

Cotter was the caretaker bishop, or vicar capitular, that year, after the bishop had died and the diocese was waiting for a replacement. At a meeting arranged by Cotter, Ryan knelt at his feet and wept as he admitted the allegations in the complaint were true.

Then another complaint came in about Ryan, this time from a parent who was a solicitor and threatened to go to the police. Cotter received four complaints in this period.

He contacted one of the diocese's resident psychologists, a nun by the name of Sister Evelyn Woodward who assessed the suitability of all priests for ministry. Upon Woodward's recommendation, Ryan would be removed from St Joseph's Primary School at Merewether and sent to La Verna Retreat House, run by the Franciscan Friars in Kew.

Woodward contacted the resident doctor, Peter Evans, who at the time was also a priest. He told her he would only do an assessment or initial diagnosis for Ryan, as Evans would be leaving the centre shortly, and there could not be any treatment at La Verna as it was not a treatment centre.[2] The nun thought nothing more of it, as the goal was to remove Ryan from the diocese as soon as possible to avoid any more disgrace. She didn't have any expertise in assessing and treating paedophilia; she later claimed she thought he would be cured.

On 16 December 1975, Monsignor Patrick Cotter wrote to the treating doctor, Dr Peter Evans:

'Father Ryan has been my assistant at St Joseph's Merewether for the past two years. The problem which now brings him under your care became known to me about one year ago. The circumstances that were such that he knew that I was aware of what happened and thinking the embarrassment he suffered from knowing – so knowing would have been more eloquent than any possible advice of mine, I decided to say nothing. Unfortunately, this was a mistake on my part, because apparently such a condition does not come right without the help of treatment. The current incident is more serious, involving altar boys and more than one.'[3]

Ryan had been deemed intellectually brilliant by the Church and had been enrolled in a doctorate of canon law in Rome. From 1962 to 1966, he had studied there with other bright trainee priests including George Pell. Now he was hurriedly sent to Melbourne, to avoid more embarrassment for the Church, to La Verna Retreat House. To update his studies, he would also attend an academic year at the National Pastoral Institute.

Woodward and Cotter abided by The Pontifical Secret issued the year before, in 1974. The investigation and allegations were to remain secret within the Church, and only the bishop of Maitland had the right to consult about this matter with the police or other civilian authorities.

Unfortunately for many children, Ryan returned after a year, receiving no treatment whatsoever and having only one assessment. Cotter had failed to stop him from being returned to ministry with altar boys, and he went on to abuse 27 more children between 1976 and 1994.

Ryan had a lovely time in 1976. He spent much of it in Melbourne, indulging himself with postgraduate courses on theology, going to the horseraces and satisfying his urbane tastes. On 6 December 1976, he returned to Sacred Heart in Hamilton. Bishop Clarke was now in charge, and Cotter informed him of why Ryan had been sent to Victoria for 'treatment'.[4]

Now, on 2 June 1996 at his holiday house in Wangi Wangi, Cotter handwrote a letter to Clarke in Maitland. 'We have had a troubled week,' Cotter began, 'with the media turning the screws on us mercilessly … I have been told the parents of the "victims" are angry with me because I did not report what was going on. Well I didn't report it because I had no firm evidence. Only one parent came to me and all he had to say was that Fr Ryan should be moved from Merewether Parish. I had no further evidence apart from rumours. Then I confronted Vince and he did admit he had a problem and that made me decide to send him for treatment.'

Cotter claimed not to have known, until he'd seen it in the newspaper that week, that Ryan had attended only one interview with Peter Evans. Cotter wrote to Clarke, 'I have been told that Dr Evans gave him the names of other psychiatrists (at least two) whom he should go to. But he did nothing about it. In that he let me down.' Cotter went on, clearly trying to justify his actions: 'I ask myself even if I had direct evidence, would I have reported to the police. Probably not. In the context and circumstances of today – yes; of twenty years ago probably no, I think I would have tried to keep it in house.' Cotter mentioned that he had discussed the matter with Monsignor Casey, who had 'agreed with what I was doing'; the matter had also come up in a meeting with a group of priests, where Cotter 'did not fully discuss it'. 'I did tell them there was a problem with Vince Ryan,' he said, 'and Casey and I had decided to send him to Melbourne for treatment. They were happy with that, and, having spoken to some of them I find they are still pleased at having heard no more about it then.'

Cotter told Clarke he was shocked by the reports of Ryan's behaviour in the local newspaper. But the complaints to Cotter from the parents and from Sister Evelyn Woodward had included startling descriptions about Ryan's sexual behaviour with the children. He wrote:

'It is a mystery how anyone with the moral and spiritual formation of a priest could act as he apparently has done. I approved your giving him an appointment when he came back from Melbourne ... But I thought he was rehabilitated having no real understanding of the depraved conduct he had engaged in, and how it could only have been done by a person very deeply flawed.'[5]

* * *

Senior constable Grant's 1995 raid on all the diocesan archives had yielded many incriminating documents, including letters between Cotter and the Vatican.

On 25 September 1975, Cotter had written to the Apostolic Nuncio in Canberra asking for a special request to be passed on to the Sacred Congregation for the Propagation of the Faith (*Sacra Congregatio Pro Gentium Evangelizatione Seu De Propaganda Fide*) in the Vatican: Cotter had wanted authorisation under canon law to set up a 'special commission ad hoc' to deal with Ryan and his offending. In response to his request, the head of the Congregation in Rome, Cardinal Angelo Rossi, wrote on 10 October 1975: 'As far as your request, made by your letter of September 25th last to H.E. Archbishop Paro, the Apostolic Pro-Nuncio is concerned, it is not judged opportune to simply permit the Maitland Senate of Priests to continue to operate. For the current affairs you mention, however (schools and education generally) you are herewith authorised to set up a special Commission "ad hoc" to deal with these matters, according to your need.' And with the stroke of a pen in Rome, Ryan had gone to Victoria, come back and been placed under Cotter's supervision in a role that gave him more access to children than ever before.

In a police statement in 1996, Cotter said that in the 1970s he'd thought Ryan was a homosexual and he'd had 'no idea about paedophilia'.[6] This contradicted testimony from Sister Woodward who said that after Cotter had asked her to deal with the situation, she'd gone to her *Diagnostic and Statistical Manual of Mental Disorders* and looked up 'paedophilia' to try to find a course of treatment for it. Father Bill Burston would later give evidence that Cotter had told him that Ryan had to be sent away because of his behaviour with young boys.[7] Ryan told police he had admitted interfering with altar boys in a conversation with Cotter in December 1975.

Cotter's police statement claimed Ryan had told him he'd been having ongoing counselling in Melbourne in 1976, and that it was a complete surprise to Cotter when he learned in 1996 that Ryan had only seen Evans once during his stay at La Verna.

Cotter lied again in this statement when he said, 'When Vince returned and was working in the bishop's office and at the Tribunal, he was living in Hamilton with me. I noticed nothing in his behaviour during that period which gave me any cause for concern. Basically, he was not with children, he was working with adults in those areas and he seemed to me to be behaving appropriately.'[8] In reality, Cotter had asked Ryan to run the Friday night youth club for altar boys. When Audrey Nash, then working as their housekeeper, had asked Ryan if her daughter Bernadette could join the club, Ryan had replied, 'There is nothing for the girls, I don't get on with girls.'[9] Cotter had asked Audrey on at least four occasions to walk upstairs to Ryan's bedroom, knock on the door, and ask the young altar boys to leave. Cotter had known Ryan was left unsupervised with children younger than twelve, in both the presbytery and during the Friday Night Clubs.[10] He lied on many occasions to protect his beloved Church and its aberrant priest.

* * *

On 27 August 1996, senior constable Grant and Detective Sergeant Mulligan travelled to Cooma Gaol, where Ryan was serving his sentence, and took him to the local police station for a formal interview. The priest, who hadn't been laicised by the diocese, was petulant and defiant – he was still a Father of the Church while being a Guest of Her Majesty. He sat in his green prison uniform and shifted uncomfortably in his seat.

The interview went on for several hours in the stifling atmosphere of a small room. Grant had just asked question number 152.

Then the emotional energy in the room shifted abruptly. All eyes were on the priest as his face contorted and his eyes started to well up. His face went very stiff, and his stare turned defiant and childlike. Soon he had descended into a tantrum, taking umbrage at minor details from previous police interviews. At the heart of his discomfort was Grant's insistence about recording every detail of the abuse. Ryan would become exasperated and say, 'I'm admitting to it, isn't that enough?' to which Grant would respond with, 'Detail is important because it goes to the proof of the offence, the seriousness of the offence, and it goes to the credibility of the evidence given by the victim and the other material that you find.'

The police officers eventually suspended the interview and gave Ryan time to sit with his solicitor. When the officers returned, Ryan threw up his hands and confessed to a further 17 victims. He claimed that 'at the time these events happened, as strange as it may seem, I didn't comprehend I was doing harm'.

'I know you can't understand,' he went on, 'but the whole thing's been lucky in the sense that I had all these months with the psychologist ... the worst day I ever had with the psychologist was the day he helped me, the day he got me to understand that I'm gonna hurt them.' He added that it was a 'burden ... to know that I hurt people whom I loved [and] since I've already hurt them, why should I now interfere with their lives. It's up to them. So I thought ... probably the best was just to let them come forward.

But this could happen the rest of me life and I couldn't put up with that. So I'd like to mention the incidents as best as I can recall them as far back as I can remember.'[11]

Grant sensed Ryan was also sick of being interviewed, and the priest must have known that more and more victims would be approaching police. Perhaps he believed he would have an easier time if he confessed to these other crimes.

Ryan told Grant that after his arrest in Taree, one of his victims had approached him and asked him not to mention his abuse at Ryan's hands to the police. In Grant's mind, this said a lot about how confused some victims were about their relationship to the priest. Victims were often boys from troubled homes or whose fathers were absent, and to them the perpetrator sometimes seemed like the most important person in their lives at the time of the abuse. It wouldn't be until many years later, sometimes a few decades – if at all – when they would come to understand what had happened and its impact on their lives.

From 1976 onwards, Father Vince Ryan had sexually abused another 27 boys. Children who could have been saved had the Church reported him to the police in 1975.

By the end of 1996, Troy Grant realised the extent of the cover-up over Father Vince Ryan.

He'd been lied to by Cotter, which was against the law. Grant had also witnessed the pain and suffering of several of Ryan's victims.

Troy Grant would keep in touch with all the victims, especially in times of despair and heartache. In the end there were 37 of them. He despised Patrick Cotter; he thought him to be the most belligerent, ignorant and condescending man he had ever met. Troy Grant held him in utter contempt.

The young senior constable decided to take on his biggest challenge yet, something unprecedented. He would try and have Monsignor Patrick Cotter charged with misprision of felony, a crime that has been on the NSW statute books since 1913. Essentially, a law that said concealment of a known crime and failing to alert police was a criminal act that could attract a jail term.

It had been used successfully before on people who had concealed information about armed hold-ups and burglaries, but never had it been used against a member of the clergy.

In 1996, Grant worked for months on his submission to the NSW Office of the Director of Public Prosecutions requesting advice on whether he could lay charges of misprision of felony against Cotter. Grant was also keen to look at the offence of attempting to pervert the course of justice.

The response from the Director of Public Prosecutions said, 'I am of the opinion that there is not sufficient evidence available which would be likely to result in a successful prosecution.'

These words would stick in Grant's heart like a bloodied arrow.

CHAPTER 8

'He did not want to cause trouble'

– Anonymous source

IN THE FIRST FEW MONTHS AFTER HIS ORDINATION IN 1996, Glen was enjoying his pastoral work and found some kindred spirits who would become lifelong friends.

Bishop Malone had assigned him the parish of Taree as his first appointment. Father Ryan had been there before Glen, so he knew the parishioners must be distressed by the scandal, and he hoped he could ease their anxiety and concerns. He'd been keeping track of it in the *Newcastle Herald*.

In the spring of that year, Glen decided to take his mother, Louise, to Floriade in Canberra's Commonwealth Park, a beautiful annual exhibition of dazzling garden displays. In 1996, it featured a carpet of pink tulips, hyacinths and daffodils, all the flowers his mother loved.

The road back to Newcastle passed by the Marist Retreat Centre in Mittagong, one of the places where Glen had been abused by Brother Coman Sykes. Glen decided to confront his former teacher in order to ask him to acknowledge and apologise for the abuse. Sadly for Glen, Sykes wasn't there, so he left the Marist Brother a note advising of his visit and asking for a response. A year would pass before he received a reply from Sykes.

* * *

By 1996, the Catholic Church's failure to protect children in its care was starting to receive widespread attention, not just in Australia but across the world as well. There were rumblings of discontent in the US state of Massachusetts and in the Republic of Ireland.

On 4 January 1996, the bishops of Ireland developed a protocol that stated all allegations of clerical sexual abuse would be referred to the police. The Vatican, under Pope John Paul II, rebuked these bishops and told them that their mandatory reporting protocol raised serious issues of a moral and canonical nature, and therefore ought to be dealt with internally by the Church under canon law and by the Vatican. The Vatican had its own judicial processes, including secret trials of clergy and religious.

The Pope's envoy to Ireland wrote the bishops a letter stating that any bishop who tried to go outside canon law 'would face the "highly embarrassing" position of being overturned on appeal in Rome'.[1]

The Vatican flexed its muscle where it could, and within the Church internationally there was still a widely held belief that The Pontifical Secret had to be obeyed.

In New South Wales, the Church was faced with growing scrutiny from the ongoing Wood Royal Commission, while the state government was under pressure to embark on significant law reform that made the definition of child sexual assault much clearer. The biggest problem for the Church was the prospect of new laws on mandatory reporting – laws that would cover all Catholic school staff along with clergy or religious who had any official connection to the schools. At this time, each parish priest was effectively in charge of the primary schools in his parish, and he was involved with the hiring and firing of school staff in conjunction with the diocesan director of Catholic Education and the bishops.

The Catholic Church would be exposed. Five decades of potential crimes committed by clergy in New South Wales had been kept in closed archives. Some of the offenders were still in parishes attached to schools. Their offending had not reached the notice of the police, but complaints against them lay gathering dust in church archives.

In 1996, Father Brian Lucas, then secretary to the archdiocese of Sydney, wrote about the safety of these archives and their vulnerability to search warrants for the Canon Law Society of Australia and New Zealand. He warned about the selective destruction of documents but suggested that in cases of great sensitivity, it would be in the best interests of the Church, not to create them in the first place.[2]

In Maitland-Newcastle, the Church didn't want a repeat of the Ryan case, during which the police had raided their archives and uncovered damaging documents of a cover-up by senior clergy. The Church was also greatly concerned by senior constable Grant's attempt to use the misprision of felony law in section 316 of the *Crimes Act*.

The Wood Royal Commission was a ticking timebomb for the Church. All the cases of priests being moved around Australia – or being sent off for treatment or to become missionaries – were just sitting in the archives, along with all the documents from bishops in every diocese that had been sent to the Apostolic Nuncio to be transmitted to the Vatican. The powerful Congregation for the Doctrine of the Faith in the Vatican was advised of every conviction and transfer of priests, and every payout the Church made to victims for their behaviour.

* * *

From November 1996, Glen became the Taree parish priest. He loved the natural beauty of the place, especially Old Bar Beach and the adjacent coastline that stretched on for miles. In the hills behind the town, verdant rainforests were rich with bird and plant life. This beauty, however, belied a very dark underbelly.

Glen became close to one of his parishioners, an elderly woman who had sent her sons to Marist Brothers schools, including in Parramatta, Sydney. A devout Catholic, she became his confidante and a source of support. They shared many beliefs and ideas, especially a love for the Virgin Mary. Their bond was unbreakable.

This woman was disgruntled about the calibre of some of the priests who had been sent to Taree. She particularly disliked Father John Denham and apprised Glen of all the scandals involving him. Some parishioners, she told Glen, had complained about Denham directly to Bishop Clarke, but he'd ignored their concerns. She was worried about her beloved Church.

At the front entrance porch of the Lady of the Rosary Catholic church in Taree was an old-fashioned plaque displaying a long list of names: priests who had served in the parish since 1958. It was like the lists of prizewinners that hang in country town bowling clubs.

Since 1958, eight of the priests listed had been the subject of complaints of child sexual abuse or cover-up allegations:

PRIESTS' BOARD[3]
1958–1959 Rev Denis McAlinden
1973–1974 Rev Lewis Fenton
1973–1982 Rev Barry Tunks
1981–1986 Rev John Denham
1982–1987 Rev Patrick Helferty
1985–1990 Rev James Hughes
1988–1990 Rev Peter Quirk
1995–1995 Rev Vincent Ryan

McAlinden had sexually assaulted kindergarten kids from St Joseph's Catholic Primary School in Taree.

From the stories he was hearing in Taree, Glen realised he might be at the centre of something dark, vast and complex. It was just a thought, an inkling. His own abuse was in the back of his mind. Could it be part of a much larger picture?

* * *

In December 1996, as the Wood Royal Commission was starting to wind up, the Church published a policy document called *Towards Healing*, which aimed to offer 'a process to make complaints known and also provides victims of abuse with a means of seeking some form of assistance or reparation from the Church to deal with the hurt suffered'.[4]

As part of the *Towards Healing* strategy, the Church needed to make a deal with the police, and the man who helped secure that deal was Father Brian Lucas, the Church's Mr Fix-It. He'd been advising the diocese during the police raids of the Ryan case, and he had been tipped off about Ryan's arrest before it happened. Lucas was also a qualified lawyer with expertise in laws relating to children.

For many years, especially in the 1980s and 1990s, Lucas was the benevolent public face of the Church in New South Wales. His jovial smile and pithy responses were part of many television reports. But behind the scenes he was a powerful negotiator with an acute intellect, who dealt with the NSW Police at commissioner level.

In the 1990s, he was also a member of the obliquely named Special Issues Resource Group, which under a Church Protocol had responsibility for investigating allegations of sexual abuse by priests.[5]

By early 1997, the NSW Church proposed a scheme to the NSW Police that could potentially compromise police investigations in relation to section 316 of the *Crimes Act*. It was known as 'blind reporting'.

The Professional Standards Office of the Catholic Church would send blind reports to the police in cases where the Church claimed the victims didn't want to go to the police themselves. The report would carry the suspect's name but not that of the victim, and its forms would have been signed by victims during their negotiations with the Church, when they were seeking compensation for their abuse, and often asking for money to support ongoing health treatments. These sessions with Church officials, hardly a level playing field, were often traumatic for the victims, many of whom were coping with mental health issues due to trauma from the abuse. Some didn't understand to what they were consenting. On one blind report sent from the Church to the police, there was a question: 'Is the victim willing to speak to the police?' The Church official wrote, 'Do not think so, said he did not want to cause trouble.'[6]

Blind reporting was a neat and tidy way for the Church leadership to control information from the victims. It also meant that each victim never found out if there were others, only if the Church official told them. And in the eyes of Church officials, they were still doing their duty by reporting the crimes to the police – they could have their cake and eat it too. From their perspective, it was an ingenious strategy to solve their problem with section 316. Eventually, hundreds of blind reports would exist in the police computers, never investigated.

As part of this strategy, Lucas and other Church officials began negotiations for a Memorandum of Understanding between the Catholic Church and the NSW Police.

* * *

The Ryan case had caused so much grief for the Church that it held an internal inquiry into his conviction. The Professional Standards Office wanted to know what lessons could be learned, given that complaints from parishioners about other priests were becoming more frequent.

In 1997, Sister Woodward, Bishop Clarke and Monsignor Cotter were interviewed for the internal inquiry. In this Church forum they happily gave lengthy answers, unlike the carefully crafted and non-committal responses they'd given to senior constable Grant the year before. At the time of her interview, Sister Woodward, the diocesan main psychologist, was on the board of the Australian Bishops Committee for Professional Standards and on the board of Encompass, the treatment facility for clergy and religious.

The internal inquiry asked Clarke whether he'd been shocked when Ryan was arrested. He answered, 'Well, not a shock, no, in the sense that about a couple of weeks before that I had a phone call from the nun who's in charge of the Josephite nuns, Sister Evelyn Woodward, she wanted to come and see me and she had had a phone call … seemingly from a mother of one of these alleged victims.'

Clarke explained that Woodward had said to him 'that she'd been down to see Father Brian Lucas in Sydney, the priest … to whom these cases were referred, and he told her to get [Ryan] to come down and see him, because Brian Lucas has a great gift of being able to interrogate some of these people and find out whether or not the allegations are true.' However, Clarke added, 'Ryan … was on holidays at the time, so before it could be arranged for him to go down to Lucas, he was arrested.'

In the end, neither Monsignor Patrick Cotter nor any of the Church hierarchy was charged with anything to do with Father Vincent Ryan.[7]

* * *

In April 1997, when Glen was still in Taree, he received a letter from Brother Coman Sykes asking him to say a mass for him and his family in the coming August. Brother Coman was very proud of his family heritage; he'd even written a book about the Sykes family history. He was very close to one of his sisters, who was a nun. Priests would often dedicate masses to people who were sick, or who were suffering.

Glen declined the request.

Sykes's refusal to apologise angered Glen. He felt cheated, as if his abuser held all the cards and was still in control.

CHAPTER 9

An Unexpected Call

OVER THE PAST DECADE, STEVEN ALWARD HAD ADVANCED quickly up the ladder at the Australian Broadcasting Corporation. He'd held senior positions in ABC News and eventually become the head of Radio National at the Sydney headquarters in the inner-city suburb of Ultimo.

Steven thought of Radio National as a national treasure. It sustained his love of the arts and literature. He came up with great ideas for programs that focused on the beauty of words and language. Literature and writing were close to his heart. At the executive producers' meetings he was in his element, laughing a lot and becoming renowned for his cheeky retorts and scathing takedowns of people and situations.

It was a normal day at the office in 1997 when Steven received a phone call from his old teacher Father Denham. After the usual pleasantries, Denham said he needed Steven to do him a favour. There had been a big misunderstanding, and the police had charged him with sexually abusing a former student. Denham said he would get off because the boy was seventeen at the time, the relationship had been consensual and they had been very much in love. According to Denham, this was an attack on a gay man and his seventeen-year-old lover. In New South Wales at the time, you could be charged with having 'homosexual sex' with a boy under the age of eighteen. He wanted Steven to write him a reference on ABC letterhead.

It all sounded legitimate to Steven, because at the time an outdated NSW law discriminated against same-sex relationships regarding the age of consent: for opposite-sex relationships it was sixteen years of age, whereas for same-sex relationships it was eighteen. There was a campaign raging by the Council for Civil Liberties and other groups to reform the law. In this context, Denham was presenting himself as a victim of homophobia.

But the call still worried Steven. He walked down the corridor to see if Lisa Sweeney was at her desk; she was one of his best friends and the talks editor of Radio National. Steven told her about the request for the reference and added that he had real concerns because of Mark's intense dislike for the man. Steven said Mark had often questioned why Denham, a much older man and former teacher, would want to remain in contact with Steven well into his adult life. Mark had even told Steven he didn't want Denham visiting them at their house in Surry Hills.

Mark just had a gut feeling about Denham. The priest was always trying to ingratiate himself into their lives, but there was also something deeper that Mark did not understand. He felt Steven was loyal to Denham because the priest had lifted him beyond his working-class roots in Newcastle. He also made Steven feel special.

In the end, Steven felt obliged to do something to help Denham, so he came up with a compromise and wrote a personal reference without the ABC letterhead. He believed he was defending gay rights.

The 'Reverend John Denham' was the chaplain at the prestigious Waverley College in Sydney from 1986 to 1994. In 1996, Denham was charged with having intercourse, as a teacher, with a male aged ten to eighteen years from Waverley College. He'd been through the trial and was acquitted of these charges.

But Denham was charged a second time. He was going through a new trial, and this time the student was from Steven's old High School, St Pius X. The boy was fourteen years old when the sexual assaults occurred. He was in Year Eight, not Year Twelve. Denham had lied to Steven to get the reference he so desperately needed. He'd told Steven the boy was seventeen and it was consensual. Steven was totally in the dark about this treachery.

Denham called another former student for a reference and told him the same story. The references before the court spoke 'glowingly of Denham in terms of his commitment and qualifications as both a teacher and a person exhibiting strong moral and religious ideals'.[1]

Denham was dismissed from Waverley College in 1994 and, in 1995, he secured an admin position at the Sydney College of Law, a postgraduate school of professional practice. This job helped him to create a veneer of respectability, as the College was a highly respected institution.

In 1997, a student who was originally from Taree walked into the admin section and saw Denham behind the counter. The student froze on the spot with fear. Denham called out to him, but he didn't reply and ran out of the room. He'd known Denham since he was seven years old, and he thought the priest was downright creepy.[2]

Denham had been appointed to the College at the same time that one of his former parishioners from Taree, Maurie Stack, became president of the Law Society of New South Wales, the parent organisation of the College. Stack was on the Law Society Executive from 1991 to 1996. He was still working as a solicitor in Taree, and his family was very close to the Catholic Church. He was a friend of John Marsden, Denham's solicitor, who had been president of the Law Society in 1992.[3]

Marsden had studied to be a priest and had friendships with some higher-ups in the Church hierarchy. He'd told one priest he liked 'rough trade', meaning young men from the wrong side of the tracks. He was accused of using the services of brothels in Sydney that supplied men with underage boy prostitutes.

In 1994, Marsden was called a paedophile in the NSW Parliament. The claims of Marsden's alleged victims were investigated by the Wood Royal Commission, which put a wire tap into the solicitor's car in an attempt to catch him with underage boys. The recording failed, and they got nothing.

Denham remained in the employ of the College of Law after he was arrested and charged with child sex offences in 1996 and 1997.[4] When Denham was charged, Marsden called Stack to discuss his client's case.

In 2019, Stack claimed to know nothing about Denham's appointment to the College of Law in 1995 or his tenure there until 2000.[5]

* * *

In 1998, Glen was moved from Taree to the Gateshead, Redhead and Windale parishes, all much closer to Newcastle. Again, he followed a priest who had been the subject of child sex abuse complaints: Father David O'Hearn.

O'Hearn's modus operandi had been to set up wrestling matches with boys between the ages of eleven and thirteen, who mainly came from one-parent families. He had victims in at least four parishes, including Windale.

O'Hearn was born in 1961 and was a close associate of Father Philip Wilson and Father Bill Burston. He was also a friend of Father James Fletcher, a priest who was particularly close with two families of Glen's acquaintance, the Feenans and the Byrnes. It was Fletcher who gave O'Hearn the reference to attend St Patrick's College Seminary in Manly.

O'Hearn's first parish was in Waratah, under the guidance of Father Tom Brennan, the former principal of St Pius X. O'Hearn was quickly transferred out of that parish after Brennan received a complaint about the sexual abuse of a child. O'Hearn committed further offences at the parishes of Muswellbrook and Cessnock (where he was the assistant priest to Father Ryan in 1990), and then from 1991 at the Windale parish.[6] He was removed from Windale in 1994. In the late 1990s, Bishop Malone ordered O'Hearn to get psychological treatment and counselling for his problems with 'authority figures'. In these sessions, O'Hearn admitted he felt 'safer' in the presence of children than adults.[7]

Glen told his brother, John, that he was beginning to feel as though he was cleaning up the mess left behind by paedophile priests. He was the one required to calm the parishioners and give them hope that these offenders were just a few bad apples.

At the time, Glen didn't know some of the details of O'Hearn's crimes. By the late 1990s, rumours were swirling around the diocese, but the whole story only came out in much later court trials. Still, Glen's suspicion about his own role as a replacement priest in traumatised parishes was growing in strength.

It was at the Windale and Gateshead parishes, in 1998, that he decided to lodge a formal internal complaint against Brother Coman Sykes. He sat at his desk and wrote a long letter to the head of the Marist Brothers for the Sydney Province, Provincial Michael Hill, whom he knew quite well from his time at the Winston Hills Novitiate. Hill had worked closely with Glen's former school principal, Turton, on the retreat teams and other matters. Hill had been on the governing body of the Marist Brothers, the Provincial Council, with Brother Coman Sykes. He and Sykes were involved in high school retreats together between 1975 and 1979.

Glen wrote the statement longhand before having it typed by a friend. It began: 'I am the Assistant Priest at St Paul's Parish, Gateshead, a suburb of Newcastle. I am 36 years old, having been born on 14 November 1961. I completed my secondary education at Marist Brothers' High School, Hamilton, at the end of 1979. I was interested in undertaking nursing studies but also attracted to joining the Marist Brothers. My parents were very supportive of my interest in joining the religious life.'

Glen then wrote about Sykes. Back in 1980, Sykes had been in charge of the Marist Brothers postulants, and he was now running the Marist Centre in Mittagong where many students, both Catholic and state, came for retreats. Glen thought about all those students still under Sykes's care; the thought made him bristle as he wrote.

He explained that early in his service in Winston Hills, he'd believed he was a favourite of Sykes. He went on to tell the whole story of his time as a postulant there, including his hospitalisations and trip with Sykes to Leura where Glen 'awakened to find Brother Coman kissing [him] hard on the lips'. Glen wrote, 'I was inexperienced sexually but because of Br Coman position in the Order, I felt bound to succumb to his advances.' Glen also wrote of how, back at the Winston Hills house, he began to be 'regularly called' to Sykes's room: 'He would kiss me and even though I physically resisted by endeavouring to pull away, Br Coman would expose himself to me and force me to hold his erect penis to the stage when ejaculation occurred. At the same time, Br Coman would run his hands over my body and would attempt to masturbate me.'

Glen added, 'These attempts were not successful as I cannot recall ever getting an erection. I submitted to these approaches from Brother Coman, and did not report them to anyone, out of fright and because of a lack of desire. This pattern of behaviour became an almost daily occurrence, generally taking place at night … Whilst I cannot be sure, I would estimate I would have been assaulted by Br Coman on at least 100 occasions.'

Glen's complaint letter was comprehensive, covering all the major events in his life until his trip to the Floriade exhibition with his mother in the spring of 1996, and his decision to confront Sykes in Mittagong. The letter reveals that Glen hadn't told his parents about the abuse 'to this day'. It ends with this stinging rebuke: 'I did not give Br Coman permission to commit any sexual assaults upon me. I submitted to these assaults because of the authority and power wielded by Br Coman over me as a very junior aspirant of the Marist Brothers.'

CHAPTER 10

The Cover-up

AFTER RECEIVING GLEN'S COMPLAINT, THE MARIST BROTHERS brought in a private investigator and former policeman, Howard Murray,[1] to do an assessment that involved interviews with Glen and Brother Coman. On 14 April 1999, Glen received a reply to his complaint from Michael Hill. Several lines provoked a visceral response in Glen.

Hill wrote that Murray's report stated: 'On the balance of probabilities, there is insufficient evidence to support the allegations made by Fr Glen Walsh and thus they are not sustained.' These words drove a stake into Glen's heart. He knew what had happened to him was wrong, regardless of him being eighteen years old – Sykes was a teacher, a superior, a man thirty-four years older, someone with power over their charges abusing that power.

According to Hill, Murray had made these recommendations:

1. That Fr Walsh be advised in writing of the outcome of this assessment.
2. That the provision of any further counselling for Fr Walsh be reviewed and professional advice be sought as to the foundation of such counselling given the result of this assessment.

3. That Fr Walsh be given the opportunity to meet with senior members of the Marist Brothers for a discussion of this assessment and its outcome.
4. That Br Coman be advised in writing of the outcome of this assessment.
5. That Br Coman be counselled as to his maintenance of professional boundaries given his current access to young people attending camps and retreats at Mittagong.

Hill concluded with: 'I have already attended to #4 and #5, and this letter obviously is a response to #1. Concerning #3 let me state once again that I am only too willing to meet with you at a mutually convenient time ... Given the outcome of this assessment, I believe it important that we do meet. In the meantime, I must suspend my formerly unconditional offer of counselling assistance.'

Glen was surely concerned about the wording of the fifth recommendation. He had been a schoolteacher and a principal, so he knew about child protection laws in civil society.

At the time, underage school students attended the Mittagong Retreat Centre at the request of Marist Brothers schools in New South Wales. Those schools and Marist centres were governed by state Ombudsman legislation, the government body with oversight over safety issues.

The NSW Ombudsman is an independent statutory authority, governed by the *Ombudsman Act 1974*, with powers to 'safeguard the community in their dealings with government and non-government agencies that fall within its jurisdiction'.[2] The Act enables the Ombudsman to keep under scrutiny the systems employed by agencies for preventing child abuse and for responding to allegations of child abuse against employees. It can investigate complaints, monitor compliance with the law and audit administrative conduct.

Following the recommendations from the Wood Royal Commission, the Ombudsman's legislation was updated on 7 May 1999, a month after Glen received Hill's response. The

Parliament enacted Part 3A of the *Ombudsman Act 1974*, which reinforced employers' responsibility for employment decisions and disciplinary investigations, subject to support and oversight from the Ombudsman.[3]

Now, Clergy and religious were considered 'employees' under the *Ombudsman Act*, and any allegation of sexual abuse against an employee was considered 'reportable conduct' by the Ombudsman: 'priests are regarded as "employees" where a priest provides a "service" to a Catholic school or other designated agency. The provision of pastoral care, the administration of the sacraments or the sacramental preparation of children are considered to be "services" to children under the Act, and Catholic Schools are regarded as a "Designated Agency" engaging in these services.'[4]

The Brothers had to be mindful of three other pieces of child protection legislation when conducting retreats for high school students: the *Commission for Children and Young People Act 1998*, the *Child Protection (Prohibited Employment) Act 1998* and the *Children and Young Persons (Care and Protection) Act 1998*. Did the Marist Brothers follow the letter of the law with regard to these acts?

But in saying that Brother Coman had 'current access to young people', Hill hadn't been honest with Glen. On 19 March 1999, a month before Hill had written to Glen, Brother Coman had been quietly removed from his position working with high school kids at the Mittagong Retreat Centre and replaced by a layperson. The Brothers couched his transfer in this way: 'The Provincial Council spoke highly of Coman's work at the Centre, but by 1999 the time had come to take a fresh look at Mittagong and it was proposed to employ another layman as manager, "though it is important to keep the spirit of the place intact".'[5]

Hill didn't tell Glen that Brother Coman had been removed, perhaps because that would be accepting there was some truth to Glen's complaint.

Hill had also failed to inform Glen that three days after Sykes had been removed from having contact with schoolchildren, the director of the centre and Sykes's very close friend, Brother Raymond 'Celestine' Foster, had suicided following the news that police were about to enter the premises and charge him with child sexual offences committed against a boy in the early 1970s.[6] Sykes had found Foster's body, and he was buried with full honours in the Brothers cemetery near the farmhouse chapel.

On 24 March 1999, just a few weeks before writing to Glen, Hill had written to his fellow Brothers to inform them of the incident. On the previous Thursday, 18 March, 'police arrived at Marist Centre Mittagong to arrest Brother Raymond concerning charges brought against him by someone who was a student in the early 1970s'. Hill claimed that neither he nor 'Ray' had any idea that this was about to occur. Foster had called him 'immediately'. 'I engaged a good solicitor without delay ... He indicated that he intended to plead guilty to the charges. I am still unaware of the details of the allegations apart from the impression that they were at the lower end of the scale of seriousness.' Hill added, 'Brother Coman [Sykes], Community Leader at Marist Centre, was aware of proceedings and he spoke with Ray several times over the weekend. At no stage did Ray indicate to anybody among the community, nor to his solicitor, nor to myself, that he was not coping as well as he appeared to be.' After discussing Foster's suicide note, Hill went on to say pragmatically, 'At this stage we have no idea what publicity, if any, this may attract, particularly in central Queensland. I have informed the bishop of Rockhampton and his CEO Director. At this stage [Foster's] family have not been informed of the above details.' Hill reflected on what the Brothers might be feeling, and how he shared in their 'devastation, anguish, deep sadness and puzzlement'. 'Our faith is sorely tested by such an action,' Hill wrote. 'Our sense of hope can be exposed as something quite fragile. Yet it is in faith, hope and love that we must support each other more than ever.'[7]

Glen, meanwhile, didn't know about the charges that would have been brought against Foster or that Sykes had been stood down. He believed that his abuser was continuing to operate as a retreat team leader, and he worried that Brother Coman might prey on students.

The anger he felt on receiving Hill's letter, at the blatant unfairness of the decision, changed Glen forever. He was no longer a priest, subservient to the Church and under the yoke of clericalism: he was a priest on a mission. He would speak the truth to Hill. He would not bow down and accept the snub graciously.

Glen stood by his claim against Sykes. On 30 April 1999, he wrote this response to Hill: 'It is with sadness that I read your letter, especially that my allegations are "not sustained". While feeling disappointed at this finding, I stand firmly by the truth, albeit fearing still the institution that provided the context for such abuse to go on undetected and still not resolved. In light of your correspondence I am of the opinion that there is no purpose in us meeting. I shall conclude the matter as best I can at this point of time.'

* * *

In 1999, Hill was a member of the National Committee for Professional Standards for the Catholic Church. Hill, a trained clinical psychologist, was also on the board of Encompass Australasia in 1997, the year before Glen had lodged his complaint.

Encompass began in 1997 and was the therapy arm of the Church that provided psychosexual 'treatment' for paedophiles and therapy for other problems as well. Before its inception, priests and religious would be sent to the US and Canada to treatment centres. Encompass is now widely discredited as an organisation that was complicit in the practice of transferring problem clergy out of view to facilities where many didn't receive appropriate treatment and very few were cured. Some returned to commit more offences. Encompass Australasia, a highly secretive operation, would quietly transition clergy and religious out of their situations with the inducement of generous compensation, often scholarships at universities across the world.

The Church held hundreds of pages of documents containing the psychosexual profiles of dozens of clergy accused of sexually abusing children and vulnerable adults. These profiles, often sent to bishops, were created as part of the Church's little-known 1997 to 2008 rehabilitation program for those it described as 'sexual boundary violators'.[8]

From 1989 to 1995, the Provincial Council had involved Hill in many sexual abuse cases because he was a psychologist.[9] The conflict of interest was patently obvious to anyone who cared to look. The Marist Brothers were a close community of Brothers, bonded through their vows and their training. Hill was close to Brother Coman; they had worked together for years.

Brother Coman had many powerful friends, especially within Rugby League. The football code was one of the biggest and wealthiest in Australia, and Sykes was part of the drive in Catholic schools to recruit League players for the game; some Marist schools were obsessed with it, especially in the west of Sydney. Brother Coman appeared in photos with the Channel Nine sports commentator Ken Sutcliffe and the much-loved Rugby League great Jack Gibson. The Voice of Rugby League, Ray 'Rabs' Warren, was a fan of Sykes, as was the former Rugby Union great Peter FitzSimons. They loved his passion for the game; he'd coached many working-class kids to achieve their dream of becoming star League players.

None of these men in the sporting fraternity knew about his dark side. Glen was taking on a David and Goliath fight, and he knew it wasn't going to be easy.

* * *

One week after Glen sent his response to Hill, on 7 May 1999, the NSW government introduced legislation updating the *Ombudsman Act*. It added Part 3(A) of the Act. Now there was no doubt that all complaints and allegations against any clergy and religious working in schools had to be reported to the Ombudsman. This included behaviour such as grooming and anything that was deemed unprofessional and a danger to students.

Before this legislation was updated, the parish priest had been in charge of the school staff in his parish. This had made it hard for staff to complain about the priest's behaviour, for fear of losing their jobs. Now the bishop in each diocese would need to forward all complaints to the executive director of the Catholic Commission for Employment Relations (CCER), and they would liaise with the Ombudsman's office.

Under the Act, there was a very important role in these processes: the Head of Agency. Whichever person at a Catholic organisation held this title – for the purposes of the Act – was required to notify the Ombudsman's office of all complaints against anyone attached to NSW schools. And here was the kicker: under the updated Act, all complaints had to be forwarded to the Ombudsman for any student under the age of eighteen.

The Head of Agency would usually be the most senior salaried officer in the organisation: for example, coordinator, director, chief executive officer or manager.[10]

Initially, the Church deemed the CCER's executive director to be Head of Agency, so the CCER relied on all the bishops, in each diocese across the state, to send in their complaints.

In 1999, all the bishops agreed to provide the CCER with support, assistance and cooperation as was necessary for the CCER to properly discharge those functions and obligations. This agreement with the CCER and Bishop Malone had been signed on 29 April 1999.

But each bishop was like a governor. He had ultimate control over his diocese apart from laicising priests, as that was done with approval from the Vatican, and following papal decrees and canon law, as that was compulsory. This meant that how each diocese kept their archives and their complaints was under the control of the bishop. In effect, the CCER could never force bishops to send in all their complaints, because the bishops acted with nearly absolute authority. The CCER couldn't force a bishop to do anything.

Meanwhile, the Church was pushing the NSW government to sign a Memorandum of Understanding including the idea of blind reporting. Letters were going back and forth between the Church lawyer Father Brian Lucas, based in the Archdiocese of Sydney, and police commissioners about the details of how the scheme would work between the two parties. One of the Church's advisers wrote to Police Minister Paul Whelan on 10 November 1999:

> Where a victim is unwilling to go to the police, then he or she must sign a written statement to that effect. The Professional Standards Office (of the Catholic Church) notifies the Child Protection Enforcement Agency (Police) of the complaint and the name of the accused but not the name of the victim ... such an agreement signed at ministerial or commissioner level will clarify procedures throughout NSW. It will also protect the Church from criticisms by courts if later a case does go to trial ... Once a workable model has been developed in NSW, it would be most helpful if you or the Commissioner were able to raise the matter at a national level, so that all other states and territories are encouraged to develop their own protocols.[11]

CHAPTER 11

The Secret Deal

BETWEEN 1997 AND 1999, THE TRIAL TO WHICH STEVEN'S reference was tendered went ahead. Denham was convicted in 2000, for the crimes committed against the boy at St Pius X but he never went to jail. For one count of indecent assault, he received a suspended sentence; for the other two counts, he received a two-year suspended sentence. There was no media coverage, and very few people knew of the outcome. Denham's solicitor, John Marsden, had done a brilliant job. Steven thought that Denham had been acquitted.

The judge remarked on Denham's lack of remorse. Justice Megan Latham said, 'There is no evidence of contrition ... from the prisoner. There is a physiological report ... it records the fact the prisoner sought counselling between 1994 and February 1995, which appears to have coincided with the period of time immediately following the disclosure of these offences to the authorities.'[1]

In 1979, Denham had attacked a Year Eight boy when the priest was his form master. He called the boy into a room and told him he would be assessing his work. He directed the boy to sit on his knee and spent the next few minutes fondling his genitals on the outside of his school shorts. Denham then told the boy that everything looked to be in order and allowed him to leave. This occurred several times, and the boy suffered considerable trauma for the rest of his life. His mother complained to the principal, Father Brennan, in late 1979 and removed her son from the school. Soon after, Denham was sent to the Charlestown parish where he offended again, although this didn't become public knowledge until a decade after his first conviction.

In 2000, Denham was stood down from his admin job at the College of Law and took up a position at the Chevalier Resource Centre library owned by the Missionaries of the Sacred Heart at their monastery in the wealthy Sydney eastern suburb of Kensington.

Denham was still a priest – he hadn't been laicised. It was almost as if nothing had happened. A great silence descended. Denham was in the clear, for now. He still kept in touch with Steven on and off, touching base with his former student as he attended to his work at the library.

For Steven, life was filled with art and music, reading and writing, and gatherings with friends. He loved language and revelled in words; he wrote stories, critiques and a book.

At work, Steven was a good listener. He was a bit of an introvert, shy at times, but treated his managers as if they were equals. He taught his peers that you didn't need to be a brash, loud personality to be a good leader. If Steven was stressed, he still projected a calm persona – even when the ABC had to cut programs or make changes to the schedule, he was calm in the face of personal abuse from some in the audience.

In early 2000, when Steven's mother became ill, he frequently travelled up to Newcastle to see her. He loved his mother and his siblings dearly, and he told a close colleague how much they meant to him. His sister, Libby, did a lot of the caring, and at times he would give her a break from looking after their mother.

Joan Alward died on 18 July 2003, after a long illness. Louise and John Walsh were at the funeral. Two years later, Steven wrote: 'My mother shaped me and taught me how to connect with others.'[2]

Glen was very close to the Alward family; he often went on their family holidays as a kid. He was also close to Steven's Aunty Mary.

When he was a young priest he would visit Aunty Mary, as she lived very close to the Sacred Heart Cathedral in Hamilton. Aunty Mary knew Audrey Nash too, they were all part of the Sacred Heart congregation. Whenever Steven and Glen came to visit her, in her small and cosy miner's cottage, she would insist on making them lunch, which was often her special bacon and corn chowder.

Glen had heard worrying stories about Denham when he was at the Taree parish several years before. However, he too was in the dark about the priest's recent conviction. The internal communication from the bishop, which went to all the priests, nuns and Brothers, hadn't mentioned it. Like some priests before Glen, the news seemed to just disappear.

* * *

The Memorandum of Understanding (MOU) between the NSW Police and the Catholic Church was taking a long time to finalise. Father Lucas had been involved from the beginning and had lobbied senior police about the virtues of the idea. Now the archbishop of Sydney, George Pell, was copied in on key correspondence, including on the final drafts of the MOU.

On 26 June 2002, a lawyer acting on behalf of the Catholic Church leadership contacted John Davoren in the Professional Standards Office of the Church and cc'd Pell. The Professional Standards Office dealt with child protection matters, and Davoren had been involved in ensuring the smooth passage of this secret deal with the NSW Police.

The lawyer wrote to Davoren: 'The draft has been provided to me by Bishop Robinson [Geoffrey] and I understand that it has not yet been finalised.'

Attached was the final draft: *Memorandum of Understanding on cooperation between the Catholic Church and the New South Wales Police Service.*

This draft was sent to the NSW Police legal department, where several clauses troubled the lawyers. Importantly, the Church got to decide whether a victim was willing to go to the police. The blind reports were second-hand, not direct, statements from the victims. 'Where a criminal offence is alleged and the complainant does not wish to make a report to police, the Convenor of the NSW Professional Standards Resource Group (Church) will report the name of the alleged offender to the police, but not the name of the complainant, and will provide such information concerning the alleged offence as is possible without disclosing the identity of the complainant.'[3]

Another clause was questioned by the police lawyers as to its legality: 'Where a complainant has indicated in writing to the Church that he or she does not wish to make a complaint to the police and the complainant subsequently makes a report to the Police, the Catholic Church will provide to the Police such information concerning the process and the outcomes of its investigation as is possible without breaching an obligation of confidentiality to any person.'

A police lawyer by the name of Treadwell sent this advice back to his superiors: 'I take this to mean that the Catholic Church will, if the draft MOU is settled, be selective about the information it discloses to the NSW Police Service when there is a criminal offence reported to them. They intend, it seems, to withhold any information in circumstances where it will reveal the name of the complainant and where that person has expressed a desire to remain anonymous.'[4] Treadwell's advice could not have been clearer: 'If the draft MOU is settled, there would prima facie be a conflict between the requirements of the MOU and the law in circumstances where a serious indictable offence is reported to [the Catholic Church] ...'

The scheme was illegal, in Treadwell's opinion, and the intelligence coordinator for the Sex Crimes Squad, Wayne Armstrong, made this clear in a memo to the head of the Child Protection Squad, Commander Kim McKay, on 30 July 2004: 'I believe the legal advice provided in May 2002 and August 2003 remains valid. Regardless of the attitude of this Command to the objectives of the MOU, the advice is that the draft MOU, if signed, "would be void on the basis of public policy".'[5]

The need to settle the MOU was again raised by the Church in 2003. Archbishop Pell was copied in on correspondence between the Church's legal advisers and its Professional Standards Resource Group. This time the Church had employed a former Labor attorney-general, David Landa, to advise them on *Towards Healing* cases and negotiations to settle the MOU with the then Labor government. The audacity of the requests from the Church suggested they had the support of powerful government insiders. They were demanding rights to withhold information from the police, and in a calculated move they simultaneously solved their section 316 'misprision of felony' problem – they were reporting everything to the police, weren't they?

The MOU was far from dead, despite the internal police legal advice saying it could be illegal. In 2003, the executive director of the Catholic Commission for Employment Relations, Michael McDonald, wrote to Commander Kim McKay seeking confirmation that the unsigned MOU with the police 'remains in place'.[6]

Within two years of this letter, new legal advice from within the NSW Police was sought, and the MOU was then deemed lawful.

Philip Wilson, by then the archbishop of Adelaide, wrote a report in 2005 titled *Bishops' Committee for Professional Standards Report*. At a national conference he advised the bishops that the previous internal police legal advice, 'indicated that the MOU would not be possible as it could involve the crime of misprision of felony. Later advice has provided an alternative opinion that such an MOU may be possible. Following the meeting (between the Police and David Landa) the police legal department is drafting an initial document for consultation. The original plan remains that when a document is finally approved in NSW it will be used as a basis for seeking a similar Memorandum of Understanding in other States.'[7]

Although Victoria Police was lobbied, they refused to enter into a similar MOU with the Catholic Church – in New South Wales, by contrast, they went one step further.

To make sure they had ironed out any issues with section 316, the Church leaders devised another brilliant strategy by appointing a serving senior police officer to the Professional Standards Resource Group, an internal Church committee. It held regular meetings where members discussed complaints and named potential perpetrators, and the police officer would give the Church advice on what to do about these issues. There was one important condition of being part of this committee: everyone, including the police officer, had to shred the notes from the meetings. It was a condition stipulated by Father Lucas that the officer would not retain any of the notes given to her as part of that role. The Church, in its view, was fulfilling all the legal requirements under the *Crimes Act*, all the while withholding information that might be required for a successful police investigation.

Lucas would interview more than thirty paedophile priests and not report any of them to the police. In the witness stand, he would testify that he had never kept notes of the conversations because of the offender's right to silence. He was a priest and a lawyer who managed to outwit the NSW Police Force.[8]

The Church believed the MOU was in operation from early 2000, though curiously it was never signed.[9] It was operating informally from the early 2000s until 2013.

Thousands of blind reports were sent from the Church to the police. This saved some in the hierarchy of the Church from successful prosecutions many years later.

CHAPTER 12

'This was my beloved son in whom I was well pleased'

– Pat Feenan[1]

THE REJECTION LETTER FROM THE MARIST BROTHERS UNSETTLED Glen. He had trouble resting; he was often agitated.

Glen had informed Bishop Malone about his sexual abuse and Malone had been informed about the complaint to the Marist Brothers. This was mandatory under church law. A priest must not keep anything from his bishop.

All of this hurt Glen deeply, and he was bitter and disappointed with the leadership. After all, he knew many of these senior Brothers from his high school days, such as his former principal, Alexis Turton. Glen felt he had been double-crossed.

Then, in 1999, Glen was offered a promotion to the prestigious role of chaplain at St Joseph's College in Hunters Hill, Sydney, a single-sex high school run by the Brothers. Glen Walsh said Bishop Malone was very reluctant to let him go, as he needed priests in the diocese, but in the end he allowed Glen to move to Sydney and take up the position at the school affectionately known as 'Joeys'. It would be a fresh start.

St Joseph's was one of the elite Catholic schools in Sydney where wealthy graziers and devout Catholics sent their boys. It was, and is, highly disciplined, masculine, obsessed with Rugby Union, and the incubator of business leaders and military officers. The role of the Joeys chaplain was a plum post for any priest, and Glen very much enjoyed his time there. He felt he had a lot to give to these boys who were searching for meaning in their lives, and it was a relief to be away from the clerical culture in Maitland and Newcastle. Years later, Glen wrote, 'The students taught me about the thirst of the young for the Lord. The boys yearned to know Christ and His Church and I was privileged to pray with them for just over two years..."[2]

This joyful period came to an end in 2002 when Glen's health started to suffer. He suffered a slight stroke, and although this didn't affect his mental capacity, he needed a break from the hectic life of teaching and coaching at Joeys. He requested Bishop Malone return him to the diocese, so he could recover.

He returned to Maitland-Newcastle in 2002, first to Singleton, on the western outskirts of the diocese, as an assistant priest. In response to his doctor's recommendations, he took on a manageable program of work as a teacher at the local Catholic college.[3]

In 2003, as Glen was recovering from his stroke, Malone moved Glen out of Singleton and appointed him as the administrator – meaning the priest in charge – of the Branxton, Greta and Lochinvar parishes, joined together as one. The towns were at the centre of the Hunter coalfields, where the Greta colliery works had employed many local men since the 1800s. There were also huge tracts of agricultural pastureland, and as a whole the area resembled rural regions in the UK and Ireland.

The administrator role was a huge task and another promotion, and Glen would be taking over from a much older priest, Father James Fletcher.

What was going on?

* * *

By the early 2000s there were more and more stories in the media about clerical sexual abuse – not just in Australia, but overseas as well. On 6 January 2002, the Spotlight investigation team at the *Boston Globe* newspaper had begun publishing hundreds of internal Church documents that revealed widespread crimes. These stories led to multiple prosecutions of at least five Catholic priests, and they would inspire hundreds of victims to come forward.

About eight months before Glen would take over from Fletcher, Daniel Feenan, a young man in Seaham, north of Newcastle, had watched a television report on a current affairs TV show, *60 Minutes*. On 2 June 2002, the show featured a story about Archbishop Pell and what he knew about Father Ridsdale, the paedophile priest who had worked in the Ballarat diocese in Victoria and been convicted of many offences against children. Immediately after watching the story, Daniel became distraught. He made several calls to his mother, Patricia, and his father, John, who were separated at the time. Daniel told his parents he had endured similar child sexual abuse by Father James Fletcher.[4] He'd made the allegation two years earlier, but this time he was determined to go to the police.

The current affairs program had featured two girls in Melbourne, the Fosters. Daniel told his mum, 'I thought I was stuffing my life up, but I am just like them.' From then on, he recognised he was a victim. To some extent this was a relief, as it helped him to accept his behaviour.

Back in 1989, thirteen-year-old Daniel had served as Fletcher's altar boy at St Patrick's church at Clarence Town. Fletcher told Daniel he needed an altar boy for a mass at Dungog, about a half an hour's drive away. Fletcher exposed his penis to Daniel on the drive there. When they arrived at St Mary's church at Dungog, there were other altar boys waiting to take part in the service. It had been a ploy to get Daniel in the car. From 1990 to 1991, the priest raped him on many occasions, and the sexual and psychological abuse continued for five years. The trauma and shame of those encounters deeply affected Daniel, and he attempted suicide in 1995.

In the hours after the *60 Minutes* program, Daniel made an anonymous phone call to Fletcher and accused him of sexually assaulting him when he was a child. Rage filling his lungs, he shouted expletives at the priest. Fletcher asked, 'Who is this?' Daniel replied, 'You used to fuck little boys!'[5] Fletcher eventually recognised his victim's voice. Daniel said that he was going to tell Bishop Malone and make a report to the police.[6]

Fletcher later told everyone he could that Daniel was after money. He spread rumours that Daniel was a big spirit drinker and a gambler.[7] He also said this to the police.

But that night, Fletcher phoned another priest, his best friend, to tell him about Daniel's call. Fletcher sounded very upset. He told his friend he didn't know who his accuser was. He lied.

* * *

Bishop Malone had first received a complaint about Father Fletcher many years before, in 1996,[8] at the same time he was dealing with the fallout over Father Ryan.

A school principal at Singleton, Patrick Roohan, had notified Malone about Fletcher's 'inappropriate behaviour with boys'. Malone had discussed the issue with Roohan, who'd told him that a previous principal – Jim Callinan, who had been made the diocesan director of Catholic Education in 1990 – had warned Roohan not to 'leave boys alone with Fletcher'. Roohan had given Malone the names of two other teachers who he claimed would know more details. But at the time, the bishop only made cursory enquiries in response to Roohan's concerns, and he didn't interview the two teachers who might have provided further insight into the matter.[9] Worse still, Malone never contacted Fletcher about this complaint. This took place one year after Daniel's suicide attempt.

One year later, in 1997, Malone received his second notification. A parishioner gave information to him suggesting Fletcher 'acted inappropriately with boys'. Bishop Malone made inquiries at the time but was unable to clarify the specific allegations or the victim. He made a file note and took no further action.[10]

Three years later, Malone received a third complaint about Fletcher on 13 December 2000. John Feenan, Daniel's dad and the diocesan business manager, had arrived at the office deflated and worried about his son. He decided to confide in his boss, Malone. John had worked for the diocese for some years under Bishop Clarke, and now he had a good working relationship with Malone.

In the past ten years, Daniel had gone from a grade A cricket player and conscientious student to a heavy drinker prone to fits of anger and mood swings. Then there had been the suicide attempt when he was nineteen.

Now, five years after his suicide attempt, Daniel had told his parents that he'd been sexually assaulted by Fletcher in the priest's lodgings.

John, as business manager, had been signing off cheques for other sexual abuse complaints. He had negotiated many of the Father Ryan settlements for the diocese, and he was a member of the management board of Catholic Church Insurance Limited, the body that paid out the money. Now his own son had disclosed to him.

Until then, Fletcher had been a very close friend of John's family and had often dined in their home. The Feenans had no idea about the 1996 complaint – they were totally in the dark about Fletcher's chequered history.

John told Malone the whole story in detail, but also raised some doubts about the veracity of the claims, because of Daniel's erratic behaviour.

Neither Malone nor his assistant vicar-general and second-in-command, trained psychological Father Burston, spoke to Daniel about his allegations, despite the fact Daniel's father worked with them full-time at the diocesan headquarters.

Malone was scared stiff about the possibility of yet another parishioner coming forward. He chose not to act on the suggestion that Fletcher was an offender, because the complaints against the man contained, he thought, very few facts – that's what he told himself, his gut feeling. He comforted himself with the idea that without more facts it would be very hard to act on these allegations.[11]

The truth was, despite any differences between Malone's and Burston's versions of events, Malone hadn't investigated the reports properly; he had only made cursory inquiries and passed on the report to the newly installed director of Catholic Education.

Malone had received three notifications about Fletcher but hadn't stood him aside or reported him to the police or the Ombudsman – and reporting such complaints to the latter had been legally mandated since May 1999, the year before.

* * *

On 4 June 2002, two days after the *60 Minutes* report that prompted Daniel's second disclosure to his parents, John Feenan informed Malone that Daniel had gone to the police and made allegations about Fletcher. John told the bishop, 'I believe that there were multiple abuses over a period of years.'[12] Daniel did not make an official statement then – that would come later.

John now knew the full story behind why Daniel had changed from a happy schoolboy to a sometime reckless alcoholic. That this victim of clerical abuse was his own son, flesh and blood, hit him hard. He'd devoted many years to the diocese and his Church, and it was an earth-shattering betrayal for this loyal foot soldier.

Immediately after the phone conversation with John, Malone jumped in his car with his then vicar-general, Father Jim Saunders, and headed off to see Fletcher in Branxton. It was normally a pleasant hour-long drive through verdant countryside and a patchwork of farms, but today the bishop and vicar-general were focused on the task ahead. Both were dreading it.

St Brigid's Church presbytery in Branxton, built in 1887, was a dark brick building with high ceilings, its architecture cold and unwelcoming. As Malone and Saunders entered, they found Fletcher waiting for them.

When Malone told him Daniel Feenan had reported an allegation of sexual abuse against him to the police, Fletcher pleaded his innocence to the two men. He denied any wrongdoing. It was an uncomfortable meeting for the three clerics, as Fletcher was shaking and jittery, obviously distressed. The priest made it clear that he did not want to stand aside.

The bishop told his priest before the police could question Fletcher or search his premises. This may have given Fletcher time to get rid of incriminating material, if any existed. When questioned about this later, Malone said he was simply following the *Towards Healing* protocol: he was obliged to advise Fletcher of the nature of the complaint and who had made it, soon after the complaint was made. However, the protocol applied only to complaints that were not being investigated by the police, and Malone knew the police were investigating Fletcher.[13]

* * *

The principal of both St Brigid's Catholic Primary School in Branxton and St Mary's Infants School in Greta was a knockabout bloke called Will Callinan. He got on well with most people, including Father Fletcher, who as the parish priest in Branxton and Greta was technically Will's boss. Will was often mistakenly linked to the Director of Catholic Education, Jim Callinan, but they were not related. The little country town schools were attached to the churches, and Will enjoyed working with the local Catholic communities. Fletcher lived in the presbytery opposite the Branxton school, so they saw each other a lot.

On 7 June 2002, Fletcher told Will that an allegation of child sexual abuse had been made against him. He looked the principal in the eye and said, 'Will, I didn't do it.' Will believed him – he liked the priest, and he hadn't had any issues with him. Because Fletcher hadn't been stood aside by the bishop, Will assumed the allegation wasn't serious.

* * *

On 20 June 2002, Detective Sergeant Peter Fox visited Malone and Saunders in Hamilton, and informed them that he was investigating Fletcher over sexual abuse matters. Fox added that the investigation would take several months and that the police wouldn't speak with Fletcher until they had finished taking Daniel Feenan's statement.

Fox looked Malone in the eye and asked him to consider standing the priest aside during the police investigation.[14] Fox also requested Fletcher be removed from parish duties and any contact with children until the investigation was concluded.[15]

Fox believed Daniel. He had no doubt that the young man was telling the truth. His tone to the clerics was firm and formal – this was a serious police request.

Malone then admitted he had told Fletcher about Daniel going to the police, and this caused Fox a great deal of concern. Why hadn't the bishop contacted police before alerting the suspect of a potential investigation? Fox had been an investigator for many years, and this flouting of procedure irked him. He told the bishop his actions might hamper his investigation.

Then Malone said to Fox, 'If I remove him it might be thought that he is guilty. Isn't he presumed innocent until proven guilty?'

Fox replied, 'Absolutely, but there is also a duty of care to the community and your parish.'[16]

In reality, Malone had interpreted canon law in his favour.[17]

John Feenan also spoke to Malone about the tip-off, saying it may have given Fletcher a chance to destroy evidence. But in the bishop's opinion, he was just following the Church's orders. Even after this barrage of criticism, he thought he would have done the same thing again had it happened again.[18]

Pat Feenan contacted Malone to ask him why he had informed Fletcher that Daniel was the one reporting him to the police. The bishop replied, 'To offer pastoral support to a fellow priest.'[19] This left Pat fuming.

But the bishop's next actions would outrage the Feenan family even more. In the months that followed the meeting with Fox, Malone did something extraordinary.

On 1 August 2002, while the police investigation was underway, instead of standing Fletcher down Malone *widened* the priest's responsibilities to include another parish, Lochinvar, in addition to Greta and Branxton. Fletcher's new parish included a primary school that had an infants' school attached to it. St Patrick's at Lochinvar.

The bishop's letter of appointment to Fletcher, dated 3 October 2002, formalised the expansion of the priest's responsibilities. It included no caveats or restrictions in connection with Fletcher's conduct near schools or children. Malone wrote, 'that the parishioners of Branxton would need to learn to "generously share you with their near neighbour"'.[20]

* * *

Towards the end of 2002, Will received a call from Fletcher. The priest sounded anxious – he said he'd found a stash of X-rated pornographic magazines and videos in the Lochinvar presbytery, and he wanted the principal to come take a look.

In the Lochinvar parish, Fletcher had replaced Father Des Harrigan. He and Fletcher were known around town to be good friends and close confidants. Now Fletcher inferred to Will that the porn belonged to Harrigan.

Will parked his car outside the Lochinvar presbytery. It was a very awkward situation, and Will thought it all seemed quite odd, as though something else was going on. However, Will still believed that Fletcher was a good priest and felt he should defer to his boss, despite the fact that Fletcher, although he hadn't yet been charged, was under investigation by the police.

Will knocked on the front door of the Lochinvar presbytery, and Fletcher ushered him in, looking around to see if anyone was watching. He took Will into the living room, where in the middle of the floor were plastic bags and a couple of small suitcases. Fletcher said to Will, 'Look what I have found!' The bags were open, and inside were magazines and videotapes with photos of nude young men, in various poses, emblazoned on the front covers.

Will was shocked. Then a thought crossed his mind. Given that Fletcher and Harrigan were close friends, why hadn't Fletcher just got rid of the material? Why had he dragged the principal into this sordid mess? It was as if the priest wanted a witness to prove that the porn wasn't his. Will thought he might be being set up – but he waved the thought away. Surely not! He liked Jim Fletcher. The man was a priest.

PART
THREE

PART
THREE

CHAPTER 13

'Father Jim isn't well at the moment and needed some time away'

– Bishop Michael Malone

PAT FEENAN WAS DEEPLY SHOCKED BY DANIEL'S DISCLOSURES. When Daniel was nineteen, Pat had found him trying to hang himself in the back shed. After he jumped, she used all her strength to hold him up to save his life. She screamed for help. One of her younger sons, only eleven at the time, heard the screams and ran in the nick of time to help his mother. That evening, as Daniel was recovering, Father Fletcher recommended the young man be sent to stay with him at the presbytery for the night. Daniel reported to police later that he went to bed in his clothes but woke up naked.[1]

After this, Daniel's behaviour spiralled out of control. He was drinking to excess, and his parents were struggling. Why had their youngest son, who had been a star cricket player and academically gifted, spiralled into this abyss?

Pat had a fierce love for and loyalty to Daniel. She was also racked with pain; she cried and cried at the thought of her boy, under the influence of alcohol, at the mercy of that priest after he had tried to suicide. Her shame and grief turned into a festering anger.

Pat was like many Catholic mothers of Irish heritage. Although slight in size, she more than made up for it in true grit. Once scorned, she was a force to be reckoned with. Nothing was going to stop her getting justice for her son.

Late in 2002, she heard from other parishioners that Fletcher was still on duty at the Branxton primary school, despite Daniel's reports to the police. She was outraged.

To get proof, she devised a cunning plan. She called up the secretary of the primary school and pretended to be a mother wanting to enrol her child. When she asked the secretary about religious education, the woman told her Fletcher was in residence and regularly spent time at the school and in the playground. Then another bit of information fell into Pat's lap: Fletcher was running a reading group for five-, six- and seven-year-old students.[2]

Pat was ropeable. She spoke to her husband, John. They made a plan to call Detective Sergeant Fox.

* * *

As a police officer with years in the force, Fox had found the bishop's defiance puzzling. Then, on 17 March 2003, Fox received a phone call from John Feenan. He was still the business manager at the diocese but now very much the enemy within.

John told him that since May 1999, the law in New South Wales stated that the Ombudsman had to be notified of any allegation against parish priests working in schools. He inferred to Fox that the bishop hadn't alerted the Catholic Head of Agency that managed Catholic schools of the complaint against Fletcher, as was required under the *Ombudsman Act*, and therefore the agency couldn't fulfil its legal duty to notify the Ombudsman.

John told Fox to notify the Ombudsman himself as a matter of urgency.

On 17 March 2003, Fox notified the Ombudsman's office of the official complaint of sexual abuse against Fletcher. Soon after, Pat alerted the Ombudsman's office that Fletcher still had access to children.

On receiving this notification, the Ombudsman's office realised it hadn't received any reports about the matter from the Head of

Agency responsible, the Catholic Commission for Employment Relations (CCER). Why hadn't they made a report as they were legally obliged to do? The Ombudsman immediately contacted the CCER's executive director, Michael McDonald, and demanded an urgent notification. They also issued an 'investigation notice'. This was seriously bad news for the CCER and the Maitland-Newcastle Diocese.

After this investigation notice was received by the CCER, Malone immediately changed his decision. The next day, on the 18th of March 2003, Malone stood Fletcher aside more than nine months after Fox had told him to do so.

That day, Will Callinan received a phone call from Malone. The bishop told the principal, 'I am just ringing to advise you that Father Jim has been stood down from his position as the parish priest. The reason I have taken this action is that I have been told that charges against Father Fletcher are imminent ... We would like to try and keep everything quiet at the moment. If anyone asks you can you just let them know that Father Jim isn't well at the moment and needed some time away.'

Malone was at the very top of the chain of command above Will. He agreed with this request.

Malone went on, 'The Ombudsman's office is also conducting an inquiry into the handling of this since June last year. The Ombudsman is not happy about the way this matter has been handled ... We have spoken about the matter when it first surfaced in a conversation through a phone call I made to you at that time. We spoke about Father continuing in his role in his capacity as parish priest within the two schools.'[3]

Will was shocked and did not respond. *Hold on*, he thought, *that conversation never occurred.* He cast his mind back to June the year before, and the months after that. He'd had a private conversation with Fletcher about his role so he could continue operating in the schools, but he had never discussed this with Malone before 19 March 2003. Will was sure of it: Fletcher had told him about the complaint, not the bishop.

The principal decided to keep a record of his conversation with Malone. On 19 March 2003, Will wrote in his diary, 'Bishop Michael rang re: Father Fletcher. Tell people he is sick. Told me he had been stood down pending charges. Ombudsman indicated he should be stood down earlier. Indicated we had a conversation about the situation then and we thought he would not be a harm to the children. I could not recall this conversation. 19/03/03.'[4]

When Glen was eventually told of these events, he felt deep sympathy for Will. Because Glen had experience as a school principal and a lay teacher, he understood the stress and anxiety the situation must be causing him. Glen also knew what it was like to be up against a powerful institution that held all the cards.

* * *

Before Glen arrived in 2003 to take over from Fletcher, two priests, who were close to Glen, contacted Bishop Malone and suggested Glen was not yet strong enough, following his stroke, to take on the administrator role. Malone dismissed the concerns but agreed that Glen could live three days a week at the Singleton presbytery and the other days in Branxton.

When he finally began the appointment, he found himself in the middle of another clerical child abuse scandal. Many years later, Glen wrote about this time in a letter to missionaries in India: 'Again my task was to take the place of a priest who had just been arrested for serial paedophilia … [and I became] involved in the case of the abovementioned priest's felonies.'[5] Glen could see there had been failures in the reporting system on every front. He had a deep respect for the rule of law – his dad had taught him that.

Glen's dealings with Fletcher in those early weeks of the crossover were far from satisfactory. On one occasion, Glen came across a stack of explicit pornography in a Lochinvar presbytery room frequented by schoolchildren for religious instruction; he walked outside and vomited. Later, a school official told police that he had also seen a stack of pornographic material when helping Fletcher move out of the Lochinvar presbytery.[6]

To make matters worse, Fletcher asked Glen to hear his confession. To Glen, who abided by the seal of the confessional, this meant that everything the priest confessed to him was out of bounds to the police. Glen was trapped in a canonical silence. Later, he told a close friend he felt as if he had been tricked into hearing this confession.

* * *

Glen soon got to know Will and the other teachers, and he heard the stories and rumours about what had gone on. Back in the day Glen had been a teacher and principal himself, so they all got along well. Will started calling him 'Walshy'.

Glen was also back in regular contact with the Feenan family – Pat and John, and their four boys – and the Byrne family (not their real surname), whom he'd got to know while training to be a priest from the late 1980s to the mid-1990s. Both families had sons who had served as altar boys, and one was Brendan Byrne (not his real name). In 1989, Glen and Brendan would sometimes meet up to have a chat. The priest admired and cared about these two families in his parish.

Back then, Fletcher was known to be a character. He was chummy with Malone, he told smutty jokes at dinner parties, and he wasn't formal or traditionally priestly at family events. During one dinner party at the presbytery, he brought out a cartoon that showed a fish biting off a man's penis, and there was some awkward giggling around the table.

As early as 1988, Fletcher had caused concern to some of the staff at the Catholic Schools Office. Not only would he tell lurid sexual jokes that were quite inappropriate, but he would use subtle threats against staff, telling them they could always transfer to another parish if they questioned his behaviour. His favourite phrase was: 'Monsignor Coolahan is a friend of mine.'[7] Coolahan was the director of Catholic Education at the time.

Daniel Feenan and Brendan Byrne had served as Fletcher's altar boys for quite a few years, and Fletcher had cultivated strong relationships with the women in their families. This was a successful psychological strategy on the priest's part. He ingratiated himself to both families, who were grateful for the extra help and guidance from a priest.

Fletcher took a keen interest in the Byrne children, and they came to think of him as a benevolent uncle. He made each child feel special, and told them to call him 'Uncle Jim'.[8]

When they went to school in Maitland, Fletcher would tell Brendan's sister, Elizabeth, that he had lollies in his pocket, and if she wanted them she'd have to put her hand in there to get them. Sometimes he asked her to kiss and cuddle him.

Fletcher bought presents for the Byrnes in order to make himself seem more important to the family. One day, two of the Byrne kids went to confession at the Maitland Pro-Cathedral, which seemed big and cold to the littlies, and they told Fletcher their sins. When the confession was finished, Brendan came running towards them, saying, 'Father Fletcher is going to buy us a television set, can you believe it?' Fletcher arrived with the second-hand TV set a week later. He also bought Brendan his confirmation clothes, and other gifts out of the family's reach.[9] The Byrnes hadn't been able to afford a TV for a long time.

Fletcher had kept in contact with the Byrnes even when he was moved to other parishes, and they visited him at Gateshead, Denman and Dungog. The whole family would go, and one time three of the brothers, including Brendan, were left to stay overnight with Fletcher when he lived at Denman.

On Tuesdays, Fletcher's day off, he would see his mother in Mayfield, a north-western suburb of Newcastle, and then he would call in for a cuppa or stay for dinner with the Byrnes. On these days he told the family he would leave at a certain time to 'follow the train to Dungog'. Every second or third weekend, he would take two sisters and Brendan to a farm in Dungog called 'Flat Tops', sometimes without their parents. Fletcher knew the owners, who were always there, and they'd have Sunday lunch and then come home.

In 1989, Fletcher and Father Philip Wilson officiated Elizabeth's wedding. Fletcher wasn't happy about sharing the moment with Wilson, who at the time was the administrator of the diocese under Bishop Clarke. Fletcher said to Elizabeth, 'I suppose you will call him "Uncle Phil" now?' She replied, 'No, you're the only one I call "uncle".'

In a very different way from Fletcher, Glen had also become close to the Byrnes, especially Elizabeth. She found him to be gentle and caring, and he always had time for her and her siblings. Even after she got married and had her own children, Glen remained a very important person in her life. This bond would endure many hardships and challenges, and propel them both into courageous acts that would light the darkness and reveal the truth.

* * *

A short time after being stood aside in March 2003, Fletcher left the Branxton parish to stay with his mother in Mayfield. He would spend his nights in the old family home while working from the Hamilton headquarters in Newcastle. Glen was left behind to mediate between those parishioners who still loved 'Father Jimmy' and those who despised him.

One day when Glen was visiting the Branxton church, he saw an ad in the parish bulletin from a group who had organised a prayer session for Fletcher. Glen contacted the group and said they could have their prayer session for the priest, but they would have to have one for the victim as well. They refused, and Glen later told Pat Feenan, 'Unfortunately, after that, the organisers went underground.'

Around this time, Pat told Glen she'd begun to receive nuisance phone calls late in the night – and one day her garage, at her home, was covered in smashed eggs. Daniel's mum was nursing a deep sense of loss and grief, and she confided in Glen about her heartache. Fletcher had groomed her so he could get to her son. He'd even made her a 'special minister', so she could be on the altar and give communion, and organised a 'commissioning ceremony' to bestow her with this title, and all their families had come to watch. Now Pat shuddered when she remembered how excited she'd been at all this attention.

* * *

On 13 May, Will Callinan was at school when he received a phone call from someone close to Fletcher, who said the priest would be charged and arrested the next day. Will thought, *Shit, is it really going to happen?!* At this point, he had hoped Fletcher was innocent. He had to run a Parents & Friends meeting that night; he didn't inform them.

Fletcher was charged on 14 May 2003. He was required to attend Maitland Police Station.

The next day, the president of the P & F confronted Will, asking him why he hadn't informed them. Will had been in shock. He still wanted to believe Fletcher was innocent.

On 17 May, the headline on the front page of the *Newcastle Herald* screamed, 'Bishop under attack, sex case anger grows.'

And then, in a move that aggravated the situation further, on 18 May 2003, Malone put out a 'pastoral letter' to all fifty-two parishes in the diocese to explain his actions:

Fr James Fletcher ... was charged with sexual assault involving a minor, following an accusation made to the Police in June 2002. In accord with normal procedures Fr Fletcher has been withdrawn from active ministry. The charges against him will now be dealt with by the criminal justice system ... There have been accusations in the media that I was negligent in not removing Fr Fletcher from his parish when the allegation was first known in June 2002. It is true that I knew of the accusation then, but at that stage it was made clear to me that it was an unsubstantiated accusation yet to be investigated by the police. I sought advice from the NSW Professional Standards Office (Towards Healing process) and others. I also consulted the Director of Catholic Schools and the local School principal at the time and informed them of the situation. Based on the advice I received and an assessment of the potential risk as per NSW Child Protection Legislation, I decided to leave Fr Fletcher in place ...[10]

Will read the letter, then let out an expletive. He had no recollection of discussions with Malone prior to March 2003, when the Ombudsman had got involved, and yet the bishop claimed Will had been consulted in June 2002. Malone's pastoral letter said Will was partly responsible for leaving Fletcher in place, with access to students, during those nine months.

Will felt anger bubble up inside him. He spoke to his wife about the allegations in Malone's letter, and they discussed whether he should speak out about the erroneous claims and risk losing his job.

Will was gutted. He immediately suspected a cover-up was going on.

* * *

In the days after Fletcher was charged, the local and state media was saturated with stories about the issue. The diocese was in shock. From Taree to Newcastle, there was great disquiet.

Glen was appalled. How many 'bad apples' were working in the diocese? He discussed the situation with Will and others in the community. Glen was particularly concerned about the principal – the pressure on him was immense and growing. The priest was also worried about how Fletcher might try to influence his supporters against Daniel Feenan.

Fletcher was a popular priest, not only with his fellow clerics but with many parishioners. Lots of them doubted his guilt.

* * *

Soon after the charges were laid, Fletcher called his old friend Elizabeth Byrne, who was now thirty-four. He started telling her about the charges, then became upset and started to cry. He was mumbling and stumbling over his words. He said, 'I just wanted to tell you that it is not true. Do your mum and dad know?'

Elizabeth replied, 'Yes.'

Fletcher asked her, 'What do you think?'

'Well,' she said, 'they're upset.'[11]

She could tell he was still crying. He said he would hang up now and call her later.

She'd known Fletcher since she was eight years old. Today, something in his voice had made her feel uneasy – she had a gut feeling he wasn't telling the truth. It was the first time she had doubted him.

She went to make a cup of tea and found herself staring out the kitchen window into her backyard. The chooks were running about, looking for worms and scraps. Her thoughts went to her brother, Brendan, and his unusual behaviour at times. Red flags popped up in her mind. When he'd turned fifteen, she had noticed a marked deterioration in his relationship with Fletcher. Dread began to settle in her stomach.

CHAPTER 14

'Look at everything
I have done for you'

– Father James Fletcher

GLEN WALSH WAS AN OUTSIDER IN THE MAITLAND-NEWCASTLE Diocese. He had entered the seminary at a much older age than most of the other priests, and he had seen quite a bit of life – his formation as a man hadn't occurred at a very young age in a seminary, cut off from civil society. Within the confines of the diocese, he had little standing. He was a nobody.

Glen was supposed to follow Church rules and only report crimes to the bishop, who then had the authority to go to the police. But the priest had nagging doubts about Malone after his poor handling of the Fletcher case. As an abuse survivor, Glen knew what these victims were going through, and he had witnessed the distress of parishioners after paedophile priests had left their trail of destruction.

He would soon find himself in an untenable situation for a priest. Would he follow his conscience or his obligations to the strict regulations of the Catholic Church?

* * *

The NSW Ombudsman investigation was now underway, and it was causing a major headache for the diocese – especially for Malone. The CCER, the diocese and the schools where Fletcher had operated were all in the Ombudsman's sights.

On 22 May 2003, Will Callinan received a call from someone representing the executive director of the CCER, Michael McDonald. The man asked him what procedures his schools had in place to report allegations to the CCER. McDonald was concerned that Will hadn't reported what he'd known about Fletcher to them, so they could notify the Ombudsman. Will told the man he'd known nothing concrete until Fletcher was stood aside by the bishop in mid-March. Fletcher had only hinted at a few things in a phone call. He knew nothing of the meeting between the police and the bishop back in June 2002. Will said the bishop had been aware of the police investigation, and he'd thought they would help to notify the Ombudsman and any relevant agencies. The CCER spokesman told Will the agency supported how he had handled the situation, and that they weren't trying to blame him.

Will's confidence in Church processes had been shattered. He would be keeping diary notes about every interaction from now on. He wrote, 'still wasn't sure what they were after or were covering up'.

On 23 May 2003, Malone called Will and asked him how he was going. Will told him he was under a lot of stress, and the bishop told the principal to contact him if he needed time off and they would work something out.

On 12 June 2003, Will was directed by the police to come to the station and make a statement. He decided to set the record straight.

Will retained his own lawyer, as he no longer trusted the Church.

On 5 December 2003, Will received a call from McDonald, who asked him what was happening with his reply to the Ombudsman. McDonald asked to speak to Will's lawyer, and Will told him he would leave that decision up to his solicitor.

. McDonald inferred they needed to 'stick together'.[1] Will informed him that he 'would be going in [his] own direction with [his] own representative'.[2]

On 8 December 2003, Will's solicitor advised him: 'It was better if they stayed away from the Church and the way they handled the matter.' His lawyer told Will that he wouldn't be calling McDonald about the matter.

Will was on his own. He was a principal of two small schools, in the middle of the countryside, and he had no one with any power on his side.

* * *

As Head of Agency, the CCER had a legal obligation under the Act to notify the Ombudsman as soon as an allegation was reported, and it hadn't done that.

The CCER relied on the honesty of the clergy to report allegations, a huge problem in its reporting system. It was an organisation made up of people who weren't clergy or religious, and it did not hold all the copies of the files on priests; they were held by bishops in secret archives.

If the CCER lost the Head of Agency status, it would be a huge embarrassment for the organisation. This state agency was telling the lay organisation that ran all Catholic schools it was under threat of losing the Head of Agency status.

This was one of the first signs to a state body that all was not well in the Maitland–Newcastle Diocese. How typical was this of other dioceses across New South Wales, which covered thousands of schoolchildren?

* * *

A month after Fletcher's arrest, Elizabeth dropped in to his mother's house in Mayfield and had a cup of tea with the priest. Fletcher's mother was there. She often talked to Fletcher in a curt and direct voice, and she only stayed for a short time. When they finally talked, Fletcher denied the allegations again. 'You can ask me any question you want. I didn't do it. I cannot tell you the name of the victim, though.'

Elizabeth asked, 'Can I tell you who I think it is?'

Fletcher replied, 'Yes.'

She said, 'Is it the boy Feenan?'

Fletcher looked at her and said, 'How do you know?'

'I knew you helped out a boy that was going to commit suicide. Mum and I thought this was a possibility?'

He then became upset and said, 'I've been looking through my diary looking for dates and what I had done. I could only see your name through it. Daniel has accused me of doing things somewhere in Newcastle near a school and near a railway station.'[3]

Elizabeth was trying to figure out which school it might have been. She felt as though he was going to ask her a favour, but at that point she didn't know what it could be. Only much later did she pick up on his double meaning: he was trying to manipulate her into backing his version of events. It was as if he was saying, *Look at everything I have done for you, look how many times you are mentioned in my diary.*

In a previous conversation, Fletcher had told Elizabeth he had been urged to sue the Feenans, when the legal issues were over. At the time, she'd had no doubts about his innocence. Now she kept running conversations through her mind. She remembered that one day when she was in primary school, Fletcher had ordered her to hug much older boys in return for lollies. It happened on the steps of the Pro-Cathedral in Maitland, where he was living at the time.

Then another memory gave her a start: she had been made captain of her primary school at the same time Brendan had been an altar boy for the priest. It had come as a total surprise to her, as she wasn't academically gifted. Could Fletcher have done it for nefarious reasons?

* * *

The Ombudsman was bearing down on Malone. Some of the bishop's reasons for not standing Fletcher aside had been contradicted by others, including the Professional Standards Office (PSO) of the Catholic Church, the internal committee that looked after child protection matters involving clergy. Malone had told the Ombudsman's investigators that allegations of abuse against clergy were managed by that office – but the director of the PSO, John Davoren, said this wasn't true once an allegation became a police matter. Worse still for the bishop, Davoren claimed that the Fletcher matter shouldn't have been dealt with under the *Towards Healing* protocol: 'We couldn't start firing shots across the bows as it would have run the danger of confusing police activity.'[4]

Davoren also contradicted another claim by Malone. The bishop had told investigators he'd called the PSO on 20 June 2002 to seek advice about whether Fletcher should be stood aside. Malone claimed Davoren had said to him, 'No, you don't have to stand him aside. It's an allegation, and that's all it is at this point.'[5] Davoren informed the Ombudsman investigators that 'his knowledge of the complaint about Father Fletcher was from two conversations with Patricia Feenan ... on 11 November 2002 and 24 February, 2003'.[6] Pat had told Davoren that Fletcher still had access to children, and she was angry about this. Davoren claimed he'd first spoken to Malone about the case after one of these conversations with Pat.

In an email Davoren sent that was produced to the NSW Ombudsman, he reported that he had spoken to Father Burston, and asked him if Malone had ever considered removing Fletcher from his parish duties earlier. Burston said that Daniel Feenan had been 'demonstrating bizarre behaviour for some years', and he 'thought ... the current matter was just another sign of his psychological disturbance'. The psychologist went on to say: 'that no other complaint of this or any other kind had ever been received against Fletcher, and the diocese still did not have sufficient information about Daniel's complaint to justify standing Fletcher down'.[7]

Burston held a senior position as the head of Centacare, the Church's welfare arm relating to children and families in the diocese. This man seemingly dismissed Daniel's behaviour as just a 'psychological disturbance'.[8] The same man who, in 1974, had told parishioners that Andrew Nash's suicide was a prank gone wrong.

* * *

On 29 May 2003, the *Boston Globe* Spotlight team won a Pulitzer Prize for their investigations into the clerical sexual abuse cover-up in the Boston Diocese. The win received massive media coverage across the world.

What was clear from the *Globe*'s investigation was that there was a pattern of sexual abuse and cover-up. Priests and Brothers were moved around. Nuns either enabled the abuse or helped to conceal it. Cardinals and bishops were implicated.

This investigation in Massachusetts was stirring an international reaction, including in Australia. New groups of emboldened survivors lobbied governments for change, and they were demanding proper police investigations into perpetrators.

The increased popularity of the internet allowed many stories about clerical abuse to become available in Australia, from small websites and blogs here and overseas. Broken Rites in Melbourne were now online, breaking stories from various court cases. Their team of researchers, some who were survivors themselves, also had access to some of the secret settlements from victims.

Glen was reading it all. Taking in every word.

* * *

Will Callinan told Glen that he no longer had any faith in the bishop or the Catholic institutions who employed him. His friend Fletcher had turned out to be a liar and a paedophile. For a principal who had devoted his life to the Church and these schools, it was devastating. And as the Ombudsman's investigators continued their inquiry, Will became more distressed by Malone's behaviour.

The interviews were in full swing by September 2003.

Malone had claimed in a parish newsletter that he had consulted Will in June 2002 before deciding *not* to stand Fletcher aside. Will vehemently denied this conversation had taken place. The Ombudsman's investigators asked Malone for a record of the conversation, but the bishop said he hadn't recorded one – he did, however, have a handwritten diary entry from the meeting with Will on 20 June 2002, and he faxed it to the Ombudsman's office. It said, 'trip to Branxton to see Jim Fletcher (+Will C)'.[9] Will couldn't remember this meeting.

The principal split his workdays between Branxton – where Fletcher was based – and Greta. Will was sure he'd been in Greta that day, so he couldn't have met with Malone when the bishop said he had.

In November 2003, the provisional report of the Ombudsman's investigation was damning of Malone, the PSO (the Professional Standards Office of the Catholic Church) and the CCER. They found there was no 'formal protocol in place between the PSO and the CCER for reporting matters involving clergy'.[10] The office that controlled the behaviour of clergy and religious had no official abuse-reporting procedure organised with the office that controlled schools, even though priests and Brothers were employees at the schools. Put simply, there was no formal Church process for reporting paedophile priests to the Ombudsman.

This situation was untenable.

The provisional findings said the CCER – the Head of Agency – had failed to put effective systems in place to ensure that child abuse allegations against clergy and religious were reported to the Ombudsman by Catholic employers. The Ombudsman demanded the CCER immediately set up training for all school principals and Catholic employers, including bishops, in the state to explain the law: that a 'child' under the Act was anyone under the age of eighteen, the child involved in the sexual abuse did not have to be a current student or program participant, and *all* historical abuse allegations against a current employee or employer required an official notification to the Ombudsman. It was a stunning confirmation of the failures of the Catholic school system to protect its students.

An extremely harsh judgment was also meted out to the bishop. His negative report included four critical points:

4.2   Bishop Malone's failure to appropriately manage the child abuse allegations against Father Fletcher. In particular;

    4.2.1 Bishop Malone failed to follow the *Towards Healing* protocol;

    4.2.2 Bishop Malone failed to notify the CCER about the child abuse allegations against Father Fletcher;

    4.2.3 Bishop Malone informed Father Fletcher of the child abuse allegations against him, knowing that the matter was intended to be or had been reported to the police and before seeking advice from police about his actions;

    4.2.4 Bishop Malone failed to adequately assess or address the risks to children as evidenced by his failure to give due consideration to the advice of police to remove Father Fletcher from his contact with children ...[11]

The findings left a dark stain on Malone's reputation, but it didn't spread widely: only the people involved in the investigation knew the results, as the report was never made public. When Detective Sergeant Fox and Pat Feenan later asked for a copy, they were denied access.

Malone realised he needed to gather people around him he could trust. He claimed to believe he was doing the right thing while following canon law and the *Towards Healing* policies. But the world had changed in the past few years – there were new civil laws and there was more scrutiny, and the survivor groups were mobilising. Journalists were becoming more aggressive in their reporting.

The NSW Ombudsman was so concerned about the CCER it terminated its Head of Agency arrangement and transferred it to the bishops in each diocese across New South Wales. The new arrangement was confirmed for all Catholic diocesan agencies, including schools and Centacares, the Church's welfare agency. The NSW Ombudsman completed three investigations and nine audits of the CCER's systems and found significant deficiencies. In the NSW Ombudsman's annual report of 2004–2005 it said: 'As a result, we decided to replace the CCER as head of agency and to consult with representatives of the Catholic Church about how to improve the arrangement. There are 11 Catholic dioceses in NSW and over 40 designated agencies founded by religious orders. We visited all dioceses twice this year and spoke separately to the bishops about our concerns and how these could be addressed.'[12]

Malone had a personal stake in this: he realised that because the laws had changed, he could be personally liable for criminal charges. He was now Head of Agency and he had to continually prove to the NSW Ombudsman that his systems were failproof. He had to lift his game and that of the diocese.

* * *

As the 2003 school year ended and summer beckoned, Elizabeth Byrne had another in-person conversation with Fletcher. He told her he was replacing his legal aid solicitor with the best solicitor in Newcastle, and he explained, 'A friend in Branxton is helping me out with the money.' He also told her the Feenans weren't to be trusted or believed; he inferred Daniel Feenan had made up the abuse allegations to get compensation. Elizabeth thought that Fletcher's comments had a nasty undertone, a slightly sinister feeling about them. She left their meeting feeling nervous and scared for the Feenans.

The rumour mill was at fever pitch. She'd heard that the Feenans' house had been egged. The family's treatment by some parishioners was ugly, and it worsened over time.

As the Christmas festivities wrapped up, Elizabeth received a call from Fletcher. 'I've got a new QC,' he said. 'The QC is one of the best, he is the one that got Lindy Chamberlain off.'

'That's good,' Elizabeth replied.

Then he told her to do him a favour. 'When I go to court, you will have to bring all your children to surround me because of the media.'

There was silence at her end. She thought, *There is no way in the world I would do that.*[13] She left his request hanging, and soon the call finished and they both hung up.

CHAPTER 15

'I am sorry I didn't look after you'

– Elizabeth Byrne

THE CONVERSATION ELIZABETH HAD KNOWN WAS COMING, that she'd been dreading, took place on 11 April 2004, on the evening of Easter Sunday – one of the holiest days of the year for the Catholic Church. She'd spent the day with her family, as it was a special day.

Father Fletcher called her again. There was some small talk, then he said, 'I was wondering if you could do me a favour. I was wondering if you could write me a character reference.'

She replied, 'What should I put in it?'

Elizabeth was buying time. She was thinking, *How do I get out of this?* She really didn't want to write the reference, but she didn't know how to get out of it.

Fletcher said, 'How I mixed with you kids. How I mixed with all of you growing up.'

Again she paused, frantically trying to think of an excuse. In the end, she just said, 'Yes.'

Fletcher replied, 'Do you think your other brother could do one for me?'

Elizabeth's other brother was a policeman, and she knew he would never do a reference for Fletcher.

The priest added, 'Another policeman is going to do one for me.'

She didn't ask who this policeman was because she just wanted to end the conversation. Why couldn't she just say no? Why did this priest have such a strong hold over her?

After the call with Fletcher ended, Elizabeth phoned her mum and asked what she thought about the reference. Her mother told her she would call Brendan to ask for his thoughts on the matter, and then she would get back to her.[1]

Later that day, Elizabeth's phone rang again. It was her mother, in tears, sobbing down the line. She had called and spoken to Brendan, but he wouldn't answer her questions. Elizabeth's mother told her that the way Brendan had spoken to her made her think Fletcher had done something to him. The two women spoke for a short time, willing it not to be true. Not their brother and son. Not him too.

In a state of anxiety and distress, Elizabeth then called Brendan. She left a message on his phone, and he returned the call around midnight.

Now she knew. There was no going back. Her beloved brother had been abused by Fletcher.

She was shaking, with the phone in her hand. She said to Brendan, 'I am sorry I didn't look after you.'

He replied, 'He was a bastard for calling you on Easter Sunday.'

The sister told her brother, 'I am sorry for what he has done to you. I feel I have been betrayed all these years.'[2]

Brendan asked her not to write the reference for the accused priest.

A dull ache entered her heart.

Five days later, on 16 April 2004, Fletcher called again.

When she told him she wouldn't be writing his reference, his voice changed from charming to irritated and angry. He said, 'Why?'

She said, 'I just can't.'

'Have I hurt you, anyone in your family or your mum and dad?'

'No.'

'Has your other brother been in your ear?' he asked, referring to the police officer.

Elizabeth became unsettled and angry herself. 'No! Respect my decision that I cannot do your reference.'[3]

There was complete silence for about ten seconds before Fletcher angrily hung up.

Elizabeth felt agitated. For the first time, she had witnessed the full force of the other side of his personality – he was like a child who wasn't getting what he wanted. He had never spoken to her like that before. She started to cry. Why hadn't she seen the signs before this?

It was as if a pit of darkness was opening up in her life. The Church and this priest had been her security, her anchor. Now she was adrift.

She and Fletcher had no contact after this call.

Now she knew there was a second victim. It was her own brother.

This crucial piece of evidence, she realised, would surely help seal Fletcher's fate in a courtroom. The Director of Public Prosecutions was preparing for the trial, and a second victim would add enormous weight to the prosecution's case.

Elizabeth knew there was only one person, outside her immediate family, whom she could trust in this situation. Someone who knew Brendan. Someone who had always listened quietly and respectfully to her concerns.

Father Glen Walsh.

* * *

Glen couldn't rest. He and Elizabeth had talked at length about the best way to handle the situation.

She was growing very concerned about her parents. They were already shocked and angry about Fletcher's arrest, and they were devout Catholics. This news about Brendan would be devastating for them on many levels.

Glen and Elizabeth came up with a plan, which would begin with him dropping in to her parents' house, wishing them a happy Easter and asking how they were going.

On Friday, 23 April 2004, nearly a year after Fletcher had been charged with offences against Daniel Feenan, Glen walked into the Byrnes' family home to find the parents upset and distressed. The atmosphere was one of sadness and disbelief.

Brendan was there as well.

Glen asked the parents what was wrong. They told him that in the previous days they had been talking to Elizabeth about Brendan and Fletcher, and that Brendan had now disclosed he was also a victim of Fletcher.

Brendan had been sexually abused as an altar boy in Maitland from 1982 to 1984.[4] The abuse had started when he was just ten years old. Fletcher had first come in contact with the family in 1978 when he was the administrator (priest in charge) of the St John's Pro-Cathedral in Maitland – he was also the master of ceremonies for Bishop Clarke at the time. From 1982, Father Wilson was, at times, residing full time at the Bishop's House along with Clarke and Fletcher.

The hurt and betrayal of Brendan's parents was obvious, and his mother was crying.

Glen told them he wouldn't be sweeping this matter under the carpet. He then gave Brendan, in a gesture of comfort and reassurance, some rosary beads that had been blessed in the Vatican.

In a quiet and firm voice, Glen told the distraught parents and their son, 'I need to go to the police. I must go to the police.'[5]

Following this visit, Glen phoned Archbishop Wilson in Adelaide. Wilson was a local boy, born in Cessnock, and a close friend of the Byrnes. Alongside Fletcher, he had officiated Elizabeth's marriage. In the early 1980s, he had lived with Fletcher in the Bishop's House at Maitland. The Byrne boys, including Brendan, had hung around that house, occasionally washing Fletcher's and Wilson's cars.

Over the phone Wilson warned Glen that if he didn't report the allegation to the state authorities, he would be 'legally liable'.[6]

Curiously, Glen thought Wilson didn't appear shocked by the allegation that Fletcher had sexually abused a second victim, and Glen made a mental note of Wilson's tone in this conversation.[7] Also, Wilson was suggesting Glen break his vows and report the new evidence to the police, but he didn't suggest he would do it himself.

Brendan's mother also called Wilson on 23 April 2004 and told him Brendan was a victim of Fletcher.

Then, that same day, Wilson called Elizabeth and told her he was 'shocked' about allegations that Fletcher had sexually assaulted her younger brother. Wilson then asked her what Brendan intended to do about it, and she said she didn't know the answer.

After Glen's meeting with Brendan and his parents, he also called Malone and told him another of Fletcher's victims had come forward. Malone replied, 'Oh, shit!'[8]

Malone instructed Glen to look after the victim over the coming weekend – by this time, Brendan was living in Sydney. Malone also asked Glen to give the victim the contact details for *Towards Healing*.

Glen didn't want to stay in Sydney that weekend because he was concerned about leaving his parishes vacant. Who would perform his priestly duties? He asked the bishop whether he should inform the priest in the neighbouring parish, but Malone said, 'No, tell no one. Just go.'

Glen was now aware of two victims whom he knew personally, and his own abuse was always in the back of his mind. He remembered what it was like to be eighteen and powerless, to be the plaything of an older person who was supposed to be a teacher, a mentor. His thoughts took him back to that awful year at the Marist Brothers Centre.

Now Daniel was in his early twenties, not much older than Glen at the time of his abuse. The young man was displaying great courage by taking on Fletcher and the powerful organisation that stood behind the paedophile. Brendan was also showing great courage. He was standing behind Daniel in a terrible fight. When Glen had tried to expose his abuser, the Marist Brothers had told him that his complaint was unsustained. He wouldn't let the same thing happen to Daniel and Brendan. Glen would support them quietly, behind the scenes, defying his Church.

That Monday, 26 April, Glen did something priests weren't supposed to do: he phoned Maitland Police Station in order to report Fletcher's abuse of Brendan.

This huge act of defiance was extremely rare among the clergy. One other priest had done something similar in a NSW diocese south of Sydney. He'd ended up suiciding in 1998.

The police officer Glen spoke to said the investigator dealing with sexual abuse matters, Detective Sergeant Fox, wasn't there that day; the officer did, however, take Walsh's name and telephone number, and said the detective would call Glen the following day.

On the morning of 27 April 2004, Glen called Malone again. The priest had some news for the bishop: the second victim was reluctant to take the matter any further, but Glen had persuaded Brendan to let Glen go to the police on his behalf.

It is from this point that Glen's and Malone's recollections of the conversation differed.

Glen later said that Malone told him it was the victim's choice not to approach the police, and it wasn't necessary to take the matter any further other than Glen looking after the victim.

The priest said he told Malone, 'Bishop, this is a second young man who has come forward ... It needs to be reported ... So if you're not intending to, I will.'

According to Glen, Malone replied, 'If anyone has to do anything, I will ... You've told me he's reluctant. We don't need to report it.'

Glen said he replied, 'Well, I am going to and I'm going to ring – when I hang up now, I'm going to contact the CCER – the police and the Ombudsman and the CCER.'

According to Glen, the bishop then said, 'If you do that, fuck off out of my diocese and don't come back.'

Glen said he did not reply to this threat, and the bishop ended the call by abruptly hanging up.

Malone later denied saying any of this, and he claimed to have instead told Glen, 'You know the police are all over the Fletcher case with Daniel Feenan you know, but go to the police if that's what you think you need to do.'[9]

Glen immediately called the police. He told the officer who picked up the phone that the matter was urgent. The officer directed Glen to go straight to the station, where Fox would be waiting for him.

For Glen, enough was enough. He wouldn't rely on the bishop to follow the law. He would do it himself.

CHAPTER 16

'The old guard rules with an iron fist'

– Father Glen Walsh

ON 27 APRIL 2004, DETECTIVE SERGEANT PETER FOX WAS
sitting at his desk at the Maitland Police Station when Father Glen
Walsh came to see him.

Fox's experiences with the clergy over the past year had
made him wary of them. But after Glen sat down and they
talked for some time, Fox realised this priest was different. Glen
told the detective he was praying for a just outcome to the case.
He said he was fearful of the consequences of his decision to
go to the police, although he knew he had no other choice.
He added that Bishop Malone didn't know he was at the police
station.

Fox called Brendan the next day and the young man came
into the Maitland Police Station to make his statement on 11 May
2004.

Over the next few months, Fox would sometimes have a cup
of tea with the priest, in his office at the police station. They
would talk philosophically about institutional sexual abuse. How
it worked on the inside, and why the hierarchy wasn't proactive
in dealing with the clerical sexual abuse issue. How he and many

other clergy wanted to see the Church change. How they wanted to see a new generation taking control. Glen told the detective, 'The old guard rules with an iron fist. They don't want things to change and it's going to continue on in the same tragic way unless something monumental happens.'

Glen asked Fox a rhetorical question: 'Do you know what it is like for a priest to give mass after your predecessor has been arrested for paedophilia?'

For months, Glen's relationship with the diocese had suffered because of his response to the Fletcher matter. Fletcher's supporters in the parish weren't happy with him.

Even before Glen had gone to the police, he'd had problems within the Church. Several weeks before Brendan had disclosed his abuse to his family, at the end of February 2004, Glen had accidently discovered he'd been removed from the casual teaching register because of 'health reasons'. Since August 2003 he had held a part-time position teaching Year Eleven at St Catherine's Catholic College in Singleton, and initially his role at the college had been defined and had included the 2004 school year. On 30 April he'd written to Malone and the Director of Catholic Education demanding to know why 'he was deserving of such treatment'.

That day he'd also written to the principal of St Catherine's demanding to know why he had been removed. 'For the record,' he wrote, 'the reasons given by the bishop (letter enclosed 2.4.2004) dismissing me as a casual teacher surrounds my "poor health". There is no evidence to suggest that this reason has any substance. In fact, I enjoy excellent health and there is no reason to doubt that this will continue.' The bishop had said in his letter of 2 April 2004 that the decision was a 'clarification' of Glen's role at the college. Glen had already begun the school year, and he protested at the unfairness of being summarily dismissed. He wrote to the principal, 'Now I resign my 0.2 position at your college, as in conscience, I cannot participate in an unjust Catholic education system at any level.'[1]

By May, Glen's resignation from his teaching position at St Catherine's had taken effect.

His decision to go to the police and disclose evidence without Malone's authority had catastrophic consequences for him. He no longer had the trust and support of his bishop, and he believed he had no alternative but to leave the Maitland-Newcastle Diocese. Later, he wrote a letter about these events to his parishioners in Singleton. He wrote; 'As it turned out, reporting this crime sealed Father Fletcher's fate – and mine. On that April day in 2004, my life changed forever ... the Bishop ordered me out of "his diocese" for disobeying his directive to NOT report Fr Fletcher's second victim to the police.'[2]

In conversations with Glen months before the Fletcher case, Malone had alluded to Glen's restlessness – this was unsurprising, given that Malone had assigned Glen to three positions shadowed by clerical sexual abuse.

Glen moved out of the diocese, to Sydney, in May 2004.

* * *

Pat Feenan was at work when a call came through from Detective Sergeant Fox. It was a busy staff development day at the school where she was the librarian.

Fox said to her, 'I have got some news. Are you sitting down?'

Pat thought, *Oh no, what can it be?* She was used to bad news. Her stomach took a tumble.

Fox said, 'There is another victim. Would you please tell Daniel? You can tell your other family members but no one else.'

Pat could hear the excitement in the investigator's voice – this was big. She felt huge relief. Daniel, her son, wouldn't be fighting this case on his own. Fox informed her that the other young man had already made a statement.

Pat called Daniel, who was initially thrilled at the news. Then the reality set in: he wasn't the only one – he wasn't special, like Fletcher had said he was. In his mind, he was just another trophy in a paedophile's cabinet.

On 10 June 2004, Glen returned to the Maitland Police Station to make a formal statement in regard to Fletcher's sexual abuse of Brendan.[3]

It was a huge win for the prosecution. It wouldn't be Daniel's word against Fletcher, but two victims, and Fletcher's behaviour to both boys was shockingly similar. Now they had a fighting chance of a conviction.

* * *

The last two paragraphs of Glen's formal police statement provide a glimpse into his state of mind. 'Since I reported the matter I have had no response from anybody within the Church hierarchy,' he wrote. 'This surprised me. Since this matter was brought to light, I have felt very cut off, and have now decided to take leave of my priestly duties. Despite this, I have felt the need to support the [Byrne family] and have kept in contact with them.' Glen revealed that he was now residing in Sydney. 'Although I am [a] fully qualified teacher and attempted to gain employment within the Catholic School System I've had a lot of difficulty gaining employment. I know that teachers with my qualifications are in demand, but I began to feel there was a problem with employing an ex-priest. I then made a direct approach to Cardinal Pell, who gave me his blessing, and I have now been able to access a temporary teaching position.'

After Glen had left the diocese, he'd lived in his car for a period of time and then moved into a friend's garage in Sydney. Despite having a loving family and many friends, those first few weeks he was very down and in shock, and he didn't want to burden anyone. He then lived with his older brother, John, in the southern suburb of Rockdale before accepting the hospitality of Father Brendan Quirk at the Rockdale parish in Sydney.

Cardinal Pell helped Glen find a position in a Sydney parish. He became the assistant priest of the Arncliffe and Rockdale parishes, and the religious education coordinator at Our Lady of the Sacred Heart Catholic Primary School in Randwick, an eastern suburb.[4]

In spring 2004, Glen became the Year Six teacher at St Catherine of Siena Catholic Primary School in the south-western Sydney suburb of Prestons. His brother's flat in Rockdale was around thirty kilometres from the school, so John would come home from work at 6 p.m. to find that Glen had already gone to bed. To his brother he seemed depressed and listless, as if a heavy burden was weighing on him.

Glen had thought a lot about what survivors of clerical sexual abuse really needed from their Church, and he wanted to communicate this insight to his bishop. So, on 10 September 2004, five months after Glen had left active ministry and the diocese, he wrote to Malone. He let the bishop know that he'd found a teaching position in Prestons and would not be returning to the diocese as a priest. 'Therefore,' he said, 'I write to you for two reasons: 1. Why I have left. 2. I need your help.' On the first point, Glen did not hold back:

> Priesthood is a calling I take very seriously, but have never felt accepted in your diocese, my home. The struggle to identify myself in the presbyterate was made more difficult by three of my appointments and their intrinsic connections to paedophilia and sexual misconduct.
>
> In 1995, before I was ordained a Deacon, I informed you of my one and half years of abuse at the hand of Brother Coman Sykes fms, hoping you would keep this information in mind when appointing me to parishes.
>
> Appointing me to Taree, (after Father Vincent Ryan) Gateshead/Redhead and Windale ... and finally at Branxton/ Greta and Lochinvar (after Father James Fletcher) while knowing I am a victim of abuse at the hands of [Sykes] meant that I was daily confronted with my own pain, as well as having to minister to those parishioners effected [sic] by abuse claims made towards their clergy. While obviously not intended, the message I received through these appointments was that the 'abusive' Church is alive and well, unsympathetic and unapologetic. I suggest it is always unwise to place a newly

ordained priest in parishes where clerical sexual abuse, alleged
or proven, has traumatised the community, especially if he is
a victim of Church sexual abuse. This, surely is a job for the
most senior and experienced priest not the recently ordained.

Michael, I write about this not because I am angry or
want to accuse, but I believe you need to know you were
right in your last letter when you stated your wonder at my
'mysterious restlessness from time to time.' I never really
settled into priesthood even though I know the priesthood
is my true vocation, my life. I remained 'unsettled' for the
reasons abovementioned. And I presumed, knowing my story,
you would understand and accommodate. My restlessness has
never been about the priesthood or the demanding ministry
within, but finds its genesis, within the abusive human nature,
found to my amazement in so many people, especially clergy.

One of the tragedies regarding all this scandalous clerical
abuse, is that the Church is rapidly losing its credibility and
its purpose. That it is taking civil law to expose these priest
predators and provide justice to the victims is unnecessary
and continues to cast a bleak shadow over a life-giving faith.
As Bishop, you have the power to drag this diocese out of
the shadow. Every victim I have counselled, simply seeks an
apology. The lies, denials and the distance by the Church
simply compounds the abuse ...

As our Bishop, you are the Sacrament who is Christ;
therefore, dare to go in persona Christi to the victims and
their families in your diocese, not with lawyers in tow and
legal rhetoric, but with the Love of God and the prophetic
faith of Jesus Christ. Making them wait for the court to rule is
wrong. You can show us what is right by spending time with
them, praying for and with them, calling them to the heart of
the faith, wherein peace and healing resides ...

Glen went on to make a request for funds, asking, 'Would
you consider helping me Bishop?' and explaining his financial
situation.

'I hope you accept my letter in the spirit in which it is written,' Glen concluded. 'I do need to acknowledge why I have left the priesthood I love so much and to seek your help to re-establish myself in a safe and fulfilling environment. I am happy teaching and thank God I have this profession to turn to.'

Several weeks later, on 29 September 2004, Malone replied. He attached a cheque for $20,000 and began by explaining that it was 'to assist with costs for getting established in Sydney'. But he went on to say:

> I am disappointed in your comments about 'the abusive Church is alive and well, unsympathetic and unapologetic.' I reject what you have written and can only put it down to the fact that you are not travelling well. You have no understanding of all the work I have done with victims of sexual abuse. To dismiss my pastoral ministry with these people, tense negotiating sessions, aggravation and grey hairs with a few scathing remarks is very hurtful.
>
> I do not expect you to know the truth of these matters but I would hope for an acknowledgement that there might be more involved than you do understand.

CHAPTER 17

'You bastard! You hurt my son'

– Pat Feenan

FOR BISHOP MICHAEL MALONE, 2004 HAD BECOME A VERY BAD year indeed.

In the Ombudsman's report on the Fletcher matter, there had been a recommendation for Malone to hand over all his archived files to the CCER. Because the bishop had failed to notify the CCER about Fletcher, the Ombudsman wanted to know if other priests might have been missed by the Church system.

The next phase of the private negotiations with the NSW Ombudsman have never been made public, but on 30 June 2004, the CCER's Head of Agency status was terminated. The bishop was now Head of Agency, and the files remained in his archives under the control of the clergy. This was the case for every diocese across New South Wales.

Malone had to prove to the Ombudsman, however, that his diocese would implement the correct processes to deal with child protection matters as determined by state law and the Ombudsman's Act. He decided it was time to set up an independent child protection unit, separate from the one operating inside the Catholic Schools Office, and staffed with people he could trust.

In the 1970s to 1990, Father Frank Coolahan, as assistant director and then director of Catholic Education, handled all complaints against teachers in the Maitland–Newcastle Diocese. He was in charge of the Catholic Schools Office that dealt with these issues. He was replaced by Jim Callinan and then Michael Bowman. Now Bishop Malone decided he needed a unit that was independent of this office and focused on child safety only.

He thought of a senior social worker, Helen Keevers, who had been managing children's services for Centacare, a diocesan welfare agency. They had first met in 1995, and Malone had been impressed by her ever since, admiring her sensitivity, compassion and patience.

Back in 1996, the bishop had felt overwhelmed by all the media coverage about the Ryan case. He had formed an internal advisory group of which Helen had been a part; it had also included a newly appointed media adviser and some other senior diocesan staff. This informal group supported the bishop through that difficult time with advice and emotional support.

Then, in 1999, Helen had dealt with sexual abuse victims as part of the *Towards Healing* process for the Church.

Helen wasn't Catholic – in fact, she was an atheist. But Malone needed an outsider, someone who would apprise him of what was acceptable outside the closed culture of the Church. And he needed to keep the Ombudsman happy with his appointment.

He was going for the best option he had. Or perhaps the only one.

* * *

Helen Keevers was completely dedicated to her work for the survivors. She studied hundreds of internal Church documents and research reports to try to understand how clericalism had exacerbated the sexual abuse crisis in the Church. As part of this quest, she pored over the Monsignor Cotter and Father Ryan cases.

Helen wanted to know if the difficulty of living up to strict canon laws such as celibacy was the main factor that led to the proliferation of abuse and its cover-up within the Church. Or was it primarily that the Church had become an institution in which illegal activities happened routinely with no consequence? Were adults with something to hide attracted to an institution that routinely ignored sexual behaviour and also had power over many children?

Malone would often take Helen into his confidence following pastoral visits with clergy and religious and nuns. She spent many hours on the road with the bishop, even visiting priests in jail. One of those men was Ryan, who was serving a jail sentence of fourteen years in Junee about seven hours south of Sydney; Malone and Helen wanted to know if Ryan could shed light on other offenders within the Church.

On another occasion, Malone came to a meeting with Helen after he had visited an elderly nun in the diocese, and he was visibly shaken by her revelation that as a young woman she had been sexually abused by Bishop Toohey: he had masturbated in front of her without her consent.

Malone gave Helen unrestricted access to most diocesan records, including the secret archives of priest and religious files. He asked her to review all the files of historical child protection concerns and to recommend further actions if needed. Whenever it became necessary, Malone allowed her to give the police access to records when they requested it.

There was one set of records – those of the Maitland Clergy Fund – that Malone did not give Helen access to. The diocese maintained this special fund in order to provide necessary disbursements for diocesan priests, such as the purchase of vehicles, costs associated with study, travel costs, and so forth. The money came from parishioners across the diocese, who would put money in the plate passed around every Sunday at mass.

During Helen's time working closely with Malone, Monsignor Allan Hart administered the Maitland Clergy Fund. At one stage, he moved the records of the fund from the Hunter Street diocesan office in Newcastle West to his home at the Hamilton presbytery. Helen always had to ask Hart for access, as he never gave her direct access. It concerned her that this fund may have been used in cases where a paedophile priest might have needed to travel and leave Newcastle.

Hart had moved quite a way up in the Church hierarchy since his time as a deacon in the early 1970s, when Steven and Glen had served as his altar boys in Shortland, and he'd taken them to the beach in his yellow car. For many years Hart had clearly seen himself as akin to a governor in the Roman Empire. Out of the blue, he would call up principals and question their decisions. He could be a bully. He was vicar-general from 1990 to 1996 and had always had ambitions to become the bishop.

Hart once invited a local Catholic family with five children to have dinner with him. They were struggling to make ends meet and grew concerned when Hart suggested a pizza restaurant. At dinner he ordered several pizzas, and the father told him he didn't know how he was going to pay for it all. Hart told him not to worry, as he had lots of cash. He pulled out and unzipped a small bag, which was full to the brim with $50 notes. As Hart went to pay, many of the bills escaped from the bag and landed on the floor.

* * *

In the spring of 2004, Elizabeth Byrne received a phone call from Archbishop Philip Wilson, her old family friend. He wanted to pop by to say hello to her and her family, as he would be visiting from Adelaide in the local area.

When he arrived at her house, her five children were playing indoors. Elizabeth and her husband sat at the kitchen table with the priest, and they sipped their tea and coffee with the noise of happy kids in the background.

Wilson asked after her parents. He raised the fact her family must be traumatised about Fletcher given how close they were to the priest.

During the visit, Elizabeth showed Wilson a letter she had written to Malone on 3 August 2004. 'You are aware that my brother [Brendan] has made a statement to the Police regarding allegations against Fr James Fletcher ... On behalf of [Brendan], my parents and the rest of my family we all feel that since my brother came forward that the Church has shunned us … In view of the hurt and alienation we have experienced my brother and all my family would greatly appreciate a pastoral message from you in respect to [Brendan]'s complaint …'

Wilson then read Malone's response to Elizabeth on 27 August 2004. 'Thank you for your letter regarding your brother's allegations against Father Jim Fletcher … On the 27th of April, 2004, I became aware through Father Glen Walsh of your brother's distress as a result of the alleged abuse by Father Fletcher …'

After reading the letters, Wilson stayed at Elizabeth's house a while longer. He seemed very interested in the case. When he'd lived with Fletcher in the Maitland Bishop's House, there had been lots of schoolkids around and some of them had visited Fletcher.

* * *

The Fletcher trial, which began on 23 November 2004, was traumatic for the Feenan family, particularly Daniel. His testimony included graphic details of his abuse at the hands of Fletcher. Daniel told the court that on one occasion when Fletcher had been raping him in his car, Daniel had focused on 'that bloody silly St Christopher medal he had hanging near the steering wheel. It was as if I just focused on that, it would take all the pain away and make me forget what was happening but it didn't.'[1]

Brendan Byrne never laid charges against Fletcher; he testified at the trial and provided a police statement. His evidence was crucial because the details of how Fletcher had abused him were remarkably similar to what Fletcher had done to Daniel. This is known as tendency and coincidence evidence. In legal terms it means a person has or had a tendency to act in a particular way.

It was now impossible for the Church's legal team to claim that Daniel was a one-off, an unreliable witness. As expected, the emergence of another victim helped lead the prosecution to victory.

The jury, and everyone sitting in the courtroom, couldn't help noticing the physical resemblance between Daniel and Brendan. They could have been twins. At one point, the sheriff mixed them up; he told Daniel to return to the witness box, but it was Brendan's turn to give evidence. When the young man walked up to the box, there was an audible gasp in the room.

Pat Feenan hadn't met the Byrnes until that day; the families had been kept separate so as not to contaminate evidence. When she saw Brendan, she thought, *Well, Fletcher has a 'type'.* She noticed members of the jury looking between Daniel and Brendan.

The Byrne family were sitting in the public seats, and they hugged each other as Brendan gave evidence. Fletcher didn't look at him once. The paedophile priest was sitting in the chair behind his defence counsel, his head in his hands.

Fletcher's legal costs were aided with a loan facility from the Catholic Church. He was helped by another priest, Father Guy Hartcher, who had donated part of the Christmas collection in his church to help pay Fletcher's lawyers. The priest's order, the Vincentians, had paid out to a victim in 1994 when he worked at the infamous St Stanislaus college in Bathurst, New South Wales. From 1999, Father Hartcher was appointed by Bishop Malone to the Gresford-Dungog parish where he became close to Father Fletcher. The parishioners didn't know their money was going to Fletcher's defence. Pat Feenan also found that Father Hartcher had been previously charged with child sex offences, although he was acquitted of these charges. Feenan complained to Bishop Malone that Hartcher should not work near children. Bishop Malone withdrew Father Hartcher from active service on 5 September 2004.

During the trial, Fletcher's defence counsel suggested to Brendan that he was lying about the abuse so he could submit a claim for compensation against the Church. Brendan denied this allegation and said that he wasn't pursuing his own charges or compensation – he had come forward simply to tell the truth.

When Pat gave evidence, Daniel was escorted from the courtroom so as not to contaminate any further evidence he would give. She took a long look at Fletcher in the dock, and he wouldn't meet her gaze. She felt like shouting at him, running towards him and putting her hands around his neck. *You bastard! You hurt my son.* Then she thought, *No, that would waste two years of diligent police work.*[2]

When Pat had finished giving evidence and gone back to her seat, she turned around and looked into Brendan's mum's eyes. Pat gave her a weary smile; Brendan's mum gave her one back. Their expressions told each other, *I know what you're going through, and I am so sorry.* Two Catholic mothers. Two beloved sons. At one point, they hugged and shed some tears. Only another mum could understand this anguish.

* * *

Father James Fletcher was convicted on 6 December 2004. When the jury returned a guilty verdict on all nine charges, which included multiple counts of oral and anal penetration, the public gallery clapped in a subdued manner. The announcement was a huge relief for Detective Sergeant Fox, the Feenans and the Byrnes.

Pat began to cry. The pressure was off. Her son had been believed.

She stood outside the court and told the waiting media that her family's sentence was 'life-long', and she praised her son's courage, describing him as 'an extraordinarily brave boy'.[3]

Had Glen and Elizabeth Byrne not encouraged a second victim to come forward, would Fletcher have been convicted?

Soon after the verdict was announced, Malone issued a full apology on behalf of the Church and also apologised for not standing Fletcher aside sooner from parish duties. The bishop set up a public hotline for any child protection issues in the diocese, and he told the public, via the television news media, that they should use it if they had any concerns about anything to do with child safety.

Despite Malone's admission of wrongdoing, the Feenans and Brendan's family were frightened there might be a backlash.

Elizabeth was worried about her children. That afternoon, at dusk, a car pulled up outside her home. An occupant of the car hurled eggs at the house, and they splattered all over the pathway to the front door.

Fletcher was sentenced on 11 April 2005 and then the Church lodged an appeal.

Pat had an in-person meeting with Malone after the original conviction. He asked her whether she felt guilty for allowing Daniel to stay overnight at Fletcher's lodgings the day her son had attempted suicide. She replied, 'I don't feel guilty, I feel angry. He was nineteen years old, and I had no idea what Fletcher had done to my son.' She then looked at the bishop and said, 'Do you feel guilty?!'

* * *

Watching all the news about Fletcher on the local TV station was a local school principal who saw Malone's appeal about the hotline on the television news.

On 9 December 2004, John Wakely rang the Maitland-Newcastle Diocese toll-free number.[4] The number went through to the Centacare switchboard, which asked for his name and number. John refused to provide these details. Eventually, they put him through to Helen Keevers.

He made several allegations to her, two of which concerned Father Peter Brock.

In the late 1990s, John had been the assistant principal and later principal of the Holy Family Primary School in Merewether (locally referred to as The Junction), a beachside suburb of Newcastle. Brock was his parish priest, essentially his boss, and had also been appointed to the diocesan Professional Standards committee – the one supposedly concerned with child protection and other issues.

After John spoke to Helen on the hotline, she recorded this file note of what he'd said about Malone and Brock: 'Bishop Malone knew of a priest in the diocese who had homosexual sex with people the priest met as parishioners. These people were not children at the time but one had sex for the first time with the priest on his 18th birthday. The priest had used the relationship he built up with the person as a child (over a period of years) to encourage him to have sex ... The caller said he had brought this matter to the bishop's attention several years ago and nothing had been done.'[5] The nineteen-year-old was a musically gifted student who John knew, a family friend whose father had died when he was sixteen. Brock's relationship had intensified with the boy from this time as the priest groomed him. When the boy reached the age of consent, Brock plied him with alcohol and had sex with him.

Brock was a local boy, born in 1945 and ordained in the 1960s. His family was considered by many Novocastrians, not just Catholics, to be akin to royalty. Many Brocks held local positions of prestige in the areas of music, journalism and religion. Two of the brothers were priests, Brian and Peter, while another, Paul, had been a Marist Brother; their sister, Megan, was a nun who rose to very senior positions in the Church, including a role with the *Towards Healing* committee at a national level. Another brother, Roger, was the editor of the *Newcastle Herald* until late June 2012.

In the 1970s, Father Peter Brock's youth groups were legendary in Newcastle. Brock would take select boys on a daytrip to a swimming hole on a friend's property in the Hunter Valley, where he would urge them to swim naked in the creek while he watched. Then he demanded the boys wrestle naked in the mud, a bit like the Ancient Greeks.[6]

In the late 1990s, there were more recent incidents that worried the principal. He'd noticed that whenever Brock became interested in a child, the priest would grow excited and become focused on that student.

In 1998, John contacted a national Church hotline and spoke to a Church adviser in Melbourne, who told him that his concerns were valid and would be relayed to the bishop of his local diocese. John then met with Malone that year and told him about the eighteen-year-old, along with some other observations including Brock's overt interest in an eleven-year-old boy on a school camp.

John assumed the conversation was confidential and his name would be protected. He did give Malone permission to engage his vicar-general, Father Burston, on the matter, because John had known Father Burston since 1971, when Burston had a done some psychological screening to see whether John was suitable for the priesthood.

Soon afterwards, Burston told John that Malone had raised his complaint with Brock, and Brock had then admitted he'd broken the canon law of celibacy by having sex with consenting adult men. From what Burston said about the meeting, John realised that Brock would be able to identify him as the complainant from some of the information that Malone had chosen to convey.

Distraught and angry, John drove over to a presbytery in the suburb of Mayfield to meet with Burston, who was the parish priest there. According to John, Burston told him that Father Peter Brock had refused to go to any psychological screening or therapy. John had suggested a treatment centre in the United States.

John no longer felt that he could access a fair reporting process within the diocese – he was a school principal whose legitimate concerns had been dismissed and whose anonymity hadn't been respected. He believed Malone had failed to comprehend the severity of the situation and, even worse, that the bishop had felt the need to curry favour with a powerful and well-connected priest. He didn't go to the police because he felt he didn't have any evidence that Brock was committing criminal offences against underage children.

John wrote to Malone on 20 August 1998: 'I raised concerns regarding Fr Peter Brock relating to the safety of children in my care, now and as young adults.' He then wrote a subsequent letter making it clear he was 'left in a very difficult position' and that he needed answers to key questions about how to work with Brock while protecting the parish's children. He added, 'I am now faced with a personal faith crisis. I have been betrayed in the process. I am bitterly disappointed.'[7]

John got on with the job of being a principal but never let the issue rest in his mind. Father Brock pretended the complaint had never happened and John kept his dislike of Brock to himself for the sake of the school, but kept his distance when he could.

Then, in 2001, Malone recommended Brock for a very prestigious position: executive officer to the National Commission for Clergy Life and Ministry in Canberra. This body advised the bishops on important issues such as the education and formation of clergy in seminaries. It was a huge promotion for Brock, and his nomination was accepted. The priest was ambitious: he wanted to be the vicar-general, second-in-command to the bishop.

The news of Brock's promotion angered John, but he still felt powerless. How could Malone have recommended Brock for this prestigious position knowing his history?

It was three years later, on 9 December 2004, that John finally decided he couldn't let the past rest and reported his concerns to Helen Keevers. He had now read all about the bishop's failure to deal with Fletcher, so he worried Brock was another example of a cover-up in the diocese.

CHAPTER 18

The Whitewash

ON 11 APRIL 2005, FATHER FLETCHER WAS SENTENCED TO NINE years and eleven months in jail.

Glen Walsh was elated. Elizabeth and Glen felt their decision to support Brendan to become a witness in the case had been vindicated. On a deeper level, this case had opened their eyes much further to the systemic clerical abuse within the Maitland-Newcastle Diocese.

* * *

In November 2004, Helen Keevers had volunteered to conduct a survey across the diocese, and Malone had enabled her to do this. It was completed in April 2005, and its key recommendation was the establishment of a coordinated diocesan response to child protection managed by a new child protection unit. It was called the Diocesan Child Protection and Professional Conduct Unit (DCPPCU).

Around this time, the diocese received a *Towards Healing* complaint by a victim who had attended St Pius X High School. The priest named in this complaint was Father John Denham.

Helen investigated Denham's status within the diocese, and she learned that he had been supported by the Maitland Clergy Fund to the tune of $874 per month and the use of a clergy-funded car. This suggested he was technically 'on leave' from the Maitland-Newcastle Diocese since he'd left in 1986. Thousands of dollars had been paid to support him over the years, in stark contrast to how Glen Walsh had been treated.

Not only had Monsignor Hart controlled the Maitland Clergy Fund for many years, but he had also taken a complaint report on Denham from a student at Waverley College in 1994.

In November 1994, Father Brian Lucas, then the chancellor of the Archdiocese of Sydney, had sent a letter to Denham instructing him to 'perform no public ministry'. But Denham remained a priest, and Lucas didn't complete any formal procedures to defrock him or to remove his faculties (ability to perform ceremonies such as mass), despite the gravity of the offences. Lucas would go on to be a key figure in arranging the informal MOU between the NSW Church and the Police.

Also in 1994, Denham was counselled by a psychologist in relation to inappropriate sexual activity on his dismissal from Waverley College. At the time he told the psychologist that his inappropriate behaviour 'was a means to comfort his victims'.[1] He told another psychologist that he'd 'engaged in the sexual behaviours as he felt that behaviour was what he would have wanted as a boy ...'.[2]

Helen wondered why Hart and Clarke hadn't acted to remove Denham from ministry (that is, remove his faculties) that year and also request that the Vatican laicise him. Laicisation can only be approved by the Pope. Why hadn't they started that procedure with the Vatican? She reported back to the bishop that this meant Denham was still technically 'on leave' from the Maitland-Newcastle Diocese. This was despite his conviction in 2000, which hadn't yet been reported in the media, for indecently assaulting a fourteen-year-old boy.

In 2005, in accordance with the law, Malone notified the NSW Ombudsman of the *Towards Healing* complaint about Denham. But it was later revealed that, back in 2004, Malone had also informed the Ombudsman of an issue involving Denham.[3]

Denham had been convicted of child sex offences in 2000 in a court of law, but it doesn't seem that Malone then immediately notified the Ombudsman that Denham was an offender. In fact, it seemingly took four years for Malone to notify the Ombudsman of this situation, even though the *Ombudsman Act* had been altered in May 1999. Meanwhile, Denham had been working in a library next to a primary school from 2000 when he had been dismissed from the College of Law, technically 'on leave' from the Maitland–Newcastle Diocese.

In 1995, when Malone was the coadjutor bishop, Bishop Clarke had informed him that Denham 'is no longer a priest of this diocese and has no faculties to minister'.[4]

But this was not the case.

It was all swept under the carpet.

* * *

In the first half of 2005, the diocese was responding to investigations by the Ombudsman and to questions from the *Newcastle Herald*. A new child protection unit was being set up, and its advisory group had been appointed. The Ombudsman would have to be notified of John Wakely's concerns about Brock, so the diocese appointed an investigator by the name of Bill Jardine. Jardine was a seasoned private investigator engaged on tricky and sensitive cases.

Then one of the most senior clerics in Australia stepped in: Cardinal George Pell.

Pell was an imposing figure. A tall man, a conservative, who wielded great power within and on behalf of his Church – in fact, back in 2005, this man was almost all-powerful in Australia. He had regular meetings with the country's most influential politicians, including those with aspirations to be prime minister. The NSW premiers had to keep him onside lest he unleash his considerable flock against the premier's political party at the upcoming elections. Pell's influence extended beyond the pulpit; he had hundreds of thousands of students enrolled in Catholic schools.

But Pell would criticise anyone who said he was the leader of the Catholic Church in Australia. He would scoff at their lack of understanding of the formal Church structures, although in truth he was the most influential Catholic on all sorts of matters, and in particular the Church's response to any threats to its clerical power.

In Pell's eyes, the Maitland-Newcastle Diocese was attracting too much attention from the Ombudsman. Malone had enemies within, who were forming alliances and armed with rumours, and there were leaks to the *Herald* along with parishioners making formal complaints about clergy and religious.

Malone and Pell weren't from the same faction. Malone was a progressive; Pell was an arch conservative. But they were both loyal soldiers for their Church. And Brock wasn't your common variety priest – he had connections among the higher-ups.[5]

Pell decided that as with many political fixes, the answer was to commission an investigation and a report. He found an expensive Queen's Counsel with impeccable credentials, while Corrs Chambers Westgarth, his preferred legal firm, would carry out an investigation into Malone and the issues raised in John Wakely's complaint.

One of the motives was to ward off the Ombudsman from removing Malone as Head of Agency and therefore to protect his archive of files. The Church needed those allegations raised by John Wakely and any others against Brock to be legally defined as *not* being 'reportable conduct' under the *Ombudsman Act*. The Church, under the leadership of Pell, went to extraordinary lengths to make sure the clergy would not be defeated.

In May 2005, Pell appointed David Jackson QC to investigate Malone's management of complaints and allegations against Brock, along with Malone's appointment of the priest to the National Commission for Clergy Life and Ministry in Canberra.[6] The initial report was for the 'Congregation of bishops in Vatican city ...'[7] It would not only investigate the handling of the Brock matter but also 'Allegations that Bishop Malone coerced a potential witness in the Father Fletcher case', and 'Bishop Malone's suitability as Head of Agency for child-protection matters'.

Malone made it clear that he didn't want the findings sent to the Congregation for Bishops in Vatican City. He had his own legal representation.

It was agreed that there should be a 'further meeting between Cardinal Pell, Archbishop Philip Wilson and Bishop Malone as to what Cardinal Pell should do as the result of the report'.[8]

Under canon law, Pell as the 'Metropolitan of the Province of NSW "was" obliged to notify the Roman Pontiff if there be any abuses'.[9]

Lawyers from Corrs Chambers Westgarth went about their investigations, which would become the *Jackson Report* and reveal much about how the Church operated behind closed doors. Once the report was done, Pell would forward it to the Congregation for Bishops in the Vatican via the new Apostolic Nuncio, Ambrose De Paoli, who had been appointed in December 2004.

The *Jackson Report* was completed in July 2005 and presented to Pell on 1 August 2005. This internal Church report was never released to the public until now.

* * *

One of the most startling revelations from the *Jackson Report* is that in 1998, when John Wakely met with Malone, Malone apparently didn't understand the concept of 'grooming'.

By 1998, Malone had been the bishop for more than two years, and his leadership had endured the Ryan and McAlinden matters. For most of 1995, he'd served as the coadjutor bishop under Clarke, before taking over in November. Despite this, the *Jackson Report* made an extraordinary conclusion: 'As a final matter, I accept that Bishop Malone was unaware of the concept of "grooming" in 1998, and that he did not understand that the complaint regarding the sexual relationship between Father Brock and 'X' may have indicated some inappropriate conduct on Father Brock's part in relation to a minor.'[10]

From 1996 to 1998, during and after the NSW Wood Royal Commission on paedophilia, Malone had been a member of the

Bert and Audrey Nash, with Carmel, Patricia, Andrew and Geoffrey, 1960s. The Nashes lived near the Sacred Heart Church in Hamilton, where Audrey worked for Monsignor Cotter and Father Vincent Ryan. *Courtesy of the Nash family*

Glen and John Walsh, with their twin sisters, Trish and Kate, and a neighbour's baby. The Walsh children grew up in a tight-knit Catholic community in Shortland, Newcastle.

Steven Alward and his sister, Libby, as children. Steven went to primary school with Glen Walsh, and they were both altar boys at the local church. *Courtesy of the Alward family*

ABOVE: Bishop Leo Clarke with the Feenan children, 1989. John Feenan, their father, was the Business Manager for the Maitland-Newcastle Diocese. *Courtesy of Pat Feenan*

LEFT: Father James Fletcher with Bernard Feenan. Father Fletcher was based in Maitland and was a close colleague of Bishop Clarke. *Courtesy of Pat Feenan*

Audrey Nash, holding a photo of her son Andrew, who died at age 13. *Newcastle Herald*

Glen Walsh in Year 7 at Marist Brothers Hamilton, 1974. The Church had already identified him as a student who had the attributes suitable for a religious vocation.

Steven Alward in Year 9 at St Piux X, 1975, where he found a mentor in Father John Denham. *Courtesy of Mark Wakely*

Brother Coman Sykes, whose real name was Geoffrey Patrick Sykes, in the 1970s. Sykes was a senior Marist Brother who was an influential member of the 'retreat teams' strategy to attract more young men to the Marist Brothers. He was very involved in rugby league in NSW and was a member of the Marist Brothers Provincial Council (Sydney).

Monsignor Patrick Cotter in 1980. Cotter was Bishop Leo Clarke's second-in-command. He lived and worked with Father Vince Ryan in the presbytery at the Sacred Heart Church in Hamilton, Newcastle. *Courtesy of the Nash family*

(L–R) Monsignor Allan Hart, Father John Gahan, Bernadette Nash (holding a book) and Audrey Nash behind Bernadette, 1980. Glen and Steven had served as Allan Hart's altar boys. Hart went on to become Bishop Clarke's vicar-general and was on his Council of Priests. *Courtesy of the Nash family*

Bishop Leo Clarke with Monsignor Frank Coolahan, 1985. Monsignor Coolahan was assistant director and then director of Catholic Education during the 1970s to 1990, and handled all complaints against teachers, clergy and religious in the Maitland-Newcastle Diocese.
Brother Peter Carroll, Provincial Marist Brother

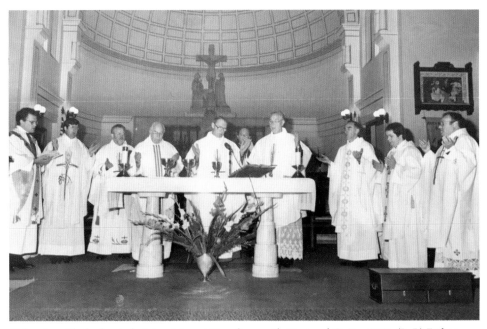

Bishop Leo Clarke (centre) giving Mass at Hamilton, with Hart and Cotter, 1980: (L–R) Father Andrew Murray, Father Graham Haggerty, Father John Gahan, Father Lewis Fenton, Bishop Leo Clarke (with Father Philip Wilson behind), then Monsignor Patrick Cotter, Father Tony Stace, Father Rufo and Father Allan Hart. *Courtesy of the Nash Family*

Glen Walsh in approximately 1989, after he had returned from Papua New Guinea and was teaching in the Maitland-Newcastle Diocese. Soon after this photo was taken he entered the priesthood and began his seminary training.

Steven Alward and his partner, Mark Wakely, in the 1980s. Both journalists, Steven and Mark met on the *Newcastle Herald* before eventually working at the ABC. *Courtesy of Mark Wakely*

The Alward family, celebrating Brian's 60th birthday in 1987: (L–R) Peter, Libby, Steven, Joan, Brian, David and his former wife, Raelene. *Courtesy of the Alward family*

Father Glen Walsh after his ordination as a priest in 1996.

Father James Fletcher, who was later convicted of nine counts of child sexual assault.

Philip Wilson, former archbishop of Adelaide and former president of the Catholic Bishops Conference.

Father John Denham in 1992, when he was chaplain at Sydney's Waverley College. Four years later, he was charged with having sexual intercourse with a person under 18 but was acquitted. By 2019, he had been convicted of multiple child sex offences against 59 victims.

Father Tom Brennan was the principal of St Pius X High School. He was later convicted of concealment charges and the Church acknowledged he was also a child sex offender.
Newcastle Herald

Inside the bell tower of the Sacred Heart Cathedral, Hamilton. Father Vincent Ryan ran a Friday Night Youth Club for altar boys. He was known to take boys to the bell tower so he could abuse them in secret. *Police photo*

Father Vince Ryan's mug shot, 11 October 1995. He is considered one of the worst paedophiles in the history of the Australian Catholic Church. *Police photo*

In 1995, at the age of 25, Senior Constable Troy Grant launched an investigation into Father Vince Ryan. Ryan was later found guilty of sexually assaulting 37 boys, some as young as nine. *Courtesy of Troy Grant*

In 2004, Detective Sergeant Peter Fox launched an investigation into allegations that Father James Fletcher had sexually assaulted children. Fletcher was eventually tried and convicted. *Courtesy of Peter Fox*

Detective Sergeant Kristi Faber is the head of Strike Force Georgiana, an investigation into child sexual abuse in the Catholic Church. The investigation has been running for 12 years and resulted in 19 convictions. *Shane Myers*

Bishop Michael Malone with Helen Keevers, the head of his child protection unit, 'Zimmerman House', in 2005. Helen Keevers changed the way the diocese dealt with survivors and their families and employed an ex-police officer to conduct investigations into the clergy and religious. *Newcastle Herald*

Father Ron Picken, the parish priest at Wingham, north of Newcastle, was a close associate of Father John Denham. Picken was present at the Wingham presbytery when Denham plied teenage boys with alcohol and sexually abused them. *Brock Perks / Sun Herald Hunter Edition*

Bishop Michael Malone held a special church service for survivors and their families at the Sacred Heart Cathedral in Hamilton on 7 August 2008. *Kitty Hill / Newcastle Herald*

By 2009, Father John Denham was facing 134 child sex offences relating to 39 boys. Detective Sergeant Faber's initial charges kept growing as more victims came forward. Here, Father John Denham is leaving Sydney Central Local Court in August 2008. *Tracey Nearmy / AAP Image*

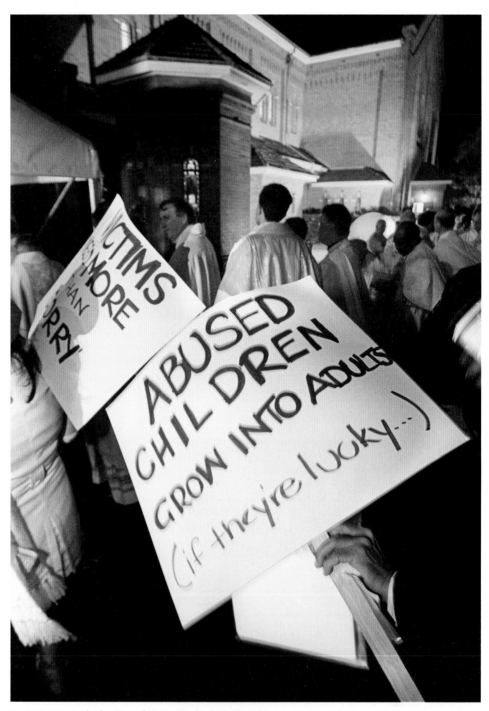

Protestors outside the Sacred Heart Cathedral, Hamilton, on 15 June 2011, on the occasion of William Wright's ordination as bishop, replacing Michael Malone. *Max Mason-Hubers / Newcastle Herald*

The *Newcastle Herald* ran a campaign for a Royal Commission into institutional child sex abuse following the death of John Pirona in 2012. *Newcastle Herald*

Troy Grant, former Police Minister and Deputy Premier of NSW, speaking after his appearance at the Hunter Special Commission of Inquiry into the Maitland-Newcastle Diocese in May 2013. *Darren Pateman / Newcastle Herald*

Bob O'Toole, the head of the Clergy Abused Network (CAN), and *Newcastle Herald* investigative journalist Joanne McCarthy, outside the Royal Commission into Institutional Responses to Child Sexual Abuse in Sydney, 2014. *Courtesy of Bob O'Toole*

Marist Brother Alexis Turton leaves a Royal Commission hearing at the ACT Magistrates Court on 18 June 2014. Turton replaced Brother Coman as the leader of the retreat teams, a strategy to recruit young men into the Marist Brothers. *Graham Tidy / Canberra Times*

Brother William 'Christopher' Wade, former principal of Marist Brothers Hamilton, leaves a Royal Commission hearing on 7 September 2016. He would later be convicted of child sex offences and making false statements to police. He was at Audrey Nash's house the night her son Andrew died in 1974. *Rebekah Ison / AAP Image*

Former Marist Brother and teacher Francis Cable, known as Brother Romuald, outside Newcastle Local Court in March 2019, where he was found guilty of abusing five boys. In 2015, he had previously been convicted of abusing 19 boys. *Darren Pateman / Newcastle Herald*

The Archbishop of Adelaide, Philip Wilson, leaves Newcastle Local Court on Tuesday, 19 June 2018, after being found guilty of concealing historical child sexual abuse. He was later acquitted. *Darren Pateman / AAP Image*

ABOVE: Father Glen Walsh, St Peter's Square, Vatican City, 2016. During this visit, Glen met with Pope Francis. He told friends he discussed his upcoming court appearance in the trial of Archbishop Philip Wilson.

Steven Alward and Mark Wakely, Chile, December 2017. This was the last photo taken of Steven Alward before he died.
Courtesy of Mark Wakely

National Committee for Professional Standards, the national Church body responsible for dealing with sexual abuse complaints against clergy – and he hadn't understood the concept of grooming!

For several years, Malone had been responsible for hundreds of Catholic school students in the Maitland-Newcastle Diocese. To be precise, the bishop was in charge of forty parishes, forty-nine primary schools, eleven secondary schools, and social welfare agencies such as Centacare, hostels, nursing homes and self-care units. The diocese also had about fifty parish priests.[11] There were the Marist Brothers, and orders of nuns, and other religious as well.

The *Jackson Report* confirms that back in 1998, Malone had concerns about Brock following John Wakely's disclosures. Malone's statement in the report reveals that in his conversation with Brock on 7 July 1998, 'Father Brock admitted that he was homosexual, admitted having a sexual relationship with 'X' (named in John Wakely's complaint) denied that he had a sexual interest in children, and asserted he was celibate.'[12] Malone accepted this and then offered Brock an assessment at Encompass Australasia,[13] though the bishop said it was up to the priest. Brock didn't want to go, and Malone didn't push it.

The *Jackson Report* says Malone 'determined that Father Brock did not pose a risk of harm to children or young persons'.[14] The report then questions this assumption, given Brock had refused the psychological assessment at Encompass. It says Malone 'did not take all reasonable steps to persuade Father Brock to undergo an assessment'.[15] Brock told the investigators that Malone 'said that had I not been so frank he would have, this is as I remember it, I think he said something like, had I not been as upfront he would have recommended that I go to the Encompass program for an assessment'.[16]

David Jackson QC revealed that John Davoren and two others advised Malone to leave Brock in place. The report is critical of Malone on a key point in this regard: 'It did not occur to Bishop Malone that because Father Brock had a sexual relationship with X at the age of 18, in circumstances when Father Brock had known X prior to him turning 18, that Father Brock's relationship with X prior to the age of 18 may have been inappropriate or involved Father Brock "grooming" X.'[17] But Jackson and his investigators never interviewed John Davoren.[18] He had given his advice that Brock didn't have to be stood aside to Malone's vicar-general, Father Burston, who had sought it on Malone's behalf.

The report says that after speaking with Brock, Malone had considered the matter closed. Jackson criticised this: 'Upon receipt of information alleging that one of his priests had posed, and continued to pose, a danger to children, Bishop Malone in my opinion was obliged to take reasonable steps to ensure that no such danger existed, and I am not persuaded that he responded appropriately to the allegations made by Mr Wakely in 1998 for two reasons; first Bishop Malone did nothing more to investigate the allegations than speak to Father Brock.' Jackson added, 'When allegations are made concerning the safety of children, it is to be expected that more would be done than simply to confront the alleged wrongdoer. It was in my view, unreasonable not to conduct even a rudimentary investigation to ascertain whether there was any substance to the allegations. It is beside the point that the investigation conducted by Bill Jardine in 2005 appears to have confirmed Bishop Malone's initial assessment. Bishop Malone's assessment was made on the basis of an inadequate investigation.'[19]

The next conclusion is even more damning: 'Secondly, Bishop Malone did not even speak to Father Brock until some two months had elapsed since he spoke to Mr Wakely. When the safety of children is at stake it is to be expected that greater diligence would be applied to ensure that they are not at risk. Should it have been the case that Father Brock posed a danger to children, the delay between the making of the allegation and any investigation being conducted by Bishop Malone could have been disastrous.'[20]

Malone had been lucky: Part 3A of the *Ombudsman Act* had not commenced until 7 May 1999, so before that date Malone had no obligations to report under it. John had raised his concerns in 1998.

But importantly, the *Jackson Report* reveals that someone else made a·complaint about Brock to Malone. On 15 May 2001, this second complaint was made by a woman calling herself 'Virginia'. The bishop's file note showed the woman had come to see him, 'to inform me of rumours she had heard about Peter Brock: her aunt had heard from a religious sister that Peter had interfered with children; her father had heard at a funeral the same rumour'.[21]

Malone had spoken to Brock on 18 May 2001. According to the *Jackson Report*, 'Bishop Malone did not make any further inquiries into Father Brock's conduct because he felt that he had "dealt with that earlier". Bishop Malone said to Father Brock, "You assure me that you are celibate and it's not a problem and you have no predilection towards children and so on and I have accepted that".'[22]

Again, according to this report, Malone hadn't considered this allegation by Virginia an official complaint but a rumour, as he had done in the case of John Wakely in 1998.

And again, Malone hadn't investigated the claims; he never contacted the 'aunt' or the 'religious sister' to get their views. The report criticises Malone for not doing these basic follow-ups; however, the report doesn't state whether its own investigators followed up on Virginia's claims, and there doesn't appear to be any evidence in the Jackson Report that they did.

In 2001, The *Ombudsman Act* made allegations of a reportable nature mandatory to report within thirty days of their receipt. So any allegation against any employee who had access to students under the age of eighteen must be reported. But because Malone considered this allegation a rumour, he hadn't notified the Ombudsman. He hadn't followed up with Virginia's sources. And his next move had been positively Orwellian in nature. He'd discussed with Brock, 'How best to "scotch" the rumours circulating about him. It was considered an article in *Aurora*, the Diocesan newspaper, would be useful. An article on the dangers of gossip was subsequently printed. The article dealt with gossip generally; not with any particular item of gossip.'[23] *Aurora* was and is a Catholic magazine that goes out to all the parishioners in the Maitland–Newcastle Diocese; Brock had been its first editor.

David Jackson's view was that Malone 'was wrong to respond to Virginia's complaints simply by attempting to "scotch" the rumours concerning Father Brock'. However, despite Jackson's criticisms of Malone's utter failure to investigate the claims, his legal opinion was that Malone had not been required by the Act to notify the Ombudsman.[24]

The report then tackles the third complaint, in December 2004, by John Wakely, which was reported to the Ombudsman while Bill Jardine was appointed as the internal diocesan investigator. Jardine's investigation had cleared Malone of any wrongdoing earlier that year.

The *Jackson Report* moves to the thorny issue of Malone appointing Brock as executive officer of the National Commission for Clergy Life and Ministry. Malone told the report's investigators that Brock was selected as a potential candidate because: 'He was a very high profile in the community … He's very musical. He conducted the University choir in Newcastle for over 20 years. He's well known in musical and artistic circles. He has always been regarded as a very fine priest amongst his peers, his peers in the diocese and by myself. He was identified as a priest with heart, with compassion and with a love for priesthood. Since his role was going to involve him in the pastoral care of priests though out [sic] Australia, it was considered that he would be ideal for such a role.'[25]

Brock was appointed in 2001, the same year that Virginia made her complaint.

The report only raps Malone over the knuckles for not advising the Canberra diocese that Brock had some allegations against him, a requirement of the *Towards Healing* protocol. This is hardly criticism.

On whether Malone coerced principal Will Callinan into backing the bishop's version of events on when he informed Will of Fletcher's offending, Malone was cleared.

Then came the question that was particularly important to Pell and the Church: was Malone an appropriate Head of Agency for the diocese?[26] David Jackson QC, in his final summation, said Malone had made some 'errors of judgement' in dealing with Fletcher and Brock: 'He had had difficulty, I thought, in recognising that in dealing with allegations of sexual abuse to children, the interests of the accused individual may have to be subordinated, as by suspension from office or duties, to other interests during the investigation of allegations.'[27] But Jackson added Malone had recognised this view must change.

Then the main resolution in the report absolved Bishop Malone; 'I am satisfied that, whatever may have been the position in the past, the bishop recognises that it is imperative that child protection issues are investigated and dealt with properly. In the result I am not satisfied that the bishop should not be Head of Agency for the diocese for child protection matters.'[28]

After the *Jackson Report*, relations soured further between John Wakely and the bishop.

John met with Brock after the report was released. Brock seemed nervous and kept saying the word 'yes', over and over. He clearly wanted to please the principal, his eyes pleading with John to believe he wasn't a paedophile. It was a tense and unsettling meeting.

John went home deflated. He told his wife, 'Priests and Brothers are unaccountable. You don't get a contract. You don't get an appraisal. You don't have surveys about how you're going. You've got the job and you've got it for life. You're ordained to it. It's like being a member of the Royal Family. It's like the Roman Empire. Same basis. Once you're the Roman emperor, someone has to stab you or you die.'

On 21 September 2005, Cardinal Pell's private secretary, Dr Michael Casey, wrote to the Ombudsman's principal investigator on behalf of Pell. Casey said that the *Jackson Report* found: '(a) Bishop Malone had at all times acted in good faith and in accordance with what he considered to be an appropriate response in relation to allegations against Father Brock ... (b) There was no reason why ... Bishop Malone should not be Head of Agency for the diocese of Maitland–Newcastle.'[29]

Malone was exonerated on all points. Nothing to see here.

The *Jackson Report* is a whitewash in many respects – perhaps it can even be described as a once-over-lightly, a sham. David Jackson QC had not overseen a thorough investigation of Father Peter Brock. The report's investigators had failed to interview all the relevant people about Father James Fletcher. Did the Ombudsman in 2005 know any of this?

John Wakely never received a copy, and he was left angry and bewildered that Malone had been exonerated. Worse still, Brock was left in a position that could influence areas that touched on child protection. Father Brock still had access to children for several years from this point.

The findings emboldened Brock. The scion of the great Newcastle family had been protected.

CHAPTER 19

Lies and Secrets

BY AUGUST 2005, HELEN KEEVERS WAS IN CHARGE OF THE newly formed Diocesan Child Protection and Professional Conduct Unit (DCPPCU), later known as Zimmerman House and after that as Zimmerman Services, intended primarily as a place where any clerical child sexual abuse survivors could receive support and pastoral care, and which would also have an investigative arm to look into complaints against Church employees, clergy and religious.

The DCPPCU was accountable only to the bishop. Malone appointed Helen as its first director, along with a staff of six people: social workers, investigators, community liaison officers and admin staff. Over time, its investigative arm included a former police officer. Together, Helen and this officer investigated abuse complaints from families and survivors, and would refer many of them to the police.

The unit was set up in an old two-storey mansion in Newcastle owned by the Church. Helen insisted all religious symbols be removed so survivors would feel more comfortable entering the property and talking about their problems. Throughout her time at the unit, Helen believed that Malone really wanted change in his diocese. In her eyes, he had taken on board the criticisms of the Ombudsman and was trying to set up the best unit possible to tackle clerical child sexual abuse. This new approach to child protection eventually saw charges being laid against four members of the clergy, and it had sparked several new Ombudsman investigations. Helen was feeding material to the police on a frequent basis, and Malone supported her in that, otherwise it couldn't have happened.

But no amount of good work could overturn decades of obfuscation. For all her authority in the diocese, Helen was still a layperson, a woman, and was not apprised of the many issues and concerns about clergy and religious. She was always an outsider. There were many secrets.

* * *

Father James Fletcher's legal team appealed his conviction all the way to the High Court, but before the decision was announced the priest died, on 7 January 2006, in jail.

More than thirty priests attended his funeral at the Branxton church, not far from where he had committed abuses against children.

The priests, all dressed in white, gathered out the front of the old brick church as his coffin was brought out and into the hearse. They surrounded the black hearse like an honour guard. Their vestments billowed in the wind.

There were only a couple of priests missing from the service – one of them was Father Glen Walsh.

Father James Fletcher was buried with full honours in the Sandgate cemetery, where deceased priests were typically interred. No mention of his convictions.

Following his death, the High Court ruled; 'We are not persuaded there has been any miscarriage of justice.'[1]

The families were relieved and happy.

Detective Sergeant Peter Fox told the media: 'The decision means that the highest court in the land accepts as correct for the district court to have allowed evidence from a second altar boy whom Fletcher abused, and that will flow on to all other courts so they too can accept similar tendency evidence.'[2]

Father Glen Walsh was elated. Not only had the ruling survived a High Court challenge, but the case changed the law in Australia. The High Court had interpreted the common law as including tendency evidence. This made it much easier to prove historical child sex abuse cases. Other victims' testimony that proved a pattern of behaviour would be allowed.

Elizabeth and Glen felt their decision to support Brendan to become a witness in the case had been vindicated.

On a deeper level, they both realised how much this case had opened their eyes to the systemic abuse within the Catholic Church in the Maitland–Newcastle Diocese.

* * *

'I want to tell you about Father Denham.'

The *Newcastle Herald* had reported on the Fletcher matter as it unfolded and had continued to investigate clerical sexual abuse allegations in the diocese throughout 2005. Its head office was in the inner city, but it also employed journalists around the region. Joanne McCarthy was based on the Central Coast, an hour and a bit south of Newcastle. The eldest daughter in a big Catholic family, she was already making a name for herself as an investigative reporter on some tough stories.

She had no idea how one phone call would turn her world upside down.

In 2006, an anonymous man called up McCarthy at her desk and asked her why no one had covered the story about Father John Denham.

She had never heard the priest's name before.

The caller told her that despite Denham having been convicted on child sexual assault charges in 2000, he was now working at a Church facility of some kind down in Sydney near children. There had been no media coverage of the conviction, and he was still a priest.

McCarthy thought this sounded like a good story. She tracked down Denham in Kensington, at the library where he was working, and gave him a call.

Denham answered with a plummy voice. McCarthy identified herself and asked whether he'd ever been charged with a child sex offence and whether he was working at a Church facility near a school. He was obviously irritated by the call, and he denied he'd been convicted of any child sex offences.

At the time of the call McCarthy had yet to receive confirmation of the conviction, so she decided not to challenge him.

The next day, an officer from the Sydney District Court Registry confirmed the details about the offences, the sentence, the file number and which judge had presided over the case.

It was everything McCarthy needed. She called up the priest and confronted him. 'You told me a porky there yesterday. You have been convicted of child sex offences. Here is the file number, the date and the penalty.'

Denham's tone grew cold and harsh. 'Are you going to write a story about me?'

McCarthy replied, 'Of course I am.'

Denham then threatened legal action and ended the conversation with a warning: 'I hope you've got good lawyers!'

McCarthy thought the priest sounded very arrogant, like someone who had never had to account for his behaviour before. He was bluffing – once someone is convicted of something in a court of law, there is no chance of defamation if you only report the facts.

Denham acted as if *he* was the victim, and McCarthy thought he was the ultimate denialist, and that this was partly why he was so dangerous to children.

The journalist called her anonymous source back and told him the *Herald* would be running an article on 6 June 2006 about Denham working near children in a Catholic Church facility despite his conviction.

When the piece went public, it was like a bomb had gone off. It let Denham's other victims know that he had been successfully prosecuted in court.

The priest was still incardinated in the Maitland–Newcastle Diocese. There had been no move to laicise him back in 2000, and it seemed the conviction hadn't even been reported to the NSW Ombudsman at the time.

Now Denham and the diocese were exposed, his victims started to come forward in large numbers. And Joanne McCarthy was there to document every one of them in the *Newcastle Herald*.

* * *

McCarthy's reportage meant Bishop Malone couldn't ignore the fact Denham was still a priest. Broken Rites, the national publication based in Melbourne, also had the story about Denham's conviction. They'd also received a call from a victim of Denham about his original conviction. Now it would get wide-reaching exposure and be shared online by hundreds of survivors around Australia and even internationally.

Malone realised he would have to begin the process of laicising Denham. The Vatican would need to be informed, as only the Pope could officially terminate a priest.

Since 2002, Denham had been working at the Chevalier Resource Centre library in Kensington, an eastern suburb of Sydney. It was right next to a primary school.

It wasn't until 3 July 2006, a month almost to the day after McCarthy's first article on the matter, that Malone wrote to Denham and formally removed his faculties to minister, taking away his right to preach, say mass and hear confessions.

But Denham was still a priest.

Malone then wrote to Cardinal Pell in Sydney, informing him of the outcome and asking him to undertake a final risk assessment of Denham.[3]

Twelve years after the diocese had received its first officially recorded report about Denham in 1994, he was finally removed from ministry. But he remained a priest for some years to come.

On 10 July 2006, Denham sent this reply to Malone:

Having been ordained for 34 years it seems a dismal and distressing ending to my priestly ministry, my only consolation being the many people God has enabled me to serve over the period and who are actively praying for my welfare.

The disgraceful *Newcastle Herald* has effectively cut me off from visiting my friends in the diocese, a penance I will obviously have to bear. This coupled to the equally obnoxious posting on the internet by Broken Rites has shaken my belief in natural justice.

Despite the half-truths and the downright lies published there is nothing I can do to defend my integrity. I will continue to maintain my innocence of the charges levelled at me until I die and go to the perfect judge who will vindicate my position.

I am deeply grateful for the marvellous support given to me financially by the diocese and hasten to assure you that I will obey without question your demands.[4]

* * *

Denham never sued Joanne McCarthy or the *Newcastle Herald* – he couldn't. He was a convicted felon. His threat was just one example of his grandiose view of himself as invincible.

From this point on, McCarthy developed and maintained a professional relationship with Helen Keevers. These two women, both passionate about child protection issues, were on a shared mission: one working on the outside, one from within.

Their chats gave them some occasional, much-needed moment of levity. Once, Helen told McCarthy that she had written to Denham without addressing him as a priest, which had infuriated him.

McCarthy realised very quickly that Fletcher and Denham were just the tip of the iceberg – there had been many offending priests in the diocese. By 2007, she'd heard that police were investigating another priest by the name of Peter Brock. This was particularly sensitive for McCarthy, because one of his brothers was her editor at the *Herald*, Roger Brock. He didn't stop her investigating and she pursued the story.

* * *

On 7 August 2007, Monsignor Patrick Cotter died. Bishop Malone conducted the funeral, which was attended by many priests across the Maitland-Newcastle Diocese.

On 10 September 2007, Broken Rites published an article online about Father Ryan and Monsignor Cotter's years of cover-up. After being briefed by Broken Rites, McCarthy and the *Herald* obtained the 1996 police files on the Ryan case.

McCarthy began reporting exclusive and detailed information on the Cotter–Ryan cover-up. The explosive material shocked the *Herald*'s readers, and the extent of the cover-up, along with the failure of the Director of Public Prosecutions to act in the matter, caused great concern throughout the Hunter Region.

She focused on concealment. How many priests and Brothers had been protected over the past few decades? The Cotter–Ryan case had revealed how it was done, providing McCarthy with the behind-the-scenes modus operandi of the Catholic Church in such cases. It was only a matter of time before she exposed other clergy and religious within the diocese who had committed and concealed crimes of sexual abuse.

Malone was angry with McCarthy's reporting of these events, especially the articles on Cotter. Soon after those stories appeared, he penned an article, 'Trial by Media', which slammed the *Herald*. He wanted it to be included in the local Catholic diocesan newsletter, *Aurora*, but it was never published.

Malone began by insulting the *Herald* with what he presumably believed was biting wit: 'Even for "The Herald" (Newcastle) described recently by one of our priests as "that grubby little rag", the concerted attack on the diocese of Maitland-Newcastle commencing late September 2007 has been quite extreme. I resent having to pay $1.20 for the paper, but I do so to learn what "the enemy" is saying!'

Malone, of course, was being perfectly reasonable: 'Readers of "Aurora" will know that I am usually happy to cooperate with the media, appear reasonably often on radio and television and have enjoyed the interaction with both presenters and audience. I cannot say the same for "The Herald" however. So called "investigative journalism" seems to demand that some members of staff be rude and arrogant. I think some of them are even dishonest in that their reporting is blatantly selective, using quotations out of context and generally writing a piece to suit their own agenda. Objective reporting is a joke.'

Recently, Malone wrote, he'd decided to refuse personal interviews 'with some of those "journalists" because I know my remarks will be used against me and, put simply, I will not get a fair go' – instead, he insisted 'on the questions being put into writing and my answers being sent back the same way'. He added that 'any interviews in future will be recorded in the presence of a member of my staff', and he went on to say, 'The recent concerted attack on the diocese came only from "The Herald". Both radio and television chose not to be involved. I found that significant since it indicates to me that even other media could see the personal nature of "The Herald's" attack and chose not to be a part of it. I think that is a credit to their integrity.'

Malone then made an astute observation: 'I also found it interesting that "The Herald" began to write these stories only after the main characters had died. Monsignor Cotter, Bishop Leo Clarke and Denis McAlinden have died in recent times. Now that they cannot defend themselves they are being put on trial by "The Herald", judged guilty and condemned. Watch the paper when I am dead! ...'[5] He didn't seem to appreciate that the paper could only report truthfully on these men *because* they were dead and therefore couldn't sue for defamation.

In conclusion: 'It was not the fault of the diocese that Monsignor Cotter failed to be charged for his alleged complicity in the Vince Ryan matter. Nor was it his age at the time of his interview with police. The truth is that Monsignor Cotter did not believe he had committed a crime and therefore had nothing to be charged with.'[6]

CHAPTER 20

Strike Force Georgiana

IN OCTOBER 2007, JOANNE MCCARTHY HAD LEARNED THAT A senior policewoman in Lake Macquarie, Detective Sergeant Kristi Faber, was looking into Father Brock at the helm of a new strike force. McCarthy called up Faber and asked her for more details. The investigator was courteous but kept their conversation brief; the strike force was confidential.

Detective Sergeant Faber had the air of a woman who meant business. Her quiet demeanour hid a steely resolve, and she cut a striking figure in her suits. She'd grown up in a male household except for her mum, and her dad and brothers had always given her a lot of respect.

By this time in her successful career, Faber had interviewed more than a hundred child sex offenders. Her first strike force had been Tolentino in 2001, when she'd ended up charging eight men with ninety-nine offences. In 2005, she was promoted to detective sergeant, and by 2007, she'd had a lot of experience with the worst of humanity. She had studied the habits of paedophiles and their psychological impulses, and she thought they were arrogant and narcissistic. Many of them had told her in interviews they believed what they'd been doing was right – in their warped view, they loved the children.

* * *

In 2007, Glen Walsh was adrift at the whim of Cardinal Pell and the Archdiocese of Sydney, and he was unsettled and traumatised from the events in Maitland-Newcastle. At least he had his teaching experience, which helped him secure jobs. Glen would also try to revive old connections in places he had worked before, but this didn't always work out – he had worked with a group of nuns in the southern part of Sydney until someone in the Church told them not to associate with him.

Glen felt he was still being punished for going to the police about Fletcher back in 2004. He was now keen to return to the Maitland-Newcastle Diocese to continue his work as a priest. He felt he had a lot more to give.

Glen had kept in touch with a priest serving in the diocese, and the two of them remained close friends.

Father James Lunn, from the St James Parish in Muswellbrook, wanted Glen to return. He decided to contact Malone about the possibility of Glen returning as an assistant priest in his parish. On 29 January 2007, Lunn wrote to Malone: 'I write to you about the possibility of inviting Father Glen Walsh to reside as an Assistant Priest in this parish … I merely wish to obtain an in-principle approval from yourself for me to write to Father Glen. I would invite him to reside in the presbytery here and have some ministerial and pastoral role … Should Fr Glen accept this invitation I would ask you to write appointing him as Assistant Priest at Muswellbrook-Aberdeen.'

On Thursday, 8 February 2007, Malone replied via email, which he labelled 'confidential': 'I know that your motives in suggesting an invitation be extended to Glen to return to ministry are inspired by your regard for him and your wish to see him settled into priesthood once more. I am sorry to say, James, that I would not welcome Glen's return to ministry in the diocese. Were he to seek a return to ministry, I would happily release him to serve in another Diocese or in some other priestly ministry.'

Lunn was angry and dismayed. He wrote again to Malone on 14 March 2007: 'I am profoundly sad to have received your letter about Father Glen Walsh. I believe that it makes you look like you have a poor spirit of collaboration: those who disagree with you or displease will be dismissed from active ministry in the diocese. I am also profoundly concerned that this appears that anyone who reports an abuser will be punished for having made such a report.' Lunn did not mince his words. 'I strongly urge you to change your decision on the matter. In regard to confidentiality, these matters are already in discussion in clergy circles and I disbelieved those who had said you would not welcome Father Glen Walsh back into the Maitland-Newcastle Diocese. I will be lodging a formal complaint in regard to these matters.'

Malone again wrote to Lunn on 21 March 2007: 'Without elaborating, I have sound reasons for my comments, none of which coincide with your own mistaken interpretation of my motives ... your own strong remarks indicate to me that you may be "testing the waters" on Glen's behalf. If that is the case, I suggest you inform Glen that I would be happy to speak with him – he will then hear my reasons himself.'

Lunn did not rest. On 8 May 2007, he wrote to Ambrose De Paoli, the Apostolic Nuncio in Canberra. In effect, he was contacting the Vatican and going over Malone's head. Lunn cc'd his letter to the president of the Australian Catholic Bishops Conference, Archbishop Wilson, and to Cardinal Pell.

... I have recently been in correspondence with Bishop Michael Malone ... over information that a priest of this Diocese would not be welcome to return to ministry in this diocese ... You will see that Fr Walsh, an incardinated priest of this diocese, has been excluded from ordinary service in this diocese. Bishop Malone himself provides no indication of any due process that was undertaken as the basis for this exclusion.

I write this letter firstly to formalise my complaint against the behaviour of Bishop Michael Malone ... Fr Walsh has sought to indicate to his Ecclesiastical superiors, his concerns about substantial injustices that have occurred either by thoughtlessness, incompetence or moral defect in this Diocese. I believe he has been unable to elicit a substantial and appropriate response from the competent authorities in regard to these matters. In fact he has found himself undermined and excluded from ordinary pastoral service in his home diocese. I write in support of Father Walsh's concerns and to register my dismay at the treatment he has received.

On 22 May, De Paoli wrote back to Lunn. He sided with Malone; he would not intervene. He said Malone had invited Glen to speak to the bishop directly to find out why the bishop had made his decision. That was that.

Many years later, Glen wrote to his lawyer and said, 'When first I was made aware of this correspondence, I telephoned Malone to ask what his "reasons" for refusing to ever appoint me to a parish. He could not/would not give me any reason for his decision!'[1]

* * *

Pope Benedict XVI was coming to Australia in July 2008 to celebrate the eleventh World Youth Day, a blessed occasion for many Australian Catholics.

With Helen Keevers' encouragement, Malone decided to make a public stand in late May 2008, and call on the Pope to apologise to sexual abuse victims in Australia. No other bishop had done this in Australia. There was criticism from some in the clergy that he was letting the child sexual abuse issue cloud the Pope's visit.

On 26 May 2008, Malone and Helen appeared on *Lateline*, a nightly current affairs television program, in a story that also featured Pat Feenan and Detective Inspector Peter Fox. Helen extolled the virtues of Zimmerman House, and Malone told the nation that he had erred badly in the Fletcher case. It was unheard of for a bishop to admit his mistakes on national television. It was an attempt to make amends for the years of mistakes and missteps.

Pope Benedict XVI arrived on 13 July 2008. On 15 July, he celebrated mass with Cardinal George Pell on the harbour at Barangaroo. Around 250,000 pilgrims slept overnight at the Randwick Racecourse in Sydney, and about 400,000 celebrated a mass conducted by the Pope on Sunday, 20 July.

Glen attended the Youth Festival events held every afternoon in the city, which included art exhibitions, concerts and seminars. He met several inspiring priests around the same age as him; some of these contacts would become lifelong friends.

Meanwhile, Malone's gesture to stand alone and demand an apology from the Pope was overshadowed by the growing number of police investigations into priests and Brothers in the bishop's diocese. Maitland–Newcastle would become notorious across Australia and the world for being one of the worst epicentres for clerical child sexual abuse.

* * *

On 7 August 2008, Bishop Malone stood in front of about five hundred people in the Sacred Heart Cathedral in Hamilton, and apologised to all the victims of clerical sexual abuse. The congregation applauded.

On 9 October 2008, only three years after David Jackson QC delivered his report to Cardinal Pell exonerating Malone's handling of the Brock matter, Father Peter Brock was charged with 22 child sex offences by Detective Sergeant Kristi Faber and her team at Strike Force Georgiana.

The *Newcastle Herald* reported:

High-profile Catholic priest and music conductor Father Peter Brock stands accused of repeatedly taking a young boy to a house and watching on as several men sexually assaulted the teen in what was described yesterday as a 'pedophilic smorgasbord'.

He faces 18 counts of indecent assault, two acts of indecency and two counts of buggery...

Father Brock, 63, is alleged to have repeatedly abused one of them while the boy and Father Brock played the game on the floor of 'counselling rooms' in two Hunter presbyteries over a two-year period.

The court was told that in the mid-1970s, when the boy was aged 15 and two years after he was first abused, Father Brock took him to a Newcastle house on at least six occasions and watched on as several men sexually assaulted the teen after plying him with alcohol.[2]

Principal John Wakely was angry. He read the reports in the *Newcastle Herald*. He had raised the alarm back in 1998 with Bishop Malone only to be brushed off. Then he had reported his concerns to the child protection hotline in 2004. He had tried twice to raise the alarm. For his efforts back then he was threatened with defamation by Bishop Malone. Now Father Brock's alleged offending was very serious.

* * *

On 16 October 2008, Glen's friend Father Lunn met with a senior official in the diocese, Gordon Quinn. Quinn confirmed to him that Malone had not discussed his request to bring Glen back to the diocese with the Council of Priests. Lunn told Quinn he was concerned at the 'lack of due process in the way Glen had been treated'.[3]

Less than a week earlier, one of Glen's closest friends had written to Cardinal Pell. She told him, '[Glen] had done nothing wrong, he did what others were scared to do, he was being treated dismally by his fellow priests and he should be allowed back to his Diocese of Maitland-Newcastle as a Minister.'[4]

She received this reply from Father John Usher, on behalf of Pell, on 7 November 2008: 'His Eminence Cardinal Pell has asked me to acknowledge your kind letter of the 10th of October 2008 about Father Walsh. The Cardinal was aware of the matters raised in your letter. He has had many discussions with Father Walsh who is now working as a Priest in the Archdiocese of Sydney, as you know. Of course, these matters have also been discussed with Bishop Malone. It is regrettable that Father Walsh is unable to work effectively in his own diocese because of the matters you raised in your letter. The Cardinal thanks you for your supportive letter.'[5]

* * *

Since late 2007, Strike Force Georgiana had been speaking to clerical abuse survivors and their families in the diocese. Curiously, along with Father Peter Brock, another priest kept coming up in their conversations: Father John Denham.

Denham stood out. When her investigation into him was over, Detective Sergeant Faber would realise he had been one of the worst perpetrators in Australia's history.[6]

During the Strike Force Georgiana investigation, which was ongoing until May 2020, police were given the names of possible victims.

One day, Faber was given a name she instantly recognised: John Pirona. He was a local fire chief, larger than life, a very confident man and very funny. Faber knew him because they'd been on a few jobs together and their children had attended the same preschool.

Faber called John at the fire station, and he agreed to come in to the Lake Macquarie Police Station straightaway. She took him to the interview room. He told her he was a victim of Denham, and then he broke down and cried.

Most victims cry. It takes days to get down their statements. Faber sat with them. From the first statement about Denham came ten more, and then others.

Suddenly Faber had forty statements in front of her.

It was as if all her years of hunting paedophiles had prepared her for this arduous investigation. She knew exactly what to do.

CHAPTER 21

'The fathers don't like that sort of thing'

– Father Tom Brennan

DETECTIVE SERGEANT FABER REALISED EARLY ON THAT THE Church had seen Father Denham as a problem for many years. She could tell from his work history: he was always 'assistant parish priest', never the top dog.

During Faber's initial investigation into Denham, she suspected he had many more victims than those who had come forward. He had offended against a boy at the seminary, and that behaviour hadn't stopped when he'd been transferred to Waverley College in 1986.

As she pored over the documents, interviews and court records, she realised that at every stage Denham had been moved, some of his superiors in the Church had known he was sexually assaulting children. After five years of offending at St Pius X High School, he'd been transferred to Charlestown as the assistant parish priest and offended again. His activities had been brought to the notice of Bishop Clarke, who had transferred him to the Taree primary school for five years. This move was particularly galling to the seasoned investigator: Denham had then had access to children in Years Three, Four, Five and Six.[1]

In one of her reports Faber wrote: 'And then they moved him to Sydney to study moral theology. So he studied moral theology for a number of years, and then eventually down there he started teaching somehow at Waverley College, and again he was reported down there to the local police and charged.'[2]

Faber also made a note of Denham's closest associates at the time of his offending. From 1975 until 1980 he had lived on site at St Pius X, and from 1978 to 1979 Philip Wilson, now the archbishop of Adelaide, had been the school's director of religious education and lived there alongside Denham for at least nine months.

Late in the evening, Faber would pore over her notes. She needed to get inside Denham's mind. She had to know everything about him. He was her prey.

One revelation for her was that Denham had known all along that he could act with impunity. He'd fully believed there would be no sanctions against him. His behaviour had been so brazen and open that surely he'd felt he had a right to offend.

At St Pius X, he had called his Year Seven and Eight classes one at a time into his office for a book review, and on each occasion he had indecently assaulted a boy, and at times he had sexually assaulted others. Denham either groped boys by their genitals or, on occasion, he anally raped some of them.

Faber usually didn't hesitate as she read over the statements of victims. But these stories were different – the calculating cruelty got to her. Some of the kids had kicked and run; others had been frozen with fear. And so many boys had done book reviews over those five years. How many kids had he assaulted in that period?

Her investigations found it had been an open secret at the school that Denham would take boys to his onsite bedroom at lunchtime and after school; the other boys would make fun of these students and call them 'Denham's bum boys'. Other classmates would come back to class after lunchtime smelling of alcohol, given to them by Denham.[3]

In 1977, Denham had gone to the Year Seven classroom, pointed out five children and told them to follow him to his bedroom in the priests' quarters. Once inside the small room, the priest made the students stand in a line, and told them, 'Drop your pants.' They all did as directed, and he forced them to stand in this position for five or ten minutes while he stared at their genitals. The boys remembered the teacher had a weird smile on his face the whole time.[4]

Faber found out that the principal, Father Tom Brennan, and Bishop Clarke had received at least ten complaints about Denham, mostly during his time at St Pius X.

In 1994, Denham had told his psychiatrist that he'd received a few 'oblique warnings' over the years; at one time, Brennan had said to him, 'The [boys'] fathers don't like that sort of thing.'

In 1978, the parents of a young teenage boy at St Pius X had complained to their parish priest and later to Clarke about Denham's behaviour towards their son. The boy's mother had found her son's notebook, and the images he'd drawn concerning Denham had frightened her. Denham phoned the parents and said their concerns were 'nonsense', then he enquired whether their complaint meant they could no longer be friends. The parents remembered the priest's tone: not worried in the slightest. A week later when they complained to Clarke, the bishop did not seem at all surprised at their revelations.

At schools such as St Pius X, along with Marist Brothers Maitland and Hamilton, clergy and religious had much more opportunity to offend than at other schools because they lived there – the school, chapel and dormitories were all connected. During, before and after school the students could be attending the priests' or Brothers' quarters, while parents and many other teachers were oblivious to what was going on. Some of the St Pius X mums would dress up for the priests and go to their quarters at the school to give them food.

But the stand-out feature of St Pius X, for this police investigator, was its brutality. The atmosphere of simmering violence gave the priests more power and authority over the students than in other schools.

Denham's reputation at the school was that he had a liking for young boys, and when some of his victims rejected his advances he behaved in an aggressive and punitive fashion towards them.[5] Sometimes he behaved this way regardless of what they did. His cruelty knew no bounds. He anally raped one boy until he was bleeding, then he coldly told the child to go and clean himself up – this was Denham's initiation for altar boys.

While he was a teacher at St Pius X, he regularly took high school kids to Wingham, near Taree, on the weekends to stay with his mate Father Ron Picken. He also saw Father Barry Tunks, whom Denham had known since their time in the seminary together. He took Steven Alward away to Taree and to Wingham on some weekends.

Picken had been well liked in the Wingham area. He would call up some of his favourite parishioners and tell them Denham was lonely, so could he come to dinner? Denham would dine with the local doctors and their wives, and regale them with his superior knowledge of wines and the classics. He would boast to other families about the expensive nature of the champagne he would consume at their friends' houses.

At one such dinner, the twelve-year-old son was in attendance. Decades later, he remembered Denham's stare: it was as though the priest was seeing through him. The boy retreated to the lounge room to eat his dinner. The feeling of being sized up, like prey being assessed by a predator, has never left this man, who was now a successful lawyer.

In the Maitland-Newcastle Diocese, there were plenty of isolated rural towns, places where laws could be discreetly broken. There were reports Denham had taken boys elsewhere in the Hunter Valley, to a property at Muswellbrook. Other rumours, not specifically related to Denham, spoke of altar boys being taken to a Hunter property where they would be abused during so-called 'sex parties' with both clerical, religious and secular members of the Newcastle establishment.

Faber wondered if altar boys had been used to recruit their peers to these events. Was that why none of them had come forward, in case they incriminated themselves?

* * *

When Faber interviewed Father Ryan, he admitted he had done something wrong. But when Faber spoke to Denham, he was arrogant, without a skerrick of remorse. From a law enforcement perspective, this caused her great concern about whether Denham could be rehabilitated. And he certainly wasn't alone in this among the offending clergy and religious in the diocese.

Strike Force Georgiana found there was an extra dimension when dealing with paedophile priests and Brothers as opposed to secular offenders. The training of the priest or Brother had taught him he was a divine being. Society put him on a pedestal. Then there was his power over a community; many Catholic parents, particularly the mothers, doted on the priests and Brothers. All of this fostered narcissism in these men.

The whole community was being groomed for decades, and this was new for Faber. She and her team had to deal with the cult-like adoration of these priests and Brothers in some parishes.

But Faber would come to the conclusion it wasn't just about their training and formation: she believed that when they went into the seminary to become priests or when they decided to train as Brothers, these men were already offenders or planned to offend. They had come to the Church because it was a perfect place to hide while accessing victims.

The Church had provided a safe haven for these criminals, and the parents' unequivocal love of their Church often bound their families in a pact of secrecy. As a rule, most parents didn't go to the police when their children told them about the abuse, and the children very rarely did. It wasn't until the victims were much older, maybe after they had kids of their own, that they sought out Faber and her team.

They would call her and say they weren't ready to talk. Then four years might pass before that person would call her again and say, 'I am ready to speak to you now because my mum's passed away.'

At this point, Faber would sit down with them. They would tell her they couldn't have spoken to the police while their mother was alive, because it would have broken her heart. They would say how much their mother had loved the Church. These cases helped Faber to understand that she was dealing with cult-like behaviour.

In the 1970s there was a boy in Taree who had lost his father, and then his mother had joined a Catholic convent and become a nun. The boy was left to fend for himself and ended up living in a tent for a while. Denham preyed on the child, and the trauma never left him.

Faber was always saddened as she watched the mothers in the courtroom. Some children had been met with incredulity and occasionally physical punishment when they had told their parents about the abuse. At the time, one parent had said to their child, 'a priest wouldn't do that to you'. Now the mothers were hearing testimony from victim after victim. The reality of what had happened dawned on them. Their anguish was palpable. They understood the depth of the betrayal.

* * *

When Faber first charged Denham on 14 August 2008, a month after the Pope had visited Australia, she and her team would eventually gather 39 victims with multiple offences including serious sexual assaults. Thirty-nine men had told Faber their stories of sexual abuse. Denham was refused bail and remanded in custody until his trial in 2009.

Little did the detective know that as more of Denham's victims came forward, the court cases into his heinous offending that began in 2009 would continue until 2019. After he was sentenced for the first trial in 2009, another 18 victims came forward. There was another trial in 2010. Faber took care of most of these cases; the others were handled by the police in Taree.

In 2009, the first of these trials was held in the District Court of New South Wales, the largest trial court in Australia. The courtroom was small, its atmosphere oppressive. The survivors, with their families and partners, were on one side and Denham was on the other, surrounded by corrective services officers who had transported him there from jail.

Denham looked dishevelled and unkempt. His hair was greasy, and he seemed uncomfortable in his prison issue dark-green tracksuit. He had a very unsettling presence. This was a far cry from his days as a powerful priest, sipping the best wines and champagnes in the wealthier Catholic households.

Justice Helen Syme read her judgment to the court. She said, 'The indecent assaults involved multiple children, often significant planning, were frequently sadistic and overall persistent, objectively serious, criminal course of conduct. The offender's actions contributed to a culture of fear and depravity especially at the school which allowed these disturbing offences to occur and then remain unpunished for years. This sentence relates to those multiple offences.'

Syme also found that Denham and Picken had been involved in criminal behaviour together at the Wingham presbytery near Taree: 'On several occasions, the offender took small groups of boys on 2-day visits to the Wingham Presbytery. The offender sought written parental permission for such trips. Contrary to all proper expectations, alcohol and cigarettes were freely provided to the boys. The Wingham priest was also in residence. Sexual assaults on some of the boys occurred on these occasions.'[6]

The court heard that even after he was transferred to Waverley College in 1986, Denham returned to Taree and the Wingham presbytery while he continued to offend against a young boy.

In 1994, he had told his psychologist that he thought his behaviour was good for the children: 'The offender's statement to his psychologist ... included "Mr Denham described himself as a person who enjoyed 'saving' people, especially young boys and men and clearly saw himself as someone whose good deeds far outweighed his sins".'

Denham pleaded guilty to all the offences including buggery. But in another psychological report tendered to the court, he put in a caveat – he did not admit to all the charges but he agreed to plead guilty in order to save the diocese from more embarrassment:

'He believed that he admitted to guilt for situations that did not occur, but pleaded guilty to avoid the pain of his victims having to testify and his desire to shield both the diocese and himself from testimony as well.'[7]

In 2009 and 2010, Denham was sentenced to a total of nineteen years and four months in prison with a non-parole period of twelve years and four months. He'd been convicted of sexually assaulting an additional 39 victims.

When his sentence was read out in the first trial, some of the survivors started shouting at him angrily, their expressions full of anger and contempt. He just stood there as the judge spoke, his head bowed so he couldn't look them in the eye.

Syme wrote in her 2010 sentencing judgment: 'There is evidence of offending since 1986. He was convicted of 2 counts of indecent assault of males in 2000, matters he categorised as arising due to the disquiet of the person's mother, rather than the complainant ... The offender has gone through the years untroubled by his offences, lacking any remorse in respect of them and feeling confident that they will never come to light because the victims never would be prepared to talk about them. The offender enjoyed over the many years unwarranted acceptance by his associates in his respectable and stable lifestyle.'[8]

* * *

In 2008, there was someone else in Detective Sergeant Faber's sights related to the Denham matter: the former principal of St Pius X, Father Tom Brennan.

Faber had presented written evidence in her submissions to the court that there had to have been some collusion between Denham and his superiors given the number of historical complaints from parents at the school: at least ten. She brought forward evidence that Brennan had caned boys who had complained to him about their sexual abuse by Denham, and that he'd told them not to repeat these stories.

On 15 August 2008, Faber charged Brennan with perverting the course of justice and knowingly making a false statement after he had denied any knowledge of child sex allegations against Denham – Brennan had told police that no one had ever reported or disclosed allegations about Denham to him.

Not only had Brennan been repeatedly told in the second half of the 1970s that Denham was sexually abusing children, but the principal had physically assaulted some kids for raising the allegations. He'd then quietly moved Denham from the school after the father of one boy confronted Brennan about what Denham had done to his son.

Brennan was convicted of the above offences. At the time he was the vicar-general, or second-in-command to the bishop. He'd known of at least ten complaints against Denham and yet he had lied to police.

In 2009, he was convicted of knowingly making a false statement to police, but he appealed the conviction. It was upheld, and he received a twelve-month suspended sentence.

There was another woman who had been trying to get Brennan to tell the truth and go to the police: Helen Keevers. One of her biggest epiphanies about the scale of the paedophilia problem in the Church was her realisation that Brennan had covered up for Denham.

In 2009, Helen asked her husband to drive her to the nursing home where Brennan was living. She told her husband she was going to convince Brennan to go to the police. When they arrived, she asked her husband to wait in the car. She returned with a spring in her step; she told her husband that Brennan had agreed tell the police everything.

Two days later, Brennan changed his mind, and Helen was angry and upset. She told her husband, 'He'd been got at.'[9] Helen had no sympathy for Brennan – he'd been responsible for every child's welfare at St Pius X.

When Justice Syme sentenced Denham in 2010, she asked an important question: why hadn't the other teachers and adults who knew about the behaviour intervene? 'For reasons known only to them, other teachers and priests did not intervene to stop the abuse of which most of the students were aware. Occasionally a child did complain of the offender's behaviour to Father Brennan, who was the principal of the school. He at best took no action, and at worst, caned the boys who complained. On one occasion this occurred even after a complaint from parents.'

The judge came to the conclusion there had been a criminal conspiracy at St Pius X: 'The facts disclose that at some level, the hierarchy of the Church was aware of his criminal offending in the past, and chose to place him in what they considered to be "safe" placements. This did not stop him offending by returning to Taree in 1983 to commit further offences against children, whose parents were unaware of his history.'[10]

* * *

Around this time, survivors in the Maitland–Newcastle Diocese realised they would have more impact if they formed an advocacy group. About five people held a meeting in a park on a beautiful stretch of river in Maitland.

This small gathering would eventually become the Clergy Abused Network, or CAN.

From these small beginnings, this group, under the leadership of Bob O'Toole would become a formidable force. Bob was a very effective operator. He created this network of survivors as a way to gather information about the clergy and religious, and he started keeping extensive files that could be used by survivors in their compensation cases. The data he kept was also very useful for journalists like Joanne McCarthy. McCarthy would direct survivors to CAN when they needed support.

CAN also received a lot of support from Helen Keevers. McCarthy, Keevers and O'Toole were in contact with Kristi Faber at Strike Force Georgiana. They were all part of a mission to expose the decades of cover up.

Helen Keevers was regularly passing on information to Faber. She recruited a top former police officer to work in her investigation arm at Zimmerman House, and she was threatening the Church hegemony at great personal risk.

But one case currently being investigated by Strike Force Georgiana was causing her considerable grief behind closed doors. Before Peter Brock was charged with 22 child sex offences in 2008, the police notified the diocese of the investigation and he was removed from active ministry.

The diocese went into a panic. By this time, Father Peter Brock had been awarded the Order of Australia medal for his services to choirs in the Hunter and the Catholic Church.

Helen Keevers went to visit John Wakely to apologise.

The principal, John Wakely, had been a loyal foot soldier in many Catholic schools, both as a teacher and a principal, and yet he had been ignored, and, worse still, threatened with defamation.

Helen Keevers was upset and angry. She hadn't been apprised of the total story. There were so many secrets. How was she supposed to do her job?

Back in 1991, Father Peter Brock, along with other child sex offenders, had been on the Council of Priests advising Bishop Leo Clarke.

It was from this moment on that Helen Keevers realised she was dealing with organised crime on a significant scale. There weren't just a few bad apples. She started to see the connections and for the first time felt slightly afraid.

There were a few clerics who might have a lot to lose.

However, Father Peter Brock had a lot of influential connections, including a family member on the national Professional Standards Office of the Catholic Church, the body responsible for overseeing child protection issues and clergy.[11]

Father Peter Brock also made attempts to influence the outcome of the investigation and he was desperate to return to active ministry.

On 12 May 2008, Father Brock paid a visit to Helen Keevers at Zimmerman House, the child protection unit's place for survivors.

He asked Helen Keevers if she would help him return to active ministry. She told him that while there was an active police investigation he would not be returning, and after the police had finished, there would be an investigation for the NSW Ombudsman done by an independent investigator with no links to the diocese.

He became agitated and paced up and down the room.

He suddenly disclosed he had been in touch with the main victim in his case, against his solicitor's advice. At the centre of the case were two brothers, whose mother would call Brock when her husband got drunk and beat her with clenched fists. As part of his claimed mission to help boys from dysfunctional families, Brock would go to the house and restrain the man.

After the drama had ended, he would offer to put one of the boys to bed, when he would undress the child and sexually assault him. This traumatised the boy to such an extent that he ended up spending most of his adult life in psychiatric institutions.

The victim, who has been given the pseudonym 'JP', was fifteen when Father Peter Brock was sexually assaulting him.

Peter Brock and JP had met twice and spoken on the phone once to 'clear the air on this matter'.

Father Brock told Helen Keevers that he told JP, 'If this matter goes to court he would not want to, but [he] would have to tell some stories about the dysfunctional nature of [JP's] family.'[12]

Father Peter Brock told Helen he had legal advice that suggested if the police did not act soon, Bishop Malone should return him to active ministry. His tone was menacing.

As soon as Father Brock left her office, Helen Keevers made a file note and informed the police at Charlestown.

She understood Father Brock was trying to influence this witness, the most important one in the police case against him.

The last thing Peter Brock said to Helen Keevers that day was, 'Since JP has contacted him, he felt a great weight had been lifted from his shoulders because he knew he could not be convicted of anything that took place with JP.'[13]

Strike Force Georgiana had charged Father Peter Brock, along with a local dentist.

Police had the evidence that was needed to go to trial.

From evidence collected, police believed there were other victims. An important witness sought by police had, unfortunately, suicided two months before they had started their inquiries. It was a terrible tragedy.

Police were investigating a paedophile ring involving a priest.

The abuse that had been committed on the victims, including JP, was horrific. Sadly, these men were not well enough to give evidence in a criminal court where they would be heavily cross-examined.

The trial was aborted. The Director of Public Prosecutions withdrew.

Helen Keevers spent the next decade championing the cause of this victim. It became her mission. She took the case to the NSW Ombudsman instead. She stayed with it until the end.

The NSW Ombudsman's office did its own investigation and found, 'The priest had committed a 'range and pattern of behaviour that constituted sexual misconduct between 1968 and 1975.'[14]

Around this time, Helen realised she had been operating in the dark. Bishop Malone had been willing to change the diocese's approach to clerical child abuse survivors, but some historical offences, before his time, were so despicable and so large, they were kept secret by the priests who committed them. No files existed on these crimes, and Bishop Malone had not been apprised of the facts in a lot of cases. It was if they had never happened.

* * *

The 2009 Denham court case had been the first time Faber had met Joanne McCarthy. They acknowledged each other across the courtroom.

McCarthy had asked victims what they thought of Faber, and they'd all said she was an excellent cop. From then on the journalist directed victims to the detective, trusting they would be treated with respect and care. The women had exchanged work email addresses.

Faber admired McCarthy's work, especially as her stories often helped the police in their investigations. The detective also admired McCarthy for her tenacity and doggedness: the journalist left no stone unturned.

McCarthy's first impression of Faber was that she was a very strong person – a police officer at the top of her game who was very clear about her mission, the law, and how to prosecute her cases. The journalist admired the fact Faber was the first cop to get a conviction for perverting the course of justice with Father Brennan: that took determination and guts.

CHAPTER 22

A Dream Fulfilled

IN 1997, STEVEN ALWARD HAD WRITTEN A SUPPORTIVE reference for John Denham. It existed in a court file regarding Denham's convictions in 2000. Steven now knew beyond reasonable doubt that he had been conned in the darkest, most reprehensible way. Words were very important to Steven, and it was as if these words were indelible.

On 18 August 2008, four days after Faber had first charged Denham, Steven had emailed the other former Waverley College student who had written a reference for Denham in 1997. Steven let him know about the arrests of Denham and Brennan; the other man replied that he was 'shocked and appalled'. Steven told him he was watching the cases closely and would report back any news.

Steven's sister, Libby, his brother David, and David's wife, Theresa, asked Steven on separate occasions whether Denham had ever preyed on him. They knew he and the priest had been friends for many years. They knew Denham had taken Steven away for weekends when he was a teenager. But Steven denied anything had happened; he told them that Denham had only preyed on the vulnerable ones.

Steven threw himself into his work at the ABC and decided to take on his biggest challenge yet: he would go for the position of head of international news. This was one of the most stressful jobs at the ABC because, at that time, it had a broad remit. He was responsible for editorial and commissioning, the welfare of the correspondents and staff in the many overseas bureaus, and the logistics of getting teams to far-flung and often difficult locations.

The stress of sending a foreign correspondent into a war zone was sometimes intolerable to Steven. He would lie awake, fretting about some of the journalists while knowing the risk of death was always there. Indeed, over the years there had been deaths of foreign correspondents and camera people at the ABC. Tsunamis, suicide bombings, genocide and war – many ABC correspondents endured these terrible events, with consequences for themselves and their families.

Steven started to suffer from anxiety. He would be up late at night, taking calls from correspondents, his head in his hands.[1]

Steven absorbed the stress of journalists on the road and suffered from vicarious trauma. He was supportive and compassionate, and he genuinely wanted to look after them. His office in the Ultimo headquarters was littered with small souvenirs of his work travels and photos given to him by appreciative local bureau staff, including fixers and drivers. He knew all their names and often some of their families' names as well. He was one of the first International Editors to visit Kabul in Afghanistan to check on the welfare of the correspondent and her producer despite the risk to his personal safety. On his desk sat a spinning globe of the world across which the many ABC correspondents worked to bring international headlines into Australian living rooms.

Steven had finally secured his dream job. While it was stressful, it was intellectually stimulating and challenging; he loved to debate editorial issues with the correspondents, and his mind brimmed with story ideas. And he was happy at home: he and Mark continued to indulge their love of travel, music and art. But many of Steven's colleagues sensed there was a deep sadness under it all. He would have long lunches with too much alcohol.

* * *

It was about this time that Glen began his long romance with India. He decided he would follow his childhood dream of being a missionary on the subcontinent.

After a chance meeting with a nun from the Missionaries of Charity outside a church in Randwick a couple of years earlier, Glen had reconnected with the Blessed Teresa of Calcutta (Mother Teresa) and starting praying with these missionaries at their convent in Surry Hills. He wrote to their representatives in India and said, 'I desire to follow Christ into the heart of Calcutta to see if he really does want to use me as one of his Missionaries of Charity Priests.'[2]

Glen would spend the next eight years, on and off, working in the missions of India. He found great fulfilment among the poor, homeless and sick people who visited Mother Teresa's charities in Calcutta, and he worked closely with the sisters and the priests at the house in Calcutta where Mother Teresa was buried. He would say mass among the dying in the hospice. Every day he also prayed with thirty nuns in white habits, kneeling on the floor with the words 'I THIRST' in big black capital letters on the wall behind them.

Glen bought a small house in one of the agricultural projects he had helped to fund. He was keen to come back as soon as possible, as he found great purpose in his work in India.

On 3 January 2009, Glen left a message on a friend's phone: 'Of all blessings God has bestowed upon me in my miserable life after priesthood, this Calcutta experience is the most powerful. Words cannot express the gratitude I have for these beautiful outcasts who are waited on by these living saints. The missionaries of charity are amazing … I am closer to home here than I have ever been … You should walk with me through the slums – such poverty is unimaginable. Yet it is good to be living with the images of the thirsty Christ … Pray much for me, as here I see just how much of a sinner I am.'

In another message, he told his friend, 'God is working on this wretched vessel.'

On 8 January 2009, he travelled to Prem Daan, a hospice run by the nuns for three hundred men and three hundred women suffering from AIDS and other serious illnesses, both physical and mental. Glen wrote, 'I love holding them, blessing them and tending to their sores. The Sisters have allowed me into their sacred work of love with such gratitude of love. Pray for me. I am put to shame by the beauty within this poverty.' In Calcutta, this poverty was always in front of him: families living on the railway tracks, babies being bathed in mud puddles, and families picking through garbage for their evening meals. Glen lived among it. He spent many of his school holidays in India, helping out where he could.

Back in Sydney, on Mother's Day in May 2009, Glen had the most amazing stroke of good luck. While he was the assistant priest at the Caringbah parish, he went out to buy a scratchie from the local newsagency. He won $5000 a month for ten years. It was just what he needed to survive, as at the time he was living off his teacher's salary.

After much urging from his family, he put a deposit on a townhouse in Terrigal, on the Central Coast, about an hour and a half's drive south of Newcastle.

In July 2009, Glen moved again to be the administrator priest at St Therese's Catholic Church in Denistone, a north-western suburb of Sydney. But he told his brother, John, he left abruptly in 2010 after receiving threatening communication from another clergyman. The message was clear: don't cause trouble in the Sydney Diocese.

* * *

On his trips home Glen would read Joanne McCarthy's articles in the *Newcastle Herald*. Every few months, another priest from the Maitland–Newcastle Diocese was charged or there were claims of cover-up. Stories about clerical child sexual abuse started to proliferate on ABC TV via *Lateline*.

Glen was particularly shocked at the scale of Denham's offending, and he remembered the stories he had heard about the paedophile priest when he was sent to his first parish in Taree in

1996. He would often talk to his close friend, an elderly woman in Taree, about all these terrible events.

Glen's concerns about concealment of crimes against children and young adults in the Maitland–Newcastle Diocese had been well and truly vindicated. But despite a chronic shortage of priests now made worse by all the offenders in the region, Glen was still not welcome back to his home diocese.

* * *

Elizabeth Byrne and Archbishop Philip Wilson had communicated a few times in the years since Fletcher's death.

When Wilson had been a younger priest in Maitland, he had been close to the Byrnes, particularly Elizabeth's parents. At one point in her correspondence with the archbishop, she mentioned that her parents needed help in the form of compensation so they could pay for their health bills. The trauma had caused them great stress, and their health was suffering.

On 15 December 2009, Wilson sent Elizabeth a letter; enclosed was a cheque for $1000 and a note that said, 'I enclose a cheque and I know that you will deal with this in the best way. I hope it will be of some help to your mother and father. With lots of love and Christmas wishes to you ... and your family. I hope that we will see each other soon.' The cheque was from the Catholic Development Fund account and dated the same as the letter.

The cheque, with Wilson's signature on it, made Elizabeth uneasy. She didn't know whether he was genuine or had some hidden motive.

Three days later, she wrote back to him: 'We have decided to be honest and open with mum and dad, under these circumstances we have come to the decision to return the cheque.'[3]

PART
FOUR

PART
FOUR

CHAPTER 23

Betrayal of Trust

FROM 2008 TO 2017, FATHER GLEN WALSH AND STEVEN ALWARD watched closely as Detective Sergeant Kristi Faber went on to convict a large number of priests and brothers with hundreds of charges relating to close to 180 victims.[1] The Maitland–Newcastle Diocese was now all over the television, radio and online media, and the two old friends read all the information they could about each offender and where he had operated. Similar teams of police were also looking at the Anglican Church in Newcastle.

Sometimes Faber would have six matters running at once in the courts. Some investigations ran for more than eleven years. And she still believed her team had only scraped the surface in the diocese.

The detective spoke to Helen Keevers and Bishop Malone about her concerns that clergy and religious were not normal offenders, and that the culture of the Church attracted and fostered narcissistic paedophiles.

Denham's callous disregard for these children was summed up by his court-appointed psychologist. 'The psychologist's report does not assist him,' Justice Syme wrote in 2010; 'There are many passages in the report that speak of Mr Denham's lack of his insight into the sheer moral depravity of his actions, even to this day.' Syme then quoted the report. 'It states, "Therefore, he felt that the boys were consenting if they did not move away or reject him. Further, he felt that he never 'chose' students, rather, that they were often 'little bastards' who were already in trouble. Mr Denham also felt that some of his victims approached him, even after he left his teaching post. He admitted that their pain aroused him. He allowed them to drink alcohol, perhaps as a tool to gain trust or as a disinhibitor. He did not have insight into the perceived difference in power and status that he held as a priest."[2]

Denham, the former German teacher, explained to one of his psychologists a process of self-forgiveness called *Abgeschiedenheit*. Essentially, it is taking the behaviour outside yourself, examining and forgiving it, then taking it back to claim as part of yourself. Syme was unconvinced. She wrote in 2010, 'Mr Denham's self-forgiveness is not a demonstration of remorse.'[3]

Many of the priests that Faber investigated asked their victims for character statements to use in their trials.

Monsignor Allan Hart, who had been close to the Alward family, was telling parishioners he had warned Bishop Toohey not to let Denham be ordained as a priest. They had been in the seminary together. Steven was bemused – why hadn't Hart gone to the police earlier with this information? He'd been high up in the Church hierarchy for a long time.

Then Steven's thoughts turned to himself. He remembered the character statement he had written for Denham. He remembered the priest's lies. His precious words, his writing, had been used in a ploy to cover up many heinous crimes. Steven felt deep shame.

* * *

By 2009, Helen Keevers was encountering serious opposition from some members of the Council of Priests, the advisers to the bishop. She'd also employed a very experienced ex-police officer who began looking at the Anglican Church offenders in Newcastle. There was some concern that maybe some of the Catholic and Anglican offenders might have committed crimes together against children. There had been estimates that as many as 80 Anglican clerics had offended against children over the past five decades.

By June 2009, Helen Keevers had left her job as director of Zimmerman House.

The following year she attended the Newcastle Police Station and spent four hours giving a long statement to one of the police officers attached to Strike Force Georgiana. She told the police where they could find critical Church documents they would need for their investigations. The three places she mentioned were: the National Professional Standards Office in Sydney; the Catholic Church Insurances Offices in Melbourne, where the payments to survivors was kept; and a storage facility near the Australian Catholic Bishop's Conference (ACBC) office in Canberra, where all the records from Encompass Australasia (the Church's in-house treatment facility for offending clergy) were taken when Encompass suddenly closed in 2008.

Helen moved on to another social work position outside of the Catholic Church. She devoted much of her time to supporting the Clergy Abused Network (CAN) and Bob O'Toole and one of Father Peter Brock's victims.

On 17 May 2010, *Lateline* questioned whether the archbishop of Adelaide, Philip Wilson, had any prior knowledge of Father Fletcher's offending when he lived with him at the Bishop's House in Maitland as a young priest. Peter Gogarty, another victim of Fletcher, alleged Wilson had seen him with the paedophile priest at the Bishop's House when he was a teenager. The story was broadcast across the nation, and it led to three people approaching the Lake Macquarie police.

Lateline did a follow-up story on 18 June 2010 questioning Wilson's involvement in a case regarding Father McAlinden. Helen Keevers had given internal Church documents on McAlinden to two of his victims, who had passed them on to Joanne McCarthy. The documents showed that Wilson had been charged with defrocking McAlinden and taking victims' witness statements back when he was working underneath Bishop Clarke.

Malone had given Helen permission to release these secret Church documents from the archive.

As part of the same story, Bishop Malone called on Wilson to 'clarify what he knew' about paedophilia among clergy in the diocese. Malone contradicted a statement put out by Wilson; the bishop said, 'There was sufficient smoke around ...'[4] for Wilson to have known a particular priest was a predator. Wilson had been in senior leadership roles for two decades while the abuse had occurred.

It was highly unusual for a sitting bishop to criticise an archbishop, and there was obvious unfinished business between these two. Malone was venting about the clergy that had preceded him in the diocese; he felt he'd been left to clean up the mess, while Wilson had moved on to Wollongong and then been promoted in Adelaide.

Wilson had been the co-chair of the Church body responsible for child protection and sexual abuse allegations against clergy, the National Committee for Professional Standards, from 2003 to 2006, and from July 2011 to July 2012. He was a member of that committee from 1997 to 2012, where he was joined at various times by two former NSW attorney-generals, a former NSW Ombudsman, and internal Church lawyers.

Malone's handling of several cases had badly misfired. In 2009, he had requested the Pope find a replacement for him as bishop in the Maitland-Newcastle Diocese. He'd had enough.

But one of his last acts as bishop caused the members of CAN to organise a protest and they were joined by Helen Keevers. The protest was called 'Silence Against Silence' and it took place in the Civic Park in Newcastle in November 2010. It was a night-time gathering; the survivors, and their supporters, lit candles and remained silent for several minutes, in the clearing, surrounded by trees in the park.

The catalyst for the timing of the Silence Against Silence protest was a public statement released by Bishop Malone about Father Peter Brock on the 12th of November 2010:

'It is with considerable joy that I inform you that Fr Peter Brock is able to return to ministry as a priest ... On advice from my Child

Protection Officer and others, there is no barrier to Fr Peter's return to ministry. After more than three years of anxious waiting Fr Peter is understandably bruised by his experience. He and I are grateful to his family and friends for their loving support of him during what has been a traumatic experience … Initially, he will focus his considerable talents on ministry to adults and supporting our clergy. Please continue to keep him and his family in your prayers.'

It would only be a few years later when the new bishop would issue a formal apology to Father Peter Brock's victims and compensate some of them. In response to the Catholic Church admitting Brock was an offender, the University of Newcastle revoked his honorary degree.[5]

Malone resigned on 4 April 2011. He was bitter and angry after his sixteen years as bishop.

Pope Benedict XVI announced that Malone's replacement was the Reverend William Wright, from a parish in Sydney.

On 5 April, Malone went on the local radio in Newcastle and said dealing with the problem of sexual abuse in the Church had taken its toll: 'It's been tough, I'd have to say.' When the presenter asked Malone whether the Catholic Church had learned any lessons from these difficulties, he replied, 'I think the jury's out a bit on that.'[6]

* * *

As soon as Malone stepped down as bishop, Father James Lunn sent the new bishop, Bill Wright, a letter requesting Father Glen Walsh be returned to the diocese as a 'supply' priest. On 7 June 2011, Lunn wrote, 'For the period of time from September the 24th to October the 9th I was going to ask Fr. Glen Walsh to do supplies in the Parish of Saint James, Muswellbrook and Aberdeen. Fr. Glen is an incardinated priest of this Diocese and has been living in Sydney in recent years. As you are aware seeking a supply priest is not something that would normally require correspondence with a Bishop, however, I thought it best to seek your permission in regard to this matter.'

Lunn added, 'I believe that there are a number of priests who have left ministry in the diocese, and have not been embroiled in public scandals, who would be interested in conversation with yourself. I do not raise those issues at this time, but merely seek your permission to allow Fr. Glen to do supplies for the Parish over the nominated time period ...'

Glen and Lunn were hopeful the new bishop might have a different view, and they waited patiently for a response.

* * *

On 4 February 2011, Detective Sergeant Faber charged Denham with further child sexual assault offences. Technically, he was still a priest.

On 30 November 2011, Pope Benedict XVI officially terminated Denham's right to be a priest by laicising him, seventeen years after Monsignor Hart had taken the first formal complaint against Denham, and eleven years after his first conviction for indecent assault against a child.

The new bishop, Wright, released a statement. It failed to mention Denham's first conviction in 2000:

John Denham was a priest in the diocese of Maitland-Newcastle from 1972 to 1986. In July 2010 he was convicted of committing sexual assaults against children. On 20 May 2011, his Holiness Pope Benedict XVI decreed that John Denham was dismissed from the clerical state. I welcomed his decision.

It has now come to my attention that Mr Denham is facing further child sexual assault charges. This may be the beginning of the legal process of unknown duration.

My thoughts are with the alleged victims and I pray that they have the strength and support to deal with the painful memories that may arise during this time. I admire their courage in coming forward and I pray for their families and friends during this difficult time. I also pray for Mr Denham that he will honour the truth. Despite his past proven crimes, he should be afforded due process so the courts can test the validity of these additional charges.

On behalf of the diocese, I acknowledge and regret the distress and the harm that Denham's past actions have caused. I encourage any person who has suffered from Mr Denham, and who wants to come forward, to do so. I encourage you to talk to the Police, to the many excellent counselling and support services offered through community health and non-government agencies and the diocese of Maitland-Newcastle. We will welcome you; we will listen respectfully and work with you to support your individual path to healing ...[7]

* * *

On 8 June 2012, Steven's Aunty Mary died. She had always been proud of his achievements, from the time he'd started school through all his success as a journalist.

Aunty Mary had lived in the Catholic suburb of Wickham; she was one of the pillars of the Church. Priests would visit her for a cup of tea, including Glen Walsh and Monsignor Hart. Her husband and son had died some years before, so she spent a lot of time in service to other people. She was renowned for her work at the Mater Catholic Hospital as a Pink Lady volunteer; they would wash patients and change the beds, doing some of the more difficult jobs to help the nuns. She'd been the messenger between Glen and Steven over the years, passing on bits of news between the two men.

Steven had loved his aunty, his dad's only sister. Her death took him back to when he was a boy, growing up in Shortland, and his relationship with his mum and dad.

On the day of Aunty Mary's funeral, Steven was going to catch a train from Central Station in Sydney to Newcastle. He called his brother David in tears and said, 'I am standing on Central Station waiting for the train and I am bawling my eyes out and I don't know why.'

David said, 'Just get on the train, I will pick you up from Broadmeadow and we will talk.' David didn't probe any further, because Steven had told him he didn't know why he was so upset.

After David picked him up from Broadmeadow Station, they drove to the Sacred Heart Cathedral in Hamilton, where Andrew had been mourned and Glen had been ordained. Steven was still upset, so David reminded him of some funny anecdotes about Mary and they had a laugh.

Hart was officiating at the funeral, and he greeted the family after the service.

Afterwards, at the wake, David suggested Steven take some leave from work and come stay with him at Pelican Waters in Caloundra, Queensland. David said his brother could do with the sun and the fresh air, in an environment a million miles from the daily stresses of being a journalist. Steven agreed.

At Pelican Waters, David and Steven walked every day along the Golden Beach foreshore. Over two to three weeks, Steven seem to recover quite a bit. He read a lot.

Then he went back to Sydney and resumed his life there, in his hectic job with its many international time zones. He was far from happy: depression had invaded his body, and it wasn't letting go any time soon.

One day, Mark received a call that Steven was crying at his desk, so Mark walked briskly from his office at Radio National to Steven's office. It was now clear he was having a breakdown. The culmination of years of anxiety, much of it hidden from view, led him to leave the ABC and seek a quieter life.

* * *

On 27 June 2012, Roger Brock, Father Peter Brock's brother, resigned as editor of the *Newcastle Herald*. After thirty-five years at the Fairfax media organisation, he was retiring.

Joanne McCarthy and her new editor, Chad Watson, decided it was time to campaign for a National Royal Commission into clerical child sexual abuse.

In late July 2012, one of Denham's victims who had worked closely with Detective Sergeant Kristi Faber disappeared. The previous Saturday night, John Pirona's wife had hugged him and said, 'We will get through this.'

Faber headed the investigation into his disappearance. This was personal for her: she and John, or 'Johnny' as she called him, had first met back in 2005.

It wasn't long before John's body was found.

On Wednesday, 1 August, McCarthy wrote an article about the note that John had left: 'too much pain'.

John's father, Lou, called for an inquiry. He said, 'Any inquiry that unearths the truth about the people who did these things to children, and those who hid it, is not only desirable, but necessary.' John's wife also called for a Royal Commission.

On 30 August 2012 Father Tom Brennan, the former principal of St Pius X, was charged with misprision of felony, the concealment of crimes. It sent shock waves through the community.

The head of Strike Force Georgiana, Kristi Faber, also charged Brennan with common assault for the caning of the boys, who had come to him, reporting their sexual abuse by Denham. She had been disgusted to find out that Brennan had received at least ten reports about Father Denham's behaviour and had done nothing. She was going to make Brennan an example for the rest of the clergy and religious. The cover-up had to stop.

Then a major breakthrough happened in Faber's investigation into Brennan. She was given evidence he was also a child sex offender.

In 2012, Faber was investigating Brennan for committing a sexual assault against a minor. This related to when he'd been based in Waratah in 1984 with Father David O'Hearn. That year, O'Hearn had been convicted of sexually abusing four boys at the Waratah Presbytery Hall, soon after he had come out of the seminary.

In earlier judgments in 2009 and 2010, NSW District Court judge Helen Syme had raised the prospect of a criminal conspiracy given the number of complaints that had been ignored and the knowledge of the offending at the very top levels of the diocese. The webs of lies and deceit were being exposed.

* * *

By 2012, the Victorian Parliament had announced a parliamentary inquiry into 'The Handling of Child Abuse by Religious and other Non-Government Organisations' following reports of 40 suicides among 620 victims, many from the Catholic parishes of Ballarat in Victoria. McCarthy believed there should also be a national Royal Commission and spent much of 2012 writing articles about the need for one.

The Shine the Light campaign was born.[8] The headline on McCarthy's 3 August opinion piece was: 'There will be a royal commission because there must be.' The piece was in response to John Pirona's suicide. McCarthy wrote: 'Next week the Pirona family will farewell John – father of two children aged 11 and 7, husband, son, brother, friend, workmate, and victim of a sadistic Hunter paedophile priest [Denham], and the system that supported and hid his crimes for decades … He is the reality of the Catholic Church's child sex crisis that has been largely hidden from the community until the last decade or so … He is the face of thousands of Australians whose childhoods collided with the ugly secrets of the church. He is one of many who struggled through adulthood until he could do it no more, despite the love of his family, and the love he felt for them.''

Commercial and public television stations were ramping up their coverage. There was a frenzy of reportage, including many exposés on *Lateline*, as well as ABC TV's *Four Corners*, and *7.30 Report*.

Detective Chief Inspector Peter Fox, the investigator who had successfully prosecuted Father Fletcher, was wrestling with his conscience on this issue. He was coming to the conclusion he would have to speak out and call for a national Royal Commission; he was convinced this would be the best way to get justice for hundreds of victims. It was extremely rare for serving police officers to go on national television and call for a Royal Commission, but Fox decided to appear on *Lateline* on 8 November 2012, and McCarthy published a story about him that day.

The extended *Lateline* report, which detailed the cover-up in the Maitland-Newcastle Diocese, and the interview with presenter Tony Jones that followed, was like an incendiary device. It became the tipping point that led the then NSW Premier, Barry O'Farrell, and the Prime Minister at the time, Julia Gillard, to announce state and federal royal commissions in the days following the broadcast. Prime Minister Gillard had been watching the *Newcastle Herald*'s Shine the Light campaign, over the previous months, with increasing concern that criminal behaviour was going unpunished. She announced a Royal Commission into Institutional Responses to Child Sexual Abuse. It would have far-reaching powers.

The day after the *Lateline* and the *Newcastle Herald* reports, Premier O'Farrell, announced a Special Commission of Inquiry with Royal Commission powers into the Maitland-Newcastle Diocese, chaired by Margaret Cunneen SC. The focus would be on two priests only: Fletcher and McAlinden. This surprised many, given the number of priests and Brothers who had offended in the diocese.

The Special Commission would also investigate claims by Fox about the police response to the epidemic of abuse. He had raised these concerns in the *Lateline* interview. The Special Commission terms of reference were drafted so that the police side of the inquiry focused on his claims about a lack of action from the police force, rather than solely on the police response as a whole.

Watching from the sidelines was a priest who had been at the centre of the Fletcher matter. Glen Walsh knew he would be called as a witness to the Special Commission of Inquiry. He would be cross-examined and have to face the priests who despised him, and he would have to testify against Bishop Malone. Glen was dreading it.

CHAPTER 24

The Price for Telling the Truth

FATHER TOM BRENNAN, THE FORMER PRINCIPAL OF ST PIUS X, died of cancer on 4 January 2013, before the charges of misprision of felony could be tested in court.

Strike Force Georgiana now moved from the priests of the diocese to the Brothers at Marist Brothers Hamilton and Maitland.

On 29 January 2013, Brother Francis 'Romuald' Cable from Marist Brothers Hamilton appeared in the Newcastle Local Court charged with multiple child sex offences. The allegations included indecent assaults and incidents of buggery on boys at Marist Brothers Hamilton, Maitland and Pagewood in Sydney between 1960 and 1974. More victims came forward over the next two years and, by 19 March 2015, he was found guilty, with 19 victims and sentenced to sixteen years in prison. The average age of his victims at Marist Brothers Hamilton was thirteen and fourteen – about the same age as Andrew Nash – and the offences were committed between 1971 and 1974. Romuald had abruptly left the school after Andrew's suicide in 1974.

Audrey Nash was sitting in her dining room, reading the reports of Romuald's arrest and charges in the *Newcastle Herald*. She caught a line in one of the stories that made her recoil with horror; one of Romuald's victims said the Brother had taken him to Bar Beach and sexually abused him – the same place Romuald's had taken Andrew, her son, in the months before his death. The memories came flooding back.

Audrey and her son Geoffrey went to the police station to make a statement. They were met by Kristi Faber, who believed that Andrew was a victim of Romuald. What made Faber especially suspicious was the lack of pastoral care from the Church following Andrew's death.

Around this time, Geoffrey called up Joanne McCarthy and asked her if she would speak to Audrey. He described his mother as a devout Catholic who was struggling with what was happening in the diocese.

McCarthy happened to be in Newcastle for a few days, so she met Audrey in a café in Hamilton. The journalist took several documents with her to show Audrey that the clerical abuse issues were real. Audrey barely said a word, and Joanne assumed she was another example of how the Church had managed to silence many of its devout women.

Audrey did not raise the story of her son at this meeting.

A few weeks later, McCarthy received a call from Geoffrey Nash. He told Joanne the story, and she was shocked.

After that, it didn't take long for Audrey to be ready to tell Andrew's story to the public. She'd had her own epiphanies about what had happened back in 1974, and how she and her family had been used by some of the clergy and religious.

The article ran on 8 February 2013. Audrey told McCarthy, 'I had no idea why it happened so I blamed myself for a long time. There was no reason, nothing. That's why it was so horrifying.'

After they read the article, some of Andrew's old mates called Audrey and Geoffrey, and told them about their own abuse at the hands of the Brother.

* * *

In 2013, the Hunter Special Commission of Inquiry in Newcastle emboldened some victims and their families to come forward and either testify or talk to the media. It took place in the Newcastle courts on Hunter Street. Each day the media would wait out the front to film the participants, especially witnesses from the Catholic Church. The media was barred from attending the private hearings.

Most of the senior Catholic clerics were cross-examined about their roles in the Fletcher and McAlinden cases. Much of it was behind closed doors.

On the police side, Detective Chief Inspector Peter Fox spent around fourteen days in the witness box. The Special Commission didn't look at the Memorandum of Understanding (MOU) that had been drafted years before between the Church and the police or the issue of blind reporting; instead it focused on Fox: his claims, were they true, was he a reliable witness, and so forth – it nearly broke him. Day after day he would be in the witness box, answering questions by senior counsel when other senior police provided medical certificates or weren't called to give testimony before the media. And frustratingly for Fox, some of the evidence he wanted to present was ruled out of order because it referred to another priest who was not part of the Special Commission's terms of reference or its predetermined parameters.

Joanne McCarthy was called to give evidence on several occasions and Helen Keevers made submissions to the Inquiry. In the public seating areas were Audrey and Geoffrey Nash; John Wakely; Pat, John and Daniel Feenan; Brendan and Elizabeth Byrne; Will Callinan; Troy Grant, who was now a member of the NSW Parliament as the sitting member for Dubbo in western New South Wales; and a number of police officers. They all gave oral or written evidence.

On the clergy side, there were public and private appearances by Monsignor Hart, Bishop Malone, Archbishop Wilson, Father Burston, Father Lucas, Father Glen Walsh and several others.

* * *

In early 2013, at the beginning of the Special Commission of Inquiry, *Lateline* had broadcast a number of exclusive reports on the MOU between the NSW Police and the Catholic Church, and the issue of so-called blind reporting. Father Lucas, Cardinal Pell and Archbishop Wilson had been involved in the Church's efforts to secure the MOU, while the NSW Police legal department had raised concerns about its legality: because the reports weren't sent directly from victims to the police, the Church was almost acting as an agent for state law enforcement.

In 2013, a Greens senator in the upper house of the NSW Parliament, David Shoebridge, had received an anonymous package of documents at his office. These were the Church reports that de-identified the victim so police could not follow up with a direct contact – reports that disclosed the existence of the informal MOU.

A series of freedom of information applications by Shoebridge, and the *Lateline* television program, yielded explosive results. For the first time, it was revealed to the public that a serving police officer had been appointed to an internal Church committee that discussed issues of child protection and potential offenders. It was a rule of the Church that all the minutes of these meetings be destroyed, and by complying with this the officer had agreed with the destruction of potential evidence.

Shoebridge handed all these documents to the Special Commission of Inquiry, which decided the issue was outside its terms of reference. This was despite the fact Bishop Malone had sent a blind report about Father Denis McAlinden, one of the subjects of the Inquiry, to the police in 1999.

* * *

The Special Commission of Inquiry was a huge story for the NSW and local media in Newcastle and the public gallery was full of survivors and support people. Helen Keevers sat there even though she no longer worked for the Maitland-Newcastle Diocese; she was there to support the survivors.

Will Callinan spent several hours testifying. He cried during the hearing and later told his friends and family he was a 'blubbering mess'. Three days later, he was still nervous and agitated.

Will's counsel cross-examined Malone and accused him of adding the '(+Will C)' to the file note months after he claimed.

Counsel Will Potter: 'What I'm suggesting to you is that you jotted down something after the event so that those words in brackets "+Will C" were added after 20 June; do you agree with that?'

Malone: 'I sort of made this little note when I got back to the office on 20 June.'

Counsel Will Potter: 'I'm suggesting it was made later than that, in fact, in September when you were asked about these events by the Ombudsman; would you agree with that?'

Malone: 'No, I would not agree with that.'

Following the Special Commission, Will retired two years early from his job as a principal. The past fifteen years had taken their toll on him mentally and physically, and his workplace had grown grubby and toxic. He had been accused of lying, and he had been implicated in a case of a priest who should have been stood aside immediately.

Peter Gogarty, a survivor of Father James Fletcher, gave evidence to the Inquiry, as did many other survivors.

Father Burston was cross-examined about what he'd known during his time as vicar-general from 1996 to 2001, and as one of the diocesan consultors[1] to Bishop Clarke in June 1987 and also from 1992 to 1997. According to the report from the Special Commission, 'In relation to his role as a consultor, Burston said the bishop called meetings irregularly and that matters of pastoral care relating to priests could have been dealt with in these meetings.'[2] This was a group of the bishop's most trusted advisers.

Burston was an uncooperative witness. He produced medical reports that said his memory had been damaged due to a general anaesthetic, and subsequently he answered, 'I can't recall' to a least twenty questions from the various barristers and senior counsel. He was therefore the subject of negative findings by the Special Commission: 'The regularity with which Burston replied "I don't recollect" was a feature of his testimony. It left an unavoidable impression that, in relation to many matters about which he was questioned, he was not prepared to consider the question fully or to examine or explore his memory in order to assist the Commission. Having regard to the totality of his evidence, the Commission found Burston to be an unimpressive witness in certain respects.'[3]

Malone was cross-examined both in private and public hearings. It was revealed that he had withheld information in 2011 from a police strike force known as Lantle about another Fletcher victim, when the officers had asked him if any other victims of this priest existed. To the Special Commission, Malone said he'd just forgotten about the Fletcher victim named Peter Creigh, even though he'd visited Creigh at his home in 2010.

Elizabeth Byrne and Glen Walsh knew nothing about Peter Creigh or the fact Malone had revealed this in private testimony to the Commission. It was not revealed to the public or other witnesses at the time.

Malone admitted he had ignored abuse allegations and apologised again for his past mistakes. He had made many apologies about his time as bishop. In a stunning revelation, he admitted he had been out of his depth and he felt compelled to defend his church.[4]

* * *

A few months before it started, as preparations for the Inquiry were underway, Margaret Cunneen SC spoke to Father Glen Walsh. He was served a subpoena and became a Crown Witness for the Special Commission. He continued to support himself by teaching at an inner-city public school in Sydney and his health was starting to deteriorate. He was ordered to attend several hearings in the evening in the lead-up to the Inquiry and then two private court appearances where he was aggressively cross-examined by the legal defence teams representing Archbishop Philip Wilson, retired Bishop Michael Malone and Bishop Bill Wright. His entire testimony regarding Father James Fletcher from 2003 to 2004 was challenged by the senior clerics and their barristers.

He told his close friends the experience had been harrowing and had affected his health. All the priests who were ordered to give evidence were offered legal representation by the diocese, except Glen. In the end, the Special Commission provided him with a lawyer from the Solicitor-General's office. Glen told another close friend the open hostility he received from his fellow clergy had caused him great anxiety, and after giving evidence he later ended up in St Vincent's Hospital because of issues with his heart. In his lifetime he'd had several major health issues, and the effects of being ostracised by his fellow clergy were affecting him mentally and physically. He had a few priests he could confide in, but he was shunned from his own diocese, didn't have his own parish in Sydney and was teaching at a local inner-city primary school. Then he received some more bad news from his doctors. They discovered some benign tumours in his stomach. They were removed but he was diagnosed a short time later with cancer in other parts of his body. Surgery followed to remove the cancer in June 2013 and his left breast and lymph nodes were removed due to a tumour on his spine. His doctors told him the stress of the past few years had taken its toll.

Glen Walsh walked in the rain, then emailed a friend and told them, 'He was pleased no one could see his tears.'[5]

His whole life he had wanted to serve his Church and its people. Now he was a pariah. He felt worthless. He told a friend it didn't matter what he did – he could never return to being a normal person.

His friends thought he had changed radically from the man they'd known when he was first ordained. His dry wit and funny one-liners had all but disappeared.

He now doubted his Church, but not his God. He told a friend that he 'still believed in God but he didn't believe in the system anymore'.

He emailed a friend to let her know that he'd undergone emergency surgery the previous evening to have a tumour excised from his mouth.[6] 'The jaw is pinned together and, where my teeth were, wire has been screwed into the jaw, onto which the doctor has sewn my gums and cemented a makeshift plastic piece in place of my front teeth. The operation took 3 hours and ... I had to remain conscious throughout which was a little challenging.' He'd then been permitted to go home, and though he admitted in the email that it was 'very irresponsible', he had driven himself back to his residence in Balmain. He had woken at five-thirty, presumably as usual, and gone off to work at the school. 'Thank God I teach beautifully behaved children,' he reflected.

When the oncologist had told him that two more operations were required and that he'd booked Glen in for these at St Vincent's Private Hospital, Glen said he had 'objected, gently reminding [the oncologist] that the private hospital was for the privileged ... I want to line up behind the poor and wait my turn.' According to Glen, it had all worked out for the best. 'The doctor was wonderful with me and will now take both remaining cancers in one big operation on 13th June [2013] in a public hospital!' He concluded by saying, 'How blest I am to have my little room as it has a bathroom with shower attached. So many do not have this luxury during illness, God help them.'

On 16 July 2013, Glen emailed a fellow teacher at his school and spoke about the stress of testifying to the Commission. He told her he was always accompanied by a doctor that monitored him during the proceedings. He wrote, 'It is so humiliating and degrading. I have been demolished by these awful people: and all because I simply did what any other decent person would do – I reported a crime.'[7]

A close friend was so worried about him, she sent a letter to Margaret Cunneen SC. It began with the declaration: 'I am writing in an attempt to find justice for my friend Father Glen Walsh.' Glen, she explained, had been a family friend for twenty years, 'a wonderful man who was destined to be a priest of great compassion and spiritual depth'.

'Due to his involvement in reporting the crimes of James Fletcher,' she claimed, 'he has not been allowed to pursue his calling to its fullest extent.' She said that over the previous eight years she'd seen 'the effect of the injustices imposed upon him'.

Glen had been 'vilified by Michael Malone and many other priests of the Maitland-Newcastle Diocese for reporting James Fletcher to the police. He has been treated as a pariah by "men of the cloth" who purport to bear witness to Christ's compassion and love. These men have made him feel unwelcome in his own Diocese and have excluded him from the everyday operations of this Diocese. This exile has forced him to seek a life away from his home and when Michael Malone continued to interfere in his life as a priest in Sydney, to abandon his vocation altogether.'

Meanwhile: 'Very few people in the diocese of Maitland-Newcastle know that Father Walsh was instrumental in the apprehension of James Fletcher. In fact, some people have been told that he just left the diocese because he was mentally unstable. Father Walsh is not here to defend his good name or character. The priests that remain have a vested interested in shoring up their own positions and sullying the character of the one who has shown them for what they are.' Glen, his friend told Cunneen, was 'not a well man. His health has suffered greatly as a result of the stress of these past years and his soul has been trampled by the viciousness of the treatment he has received at the hands of his Bishop and fellow priests. He feels that he is alone, that he is the voice crying in the wilderness. Yet all he did was follow his conscience ...'

According to Glen's friend, 'All that Father Walsh desires is an apology from the priests of this Diocese – an acknowledgement that he did indeed do the right thing ... Nothing can compare to the horror that the victims of James Fletcher's crime have undergone or to the terrible consequences of their abuse but I feel that Father Walsh is a forgotten victim in many ways. Very few people know the price he has paid for telling the truth ...'

CHAPTER 25

'I regret opening my mouth. Never again'

– Father Glen Walsh

GLEN'S HEALTH IMPROVED GREATLY. ON 9 AUGUST 2013, HE wrote to a friend: 'The interventions I have received this year for both physical and mental troubles have been so beneficial. I am cancer free at last and have ceased more treatments related … I fortnightly consult with a very experienced psychologist. She's a toughie, but very understanding.'

He continued to teach and got some pleasure out of his daily ferry rides on Sydney Harbour to the school where he worked.

* * *

In August 2013, John Denham pleaded guilty to offences against another 18 boys. This brought his victim count to 58 boys aged between eleven and thirteen. Justice Helen Syme eventually sentenced Denham, this time to nineteen years in jail. He would eligible for parole in 2028.

A month later, on 20 September 2013, Brother Coman Sykes passed away.

The tributes were many, lauding his achievements and service to others.

'Brother Coman Sykes, "Coey" to many, passed away peacefully in his sleep in the evening of 19th September 2013. We have lost a terrific, industrious, honest and caring man in Coey. Rest in Peace Brother.'[1]

There was a memorial dinner in his honour. The Marist Brother was praised for his commitment to sport, especially Rugby League. The sports journalist and former Rugby Union great Peter FitzSimons noted Sykes's death in his regular *Sydney Morning Herald* column: 'Brother Coman Sykes. The beloved teacher at Parramatta Marist who coached league, cricket and athletics for many and many a moon passed away this week. Well done, oh good and faithful servant of the games.'[2] Ray 'Rabs' Warren, the Voice of Rugby League, noted his passing during a live television broadcast, at half-time during a match. This sort of tribute was usually made for the greatest players in the sport. 'Coey' Sykes was an esteemed member of the rugby fraternity.

But for Glen, he was his abuser. Their memories of him were dark and disturbing. Glen was reminded of his complaint letter to the Marist Brothers, the one that had been so soundly rejected. In so many cases, such predators within the Church were loved by many and loathed by a few.

The light Glen had felt in India was fading quickly.

* * *

The Hunter Special Commission of Inquiry report was due on 28 February 2014. Earlier that month, Glen retired from teaching due to ill health. In the monthly newsletter to priests and religious, Bishop Bill Wright relayed the news of Glen's retirement and added that he might return to the diocese to help with 'supply' or backing up priests on leave. That gave Glen a glimmer of hope.

Glen emailed Wright with a health update: he'd had heart surgery the day before and was scheduled for another procedure in a few days. In recent years, he said, his health had become 'more of a mate with whom I wander between rests, rather than that limitless energy source, resting only for sleep'. But he added, 'I am happy with my lot.'

He then mused about the teachings of one of his lecturers from St Patrick's College in the early 1990s: 'Father John Cowburn SJ taught that the value of a human person can be both defined by and found within the ACT OF LOVE.' These reflections led into an anecdote that reveals much about Glen's values and character: 'My hospital room overlooks the Hospice for the Dying. For two days running, an elderly woman has been sat upon a chair facing outwards to catch the sun's warmth; the morning's minion ... I plucked up the courage to widen my smile and wave at this elderly woman. She returned my smile in kind and blew me a kiss! Our exchanges went into the afternoon, throughout the day on Monday and before my operation on Tuesday morning.' Glen was then confined to his bed, but he managed to sit up enough to exchange glances with the woman, his 'new friend'. By that afternoon, however, her room was dark, the bed stripped.

'God rest her soul,' Glen wrote. 'I never knew her name ... However, I am grateful for the reminder that the worth of a person lies not merely in liking, but rather, in loving; the former being an act of wo/man, and the latter, a human act.'

Wright reached out to Glen, but other clerics in the diocese had not forgiven him for going to the police about Brendan Byrne. And his hopes of being released from the consequences of his actions in the Fletcher case were short-lived.

The Special Commission of Inquiry produced four volumes, and Volume Four was suppressed until 2019. A team of police from Newcastle had been given all the evidence from the suppressed volume and they used it to charge Archbishop Philip Wilson with misprision of felony, the concealment charge over the Fletcher matter. He would be the highest cleric in Australia to that date to be charged with such an offence.

Volume Four includes this determination: 'Considering the totality of the evidence likely to be available and admissible in any future criminal proceedings, the Commission is satisfied that there is sufficient evidence warranting the prosecution of a specified person – namely, Archbishop Philip Wilson – for two specified offences: first, misprision of felony ... second, a breach of s. 316(1) of the *Crimes Act 1900* (NSW) ...'[3] The police used this information to prepare a brief for the Director of Public Prosecutions.

A priest had helped the police charge an archbishop. There was no precedent in Australia, and very few elsewhere.

Glen had told the Special Commission that he had reported the second victim in the Fletcher case to Wilson, and the authorities then confirmed Wilson had failed to report what he knew to the police. There was other evidence gathered as part of the Special Commission that, with Glen's evidence, helped seal Wilson's fate.

The reverberations were felt across the world as this became global news. As was the normal procedure, Pope Francis was informed about all these developments, via his representative in Australia, the Apostolic Nuncio in Canberra.

* * *

The conclusion of the Special Commission of Inquiry was bad for Malone, Hart, Lucas, Burston and Cotter. On the matter of Father Denis McAlinden, they all received a negative report.[4]

Malone received a devastating report on the findings related to Father James Fletcher. The Inquiry questioned why he had failed to notify Strike Force Lantle about Peter Creigh, and criticised his actions about standing Fletcher aside:

Some of the evidence Malone gave was untruthful. In a statement adopted during his evidence he asserted that, after the allegations about Fletcher arose, he had a conversation with Mr William Callinan, the principal of Branxton primary school, on 20 June 2002, warning him that Fletcher 'shouldn't be alone with kids and should stay away from the school' and urging him to be vigilant in his supervision of Fletcher. Callinan firmly denied that any such conversation had occurred ... The Commission rejected Malone's evidence about his asserted discussion with Callinan. It considers that Malone's evidence on this was in effect an attempt to disperse responsibility for his decision not to stand Fletcher down in June 2002 after becoming aware that the police were investigating him for child sexual abuse. As a corollary to its finding that Malone did not meet with Callinan on 20 June 2002, the Commission formed the view that Malone had at some later time added the words '+Will C' to an entry in his diary for 20 June 2002 with the intention of creating a false record to support his version of events – that is, that he consulted Callinan about the decision not to stand Fletcher down. That Malone would falsify documentation in this way reflects poorly upon his credibility.[5]

But the Special Commission left their findings open on whether Malone had told Walsh to 'fuck off out of the diocese', which was another blow to Glen. Bishop Malone denied the allegation that he had forced Glen out of the diocese but he admitted he stopped the priest's return in 2007. Malone told the Inquiry: 'I found him a very difficult priest to deal with, frankly ... he found it very difficult to stay in one place for very long. On average, I'd say about once every 18 months he'd want to move to another parish or leave the priesthood so he could go teaching, and then he was wanting to come back to the priesthood ... whilst he did good work as a priest, I just found that inability to settle down ... rather difficult.'[6]

A close friend of Glen's received an email from him after the Hunter Special Commission of Inquiry released its report in 2014. The vicar-general of the diocese, Father Brian Mascord, had warned Glen not to talk to the media. According to Glen, Mascord said, 'We all have our own truths.' 'What bullshit,' Glen wrote. 'Where I come from something is either truth or not.' Mascord was soon promoted to become the bishop of Wollongong.

In the email to his friend, Glen wrote:

Selfish as it may seem, I don't want to see or talk to anyone. Not sure if I ever will. This has all killed me. I am gutted. No one has helped me. No one has explained what I did and what it has cost me, done to my life. I am so disappointed in the whole thing and those involved … I still look the fool I've always looked and nobody has had the guts to get up and voice what they have done to me for being the only one to take on Malone and his filthy cover-up culture, and report a horrible crime.

From now on they may be cleverer when they interfere with kids, but their abuse will continue in every way. Nothing will change. They will delight in knowing I will now slowly die isolated and voiceless … I regret opening my mouth. Never again.

Take care. Forget about me.

Following his email, Glen pasted a black-and-white picture of a man standing alone at the end of a pier.

CHAPTER 26

A Meeting with the Pope

ON 17 MARCH 2015, ARCHBISHOP PHILIP WILSON OF ADELAIDE was charged with concealment, or misprision of felony, and took indefinite leave three days later. Glen would be a key prosecution witness in the court case.

In the secret testimony to the Special Commission under Margaret Cunneen SC, another victim, of Fletcher's, Peter Creigh, had come forward and testified that he had reported his sexual abuse to Wilson in 1976. A second victim, whose name was suppressed, also alleged that he had reported his abuse to Wilson in 1976. The Special Commission had concluded the testimonies of these two men were true.

The news of these two more victims only became public after Wilson was charged. The Special Commission's Volume Four, which contained this information, had been suppressed because of the upcoming court case.

Both Elizabeth and Glen were shocked – they hadn't known anything about the other two victims of Fletcher's from 1976, the year Daniel Feenan was born. If Wilson had reported Fletcher to the police back then, maybe Daniel and Brendan could have been saved. The thought was chilling.

Glen told Elizabeth they could no longer talk about the

Fletcher case in case they contaminated their evidence. He became increasingly worried his phone might be tapped.

Glen had become a whistleblower priest, a very rare creature. He was a Crown prosecution witness against an archbishop – that was even rarer.

Although he was still an outcast, an event was coming up that all priests who belonged to a diocese had to attend every year: Chrism Mass. It falls on a special day each year, and the priests meet at a church in the diocese, carrying their oils to be blessed. These sacred oils are then used in the church during the year. Glen would have to face all his fellow priests and walk in a procession with them. On 23 March 2015, a week after Wilson was charged, Glen emailed some close friends: 'I am writing to let you know that after resisting and resisting God's prompt to attend Tuesday night next CHRISM MASS at Hamilton, I have decided I ought to go.' He asked them to 'please look out for me and, more importantly before and after the Mass, please find me and stay with me so that I will be safe'. In subsequent emails, Glen told his friends another priest would help him walk into the church. He added, 'I will be VERY ANXIOUS the whole time, but this is another demon I must face and stare down. God Help me.'

Glen attended the Chrism Mass, and his friends came to offer him moral support. When the mass was finished, they met him outside the church. Glen was visibly shaken and unsteady on his feet, so they helped him to his car. He later told his friends that he'd been verbally abused with foul language during the procession. As he'd walked in the long line of clergy towards the altar, the two priests behind him had whispered horrible words of ridicule and abuse just loud enough for him to hear.

* * *

A month later, on 25 April 2015, a violent storm hit Terrigal, where Glen was living at the time, and a big tree fell on his townhouse. He called 000, and when the operator asked him what service he wanted, and he said, 'You better send all three, I am pinned under a huge tree.' The fire brigade got him out; he wasn't physically injured, apart from shock. At eleven o'clock that night, Glen called a nearby friend and asked him to pick him up from Gosford Hospital.

While his home was being repaired, Glen lived with a friend in Sydney. His health required weekly treatments at St Vincent's Hospital in the inner-city suburb of Darlinghurst as he travelled between the heart, lung and pain relief wards.

The repairs to his townhouse took thirteen months. After it was fixed, he applied to the body corporate to allow it to be used for the resettlement of refugees, but they refused.

* * *

In 2015, a man now in his early forties decided to make a claim against a senior Marist Brother. At the age of twelve, he had been sexually abused by Brother Coman Sykes in 1972, while he was a student at Marist Brothers Kogarah, a southern suburb of Sydney.

Matthew (not his real name) was nearing the end of his first year of high school. The long summer break was just around the corner, and he was finishing off his final assignments and exams while looking forward to Christmas.

Then tragedy struck: Matthew's father died suddenly, in November 1972. His mother had to care for the large Catholic family on her own.

Sykes was involved with Marist Brothers Kogarah at this time. Although he did not teach Matthew at the school, he was a family friend and knew Matthew's mother well. She turned to the Brother for guidance, and he stepped in to offer pastoral support. He offered to take the boy away for the weekend, to the Marist Brothers Retreat Centre in Mittagong.

Instead of providing a weekend of healing, he sexually abused the child. Sykes told Matthew to keep it a secret.

Sykes was on the Marist Brothers Provincial Council from 1968 to 1994 and was one of the senior leaders in their community. In the 1970s, he had come up with the 'better boys' strategy to recruit schoolboys for retreats, and teenagers would come to Mittagong from all around New South Wales and the ACT, giving the Marists a bigger pool from which to choose trainees.[1]

By 1978, four Brothers had been employed full-time on retreat work: Brother Coman Sykes, Brother Michael Hill, Brother Michael Prest and Brother Paul Hough. By mid-1978, Glen's former principal, Brother Alexis Turton, was appointed to lead the team and replace Sykes.

Sykes moved to Winston Hills, to focus on the postulants. Glen would become one of his 'better boys'.

Glen never found out about Matthew, the twelve-year-old boy whom Sykes abused in 1972. The Marist Brothers paid out compensation on this case.

* * *

After the Special Commission of Inquiry had informed Senator David Shoebridge that it would not look at his documents on the MOU, he had given them to the Police Integrity Commission (PIC). On 3 October 2014, the PIC announced Operation Protea, a public inquiry that would look at whether these arrangements contravened section 316 of the NSW *Crimes Act*. Although the NSW Police denied this MOU had ever been signed or put in place, hundreds of these blind reports were found to exist, including ones from the Maitland-Newcastle Diocese.

Two had been made about Father Fletcher and Father McAlinden. Bishop Malone had made a blind report about Father McAlinden in 1999.

The uncovering of these reports meant several senior clerics could argue that they had abided by section 316 and reported a crime. Father Brian Lucas and his lieutenants had done a great job protecting the Church's interests.

Shoebridge told the media, 'If you wanted to design a process that gave as much legal protection to the Church, bishops and priests, and zero justice to victims and survivors of abuse, then you would design this obscene practice of blind reporting.'

The PIC inquiry found that many of these so-called blind reports had been added into the police database as information reports, purely for intelligence purposes, with many not being investigated by police. It recommended an urgent review of blind reporting. In fact, the final PIC report, released on 19 June 2015, said that this reporting process was technically illegal: 'The Commission is of the opinion that these matters relied on as justifying "Blind Reporting" would not, in general, amount to a reasonable excuse within section 316 (1) of the *Crimes Act* and that in general Blind Reporting contravenes section 316.'[2]

* * *

Sometime after Archbishop Wilson was charged by police in 2015, Glen told his closest friends and family that he'd received a request from the Vatican to have a private interview with Pope Francis. Despite his ill health, in early 2016 Glen flew to the Vatican to meet Pope Francis. He later said he met with the Pope on 9 February 2016.

Glen was still a Crown witness who would be testifying for the prosecution in the Wilson case. He told one of his closest friends that the Pope wanted to know why a priest would be involved in a court case against an archbishop in Australia – and that the pontiff wanted to know what Glen was planning to say in court.

Glen loved Rome and the Vatican, and he sent postcards back to friends. He picked a photo of St Peter's Square in the early evening light; the beauty of the architecture and the avenue leading to St Peter's Basilica enchanted him. Outside his bedroom window was the 'Church of the Holy Spirit',[3] rebuilt in 1475, and inside its main chapel were paintings of scenes associated with the healing of the body and spirit.

Glen told his closest friends that he had given Pope Francis only a brief summary of why he needed to testify against an archbishop. He had wanted to say more and express his concerns about elements of the Church, but he was concerned about the interpreter, who was translating his every word, and decided only to skim over the facts. Glen thought the interpreter had links back to the Maitland-Newcastle Diocese, but he couldn't be sure. He didn't trust the situation, even inside the Vatican. After what he had seen and been through, he only trusted his God.

The Pope listened and asked him who had been supporting him on this journey. Glen replied again with the scantest of details.

On 3 May 2016, Glen wrote to two friends in Singleton about his meeting with the Pope in February: 'On doctors' advice, I will not be returning to Rome for the four day retreat to be given by the Pope for Priesthood Jubilarians (1–4 June). At the end of my last meeting with him on 9th Feb, the Pope asked me to come back to Rome for this special event given I am 20 years a priest on this 1st June 2016. I will be just as happy to celebrate a Mass of Thanksgiving for the people of our Diocese here in my room on 1.6.16.'

Glen told several close friends that when he'd left his meeting with the Pope, Cardinal Pell had been waiting outside. He had said to Glen, 'Look what I have done for you,' and lifted his hand towards Glen's face so the priest could kiss his ring, the ritual expected when one met a cardinal of the Catholic Church. But Glen said he had refused to kiss the ring and just walked out of the room, out of the Vatican offices, and into the daylight.

* * *

Less than two weeks later, the *Herald Sun* newspaper broke the story that Pell was being investigated by the Victorian Police for alleged historical child sex offences.

The following month, Pell appeared on television screens across Australia as he gave evidence, via satellite from Rome, to the Australian Royal Commission into Institutional Responses to Child Sexual Abuse. He'd said he was too ill to travel home to Australia, and he had produced medical reports that claimed his heart was not strong enough for the journey.

This caused outrage among survivors of clerical sexual abuse generally, and several travelled to Rome to watch him give evidence.

By June 2016, Pell was charged with multiple child sex offences including against two altar boys.[4]

* * *

Later in 2016, Audrey and Geoffrey Nash testified at the Royal Commission into Institutional Responses to Child Sexual Abuse. They finally had the legal support to face the Church that had betrayed them.

Prime Minister Julia Gillard appointed Justice Peter McClellan, a distinguished judge from the NSW Court of Appeal, to head the Royal Commission. It held two major inquiries into the Maitland-Newcastle Diocese: one on Father Ryan and the other, in 2016, on several of the Marist Brothers in Hamilton, which included the case of Andrew Nash.

Out of the many documents subpoenaed by the Royal Commission from the Church archive, one revealed that Brother Francis 'Romuald' Cable had sexually assaulted a boy back in 1957 at the St Vincent's Boys Home in Westmead run by the Marist Brothers; the document was a Catholic Church Insurances spreadsheet that revealed it had paid out a claim from that time in 1993.[5]

Had the Catholic authorities dealt with the rampant abuse at that boys' home in the late 1950s, Andrew might have been saved.

The Royal Commission also revealed Romuald had at least 19 victims at schools in Sydney and Newcastle. The Marist Brothers had previously said the first complaint to the order, about Romuald, had been in 1993. But this wasn't true: they had received a complaint about him at St Gabriel's School in Sydney in 1967. He had remained a Marist Brother until 1978, then in 1979 he'd gone to the ACT and become a teacher at St Edmund's College for a decade; he was in constant contact with teenage boys throughout that time.

On the issue of her son, Andrew, Audrey got her vindication in spades: a Royal Commission with powers to recommend prosecutions was going to ask the questions she so desperately wanted answered.

The former principal of Marist Brothers Hamilton Brother William 'Christopher' Wade, who had turned up at her house the night Andrew died, was subpoenaed by the Royal Commission and cross-examined.

A year before Andrew's death, in 1973, Wade had received a direct report about the behaviour of his staff, including Romuald. But he had not gone to the police.

Under intense cross-examination by the barrister Hilbert Chiu, Wade admitted he'd been frightened of Romuald, and he conceded the children in his care probably had been too.

Wade, however, denied he had received complaints about Romuald's behaviour – except on one occasion. He conceded Romuald had admitted guilt to him, and his answers shocked everyone in the hearing room.

Chiu asked, 'Do you recall there were some questions yesterday about the one time you did confront Brother Romuald?'

Wade replied, 'Yes.'

'And his response to you,' said Chiu, '"I thought I had been good in that area recently"?'

'Yes,' said Wade.

'And you agreed that that was an admission by him to you of past interference with boys?'

'I agree to that interpretation – yes, I do agree.'[6]

Wade had been Romuald's superior in the Marist community as well as his principal, but Wade hadn't wanted to cause any animosity with this difficult Brother, especially as they lived in the same quarters. The principal accepted his teacher's denials, even though this man, who had admitted past crimes against children, was in charge of large numbers of boys under the age of fifteen.

Wade had ended up as the principal of Marist Brothers Canberra from 1993 to 2000, when he'd retired. It was announced at the Royal Commission that *this* school had the highest number of sexual abuse claims of any Catholic school.

About one year after his testimony before the Royal Commission, Wade was convicted of indecently assaulting two children that included one victim from Marist Brothers Hamilton.

He subsequently pleaded guilty and was convicted of making false statements and perverting the course of justice after he lied during a police interview with Detective Sergeant Kristi Faber; he falsely informed her he hadn't received any complaints about Romuald and Brother Darcy 'Dominic' O'Sullivan during his time as principal at Marist Brothers Hamilton.

Romuald and Wade had turned up at the Nash home the night Andrew suicided, 8 October 1974. Under questioning about why he'd done that, Wade told the Royal Commission he couldn't remember that night.

Chiu asked him, 'How many times do you recall being in a room in a house with a wailing mother whose son has just died?'

Wade replied, 'I don't recall ever having been in that set of circumstances.'

Chiu said, 'Isn't it implausible, Brother, that you've got absolutely no memory of visiting the Nash household on the evening of 8 October 1974?'

Wade replied, 'I can't say whether it is implausible or not. All I can say is that it's the truth.'

Chiu said, 'You're pretending you don't remember that evening because you're a coward and you're a liar.'

Wade said, 'That's not true.'[7]

Four decades earlier, thirteen-year-old Andrew Nash had been living in a private hell of the school's making, and had decided there was no way out but to suicide.

Audrey's anger would boil up from time to time. She spent nights wondering why her? Why Andrew?

CHAPTER 27

'I am starting to think this is what happened to my Andrew'

– Audrey Nash

ON 6 SEPTEMBER 2016, AUDREY GOT HER DAY IN THE WITNESS stand. She looked some of the Marist Brothers in the eye and asked about her son Andrew. This slim woman in her eighties stood tall and strong, and stared down her former bosses and priests. Her former masters.

What happened to my son?

She was permitted to read out her statement from the witness stand. This was her chance to tell the world what had happened to her son and her family. To her and Bert. To Geoffrey and Carmel, and Patricia and Bernadette.

At first, Andrew's mum looked nervous. But when she spoke, she commanded everyone's attention and respect. With all eyes on her, she read her statement to the crowded gallery in Newcastle.

Audrey began by saying that in 1998 she had spoken to Monsignor Hart, who was then her parish priest, and told him, 'You must have known something was going on with Father Ryan. You knew he got sent to Melbourne.' According to Audrey, Hart had replied, 'Oh, no, I knew nothing.' She'd responded by saying, 'You know, I am starting to think this is what happened to my Andrew.' Hart had said, 'Yes, I think so too.'

Later in her statement, Audrey said, 'In February 2013, a school friend of Andrew's wrote me a letter saying he believed Andrew had been sexually abused at Marist Brothers Hamilton and that is why Andrew committed suicide. I now believe that Andrew was sexually abused and that he took his own life because of the abuse. I also believe that the reason that Brs Romuald, Christopher and John came to our house the night of Andrew's death was to try to find out if there was any evidence that Andrew left behind in relation to the abuse, such as a note.'

After the arrest of Brother Romuald, Audrey had asked Detective Sergeant Faber, 'Can you go and ask Brother Romuald if he did abuse Andrew? It would provide a lot of peace of mind to actually know what happened.' Faber got back to Audrey and told her that Romuald's lawyers wouldn't let Faber speak to him, but one of them would ask Romuald about Andrew's abuse. 'I never heard anything more about it,' said Audrey.

In early 2012, a Sister of Mercy had arrived at Audrey's house after seeing a photograph of Andrew published alongside a newspaper article. The Sister had burst into tears. Audrey said, 'She told me that she knew nothing about any sexual abuse or that anything had happened to Andrew. She then left. The next day, another Sister from the Sisters of Mercy arrived at my house. The Sister had been Andrew's teacher in primary school. She also started crying and said she knew nothing about any abuse. She also then left. By this time I was very upset ...'

Soon after, Audrey had arranged to speak with Hart again and she began talking to him about Andrew. 'I think he got a bit fed up,' Audrey told the courtroom, 'and he said something like, "Look, it's been going on forever. The Romans had their little boys, the Greeks had their little boys, the English aristocrats had their little boys." I said, "So that makes it alright, does it?" I have not spoken to him since.'

Audrey had subsequently heard that the Catholic Church hierarchy had been saying that Andrew did not commit suicide.

She'd spoken to Father Cahill, her former parish priest in August 2013. 'I wanted to ask him why he hadn't visited me. He said, "I didn't come because you were too upset." He then told me that what happened to Andrew was a prank gone wrong.'

In January 2016, Audrey had spoken to a local priest she called 'a friend of mine', Father Dom Carrigan. He'd told her 'he had been speaking to a group of priests and that they had told him that Andrew didn't commit suicide, but had been playing hide and seek with his sister'. Audrey had insisted Carrigan tell her who had said that; finally, he'd informed her that it was Father Bill Burston.

'I have no understanding of why they would say this; it is not true,' Audrey told the courtroom. 'They simply have no compassion at all.' She continued reading:

> I spent my whole life committed to my Catholic faith and working for the Catholic Church. At my time of greatest need, after Andrew committed suicide, the only pastoral response I got from the Church was Fr Hart telling me that sexual abuse of boys has been going on for thousands of years. I don't go to Church now. I still have my beliefs, but I am appalled at the lack of empathy, the lack of support, and the lack of concern for all of the people affected by child sexual abuse. I am disgusted by the efforts of the Church to cover up the abuse, and to protect the abusers … I have been left feeling empty. I also feel so stupid that I used to fear and revere these people, and that I used to respect them and look up to them …

When Audrey finished reading out her statement, you could have heard a pin drop.

The uncomfortable silence lasted for a few seconds. Some of the clergy and religious shifted in their seats.

Audrey had the final word. She had explained what it felt like to be betrayed. There was at least some relief in that.

Joanne McCarthy was in the room when Audrey gave her speech with dignity and poise. The journalist thought Audrey had transformed before her very eyes; Andrew's mother had come a long way from the day she'd met McCarthy for a coffee, when she'd seemed submissive and subdued. Now she was a champion for survivors.

* * *

On 8 September 2016, Chiu cross-examined Father Burston, the trained psychologist, about that terrible night.

Chiu asked, 'Father Burston, this was a 13-year-old boy who had hanged himself; isn't that right?'

Burston said, 'Yes, who – yes. Who had died.'

'Well,' said Chiu, 'he had hanged himself in his own bedroom; isn't is that right?'

'Yes,' was Burston's response.

'And you knew that on the afternoon?'

'Yes, mmm.'[1]

A short time later, Chiu asked, 'Father Burston, did you tell other people that Andrew's death was a prank gone wrong?'

'I may have,' Burston replied. 'I don't remember the phrase and I don't remember telling anybody, actually, about it, but it seemed to me at the time that I could well have used that phrase that word, yes, those words, yes.'

'"A prank gone wrong", those words?'

'Yes,' said Burston.

'On what basis would you have come to that conclusion, that it was a prank gone wrong?'

'My recollection is that there was no – now, this is a recollection of 40 years ago, that there was no sign of any anxiety or trauma; that he had planned the next day what to wear, so it looked as though – and he had been playing hide and seek with one of his sisters, so it looked as though that could have been what happened.'

Chiu asked, 'So does that mean you applied some form of psychological analysis at the time to understand why he killed himself?'

'I didn't see it as having killed himself,' was Burston's response. 'I saw it as having – having died, you know.'

'So you didn't even consider that he'd killed himself?'

'There didn't seem to be any indications that he had. That was my –'

'And then you went and told other people that it was a prank gone wrong?' Chiu asked.

'I don't know,' said Burston. 'That – that – as that question comes to me, that sounds as though I spread it abroad. I don't recall doing that.'[2]

Two months later, on 17 November, Audrey Nash received a letter from Burston. 'Some time ago after a meeting, one of the priests, Father Dom Carrigan, asked about Andrew, and I told him briefly the story as I knew it at the time,' the priest wrote. 'Since then further information has come to light. So I would like to apologise for any hurt that my doing this has caused. I had, and have, no desire to cause any further pain in such a tragic situation. I regret also because my work situation took me out of parish work a few weeks later I was unable to be of more assistance to you and your family. It would be good if we could meet over a coffee and have a chat about this, but it may not be feasible.'

A woman had lost her thirteen-year-old son when her husband was away at sea, and the only excuse her parish priest could give for his lack of pastoral care was that work had taken him out of the parish a few weeks later – pathetic excuses for abominable behaviour.

This was the same priest who, as a psychologist, had assessed some of the most dubious priests and deemed them suitable for ministry.

The only priest who had given her regular pastoral care after Andrew's death was Father Glen Walsh. He was a regular visitor to the miner's cottage at Hamilton. In an email, after one of his visits, Glen wrote:

'When last in Newcastle, I was privileged to sit with Audrey Nash in the simple surroundings of her Hamilton home: an old, well lived-in home with the ambience of that beautiful patina found only in a house of love: A patina all too often absent within our grand Presbyteries, Monasteries, Convents/ Units and Churches. It would do all us "religious" figures good to sit awhile with Mrs Nash and mums/dads throughout the Hunter Region like her.'[3]

* * *

In September 2016, the Marist Brothers Provincial Peter Carroll made an opening statement to the Royal Commission that delivered an apology to Nash family.[4] 'I want to say something specific about the evidence I have heard about the death of Andrew Nash. I acknowledge the pain carried by the Nash family for the past 40 years. I express my admiration for the way they have summoned the courage to give evidence this week ... I want to acknowledge today in public that I accept on behalf of the Marist Brothers that all the evidence points to Andrew having been sexually abused, and the evidence also points to Andrew having taken his own life.'

Carroll continued: 'Importantly, it's obvious that many things have been said about the circumstances of Andrew's death, some of which must be corrected. It has been suggested in some places that Andrew's death was a prank gone wrong involving a family member, and yesterday we heard that the school at the time told the students that Andrew might have died, by an accident involving another family member. To me it is obvious that no member of the Nash family was involved in causing his death. Any suggestion that they were is completely wrong and hurtful to the family. These ideas must be totally rejected ...'

Carroll admitted that he was 'concerned about what was said at the school at the time about Andrew's death, and what information was given to the students'. 'I have agreed with the Nash's [sic] request to look into this further,' he said, 'and find out what I can for them. I have already taken steps to start that process.'

Carroll went on, broadening the scope of his statement:

I want to speak now to all the survivors, and all those who have been affected by sexual and physical abuse by the Marist Brothers. We cannot deny the unpalatable truths that have been revealed about the Marist Brothers' responses to child sexual abuse; vulnerable young people were sexually abused by Brothers, criminal activity took place, our response was entirely inadequate, the serious effects of sexual abuse were unrecognised, leaders failed to take strong decisive action, victims were offended against by means of aggressive legal processes. Our responses were naive, uninformed, even callous at times ...

As a Religious Order we have failed to protect the young people for whom we were founded and for whom many thousands of men have dedicated their lives. Those who have offended against young people have betrayed the trust placed in them by children and their parents, and by their own fellow Brothers. Our commitment today is what it should have been in the past: full cooperation with authorities, thorough, professional and effective processes and protocols to protect children and ensure their safety, compassionate responses to victims. We ask forgiveness for ourselves in our failure and we hope for the healing of victims of past crimes ...[5]

By the end of 2016, another Marist Brother who had attended Audrey Nash's house that night would be convicted of child sex offences. Brother William 'Christopher' Wade, Andrew's school principal in 1974. Once all the court cases were finished, some of Andrew's teachers would also be convicted. Brother Darcy 'Dominic' O'Sullivan was jailed for sexually assaulting 15 students, including during his time at Marist Brothers Hamilton. Later, the Marist Brothers would admit that Brother Thomas 'Patrick' Butler was also a child sex offender.

* * *

As 2016 progressed, Glen's health deteriorated. On 24 October, he texted a friend, giving them an update. Three weeks earlier, he'd had two large tumours removed from his abdomen along with five hernias caused by the tumours; when he'd been waking up from the anaesthetic, his lungs had collapsed and he'd suffered renal failure. The specialist had called his parents, who had begged the doctors to keep him alive. 'I am still in bed,' he added, 'on a liquid diet, cannot drive for months but now am allowed to walk a couple of hundred metres per day.'

Glen said, strikingly, 'It is selfish of me, but I wished they had allowed nature to take its course – but my family were having none of it, and those miracle workers brought me back to life.'

At his home in Terrigal he was being attended by family and friends, but although his surgeon had 'informed that bishop about the operation ... not the bishop, nor 1 priest has visited, nor emailed, telephoned, texted, wrote or enquired about my well being at all. Such cruelty meted out by men who are ordained to be "carers of the souls".' Glen mentioned 'they were all on "retreat" last week in Kincumber (6 kms from Terrigal) and still no contact'.

'I know I need to forget about them,' he said, 'but it still hurts – more than all this physical pain. I think I will miss my Church Family until the day I die.'

During his visits to St Vincent's Hospital in Darlinghurst, Glen stayed at a lodge nearby, normally frequented by women, men and students who lived close to the breadline or with limited incomes. It had rows of individual rooms and some shared bathrooms.

Glen would always stay in his favourite room on the second floor. Its furnishings were simple: a single bed, a TV and a sink. There was a shared bathroom down the hall. Glen had one window that looked out onto a busy city street.

On his floor, Glen found that quite a few older men needed help with their shopping and washing, and he could often be seen carrying their bags up the stairs to the second floor. He would trudge up to St Vincent's Hospital from this hostel every day for his treatment. The pain was excruciating at times. One day, Glen accidentally left his bedroom door open and returned to find one of the older men inside his room, drunk and aggressive. The man threatened Glen, so the priest had to find somewhere else to live.

Glen's loved ones were becoming increasingly angry with the Maitland-Newcastle Diocese. He was still a priest and entitled to some support from the diocese, particularly for accommodation, and his anger at his treatment would erupt every time he had to call the diocese to undertake whatever admin tasks were required of him. Under Church law, he was 'incardinated' in the Maitland-Newcastle Diocese. He belonged there and they had a responsibility to look after him.

In late 2016, Glen was trying to sort his registration as a priest with the diocese so he could finalise his curriculum vitae. After several attempts to do this, he fired off an email complaining about twice having to travel to Hamilton to fill out 'wrong forms'. 'On each occasion,' he wrote, 'I have been in obvious poor health and in even worse condition upon my return "home". None of this, whilst well known to those in "servant leadership", have taken my limited mobility into account.' He said he refused to go on a third trip but that 'as one of the few priests still with faculties and in "good standing", I would insist upon being included within the same register (and all other required registers) lest I be deleted from files and hidden again as though non-existent as I was by Malone and Doyle in the 1990s.'

Later in the email, Glen wrote, 'Sadly for some priests, this current "process" of having to be registered has been a long time foreseeable consequence of the doomed-to-fail, "Towards Healing" publication and resulting bureaucracies, set up by the Australian Catholic bishops and their quarrel of Lawyers who, with much reluctance, in the early 1990s, determined to protect their own collective cowardly arses.' He said that in spite of the well-documented flaws of the publication, 'not one bishop has had the courage to demonstrate significant servant leadership in this matter. Rather, the well-known modus operandi has allocated vast funds and has newly established "Centres of Care and Advice" to legally distance bishops and Congregational Leaders from their many Suffering people by lying about and denying the truth, omitting the truth and protecting criminal clergy (with the exception of those chosen ones whose filthy, scandalous and illegal behaviours are protected and rewarded by Bishop Wright and his confidants – —, —, Hart, Ryan, —, —, just to name a few).'

Instead of 'finally grasping with open arms an opportunity for conversion', Glen wrote, 'the bishop/s of our diocese handle/d criminality as an uncomfortable truth'. In his opinion, it had been 'known by many priests … and hidden for years. After this they painfully and forcibly exposed in the early 1990s by which time the Church determined to further quash these already crushed ones by failing to accept their stories of abuse. They refused to thoroughly investigate, to accept the truth findings and punish the offenders. Both canonical and legal avenues were bypassed, leading to avoidable ongoing abuses and gross scandal (not the least of which have been victims attempting to and successfully committing suicide) and with those Ordained bishops and Priests as well as Religious Sisters & Brothers adopting the "grand silence" around these matters – mafia behaviour indeed!'

Glen continued, not holding anything back:

Worse still, despite being put under obedience to cooperate by our own Bishop Wright if called by police to contribute to investigations or called before Commissioners and Judges, several of our own senior priests further harmed our victims, their families, the Church, the judicial system by their recalcitrant, uncooperative and even untruthful answers. Such venerable witnesses included, but were not limited to: bishops, priests and religious; reports scandalously expose vital omissions of evidence; uncooperative clergy witnesses who were under oath; giving implausible excuses; failing to recall repeatedly; presenting misleading medical reports (Burston's disease); submitting false documents and forging signature/s and admitting making available vast amounts of diocesan money in defence of the indefensible.

All the while, I, as a priest of the presbyterate I was never made aware of the same opportunities offered to every other priest, deacon and diocesan employee – to be offered pastoral care, support, financial assistance and/or legal representation. I would like to know why they unnecessarily took victims and Crown Witnesses to trial without personal support, compassion, connection nor so much as offering a shred of professional assistance nor pastoral care (in my case).

The past 13 years, since the Fletcher trial and my expulsion from the diocese by Malone, the indifference shown to my plight by Bishop Wright and the subsequent lack of support from the (collective) presbyterate, the impact of the imprisonment of our own Priest child abusers, as well those continuing to cover-up for sexual deviates ordained and non-ordained working/employed within the diocese of Maitland-Newcastle has been, and remains so significant, that it has practically ruined my life. Certainly, over these past years I have been alienated from my home (Church, parishes and God's people). For 13 years, I have been denied my canonical rights, even though I have always known and accepted my place as the lowest of the priests in our diocese (where faith once ran strong and deep).

Since my expulsion from the diocese in 2003 [sic] by Malone, neglect by my diocese of my human rights to be cared for and supported, as well as my Canonical rights to be sheltered, sustained and spiritually accommodated, has had a devastating impact on me, but even more tragically, on my birth family, my friends, my ex-students, many extended relatives and acquaintances and many rank & file members of the Catholic Church here in Australia and way beyond. I must, in charity, mention my bishops and brothers clergy whom I predominately experience as overtly hostile, rude, passive aggressive and/or simple ignorant.

Glen added, 'so that the bishops and clergy comply with this latest governmentally imposed bureaucracy we must all "register" and be tracked – adding further personal lament and indignity to an already irrelevant and shameful Church'. He again stated that he refused to 'come back to that haunted house to sign more forms'. 'I expect one of the appropriate clergy to get into their comfortable, air conditioned cars and drive to visit me for the first time in over 13 years! When was the last time David O'Hearn and Vincent Ryan were visited in jail I wonder?' Glen then asked, 'Would you kindly get back to me regarding my request that I be visited for once in order to acquiesce to this most humiliating requirement born of systemic corruption, neglect, arrogance and decay?'[6]

Bishop Wright eventually welcomed Glen back to the diocese in early February 2017. He'd been well enough to make one last trip to India before returning to Newcastle. The bishop gave him access to a house right next to Marist Brothers Hamilton. That same month, Wright sent out a message to all clergy, which was published in the *Newcastle Herald*: 'Glen has for some time expressed a desire to come home to the diocese … we waited around for too long on a prospect of accommodation that ultimately fell through.' Wright also acknowledged that in 2004, 'Glen had to act on his own in reporting Fletcher to the police. By doing so, he became something of a whistleblower and he encountered the opposition and ill-feeling that whistleblowers often do, Bishop Wright told the Hunter Priests.'[7]

CHAPTER 28

The Jail Visit

IN 2016, THE ROYAL COMMISSION INTO INSTITUTIONAL RESPONSES to Child Sexual Abuse released Church data about John Denham. The scale of his offending was breathtaking:

> Sixty-two people made a claim of child sexual abuse against John Sidney Denham. His crimes made up 39% of all claims received by the diocese of Maitland-Newcastle. The 62 claims of child sexual abuse against John Sidney Denham related to alleged incidents of abuse occurring in the period from 1970 to 1987. The gender of the people who made a claim of child sexual abuse against John Sidney Denham (where the gender was reported) was 100% male. The average age of the claimants at the time of the alleged child sexual abuse (where the age was reported) was 13 years of age.[1]

Steven Alward decided it was time for him to go and see his former teacher in jail. He wanted to confront Denham about his behaviour. And he needed answers.

Steven's brother Peter was visiting family in Adelaide for Christmas when Steven's texts came through. 'Look you know, given what's happened with Denham, and with everything blowing up, I'm thinking of going to see Denham, what do you think? What should I do? What would you do?'

Peter responded, 'Yeah, well, you know, if that's what you want to do, you should do that. You should face him, if you want to face him? I would go and see him, and I will come with you.'

Eventually, in between Christmas festivities, Peter called Steven and they talked for a long time about going to see Denham in jail. Steven told Peter that Mark was 'dead-set against it'. Mark had always found Denham creepy and unsettling, a perplexing presence in the background of Steven's life. Mark worried about the potential impact on Steven's mental state from visiting his former teacher, a paedophile, in a horrible jail. Mark thought Steven was just complicating his life more after being grossly deceived by his former mentor.

There was some deep reason for this urge to visit Denham, not yet revealed to Peter or Mark. Something very important was driving Steven's eagerness to face Denham.

Peter knew that as a teenager and young man, Steven had looked up to Denham as a mentor. Steven told Peter that Denham had treated him as one of 'his boys'. Denham would constantly praise Steven for doing so well in his career, and then emphasise his own role in that success. He'd kept reminding Steven that he owed his former teacher.

Rather than trying to stop Steven from going through with this, Peter decided to help make the visit as smooth as possible. He was a senior executive manager at the Salvation Army, which had a long history of helping prison inmates, and he organised a meeting with a Salvos prison chaplain so he could talk through the process of visiting someone in jail.

Steven told Peter he wanted to impart a message to Denham; he wanted to confront him and look him in the eye and ask him, 'Why have you deceived me?' Apparently it was all about the deceit, the fact the priest had got him to write that reference, but Peter was starting to think there might be other reasons. He started to wonder if there was more to the story than Steven had shared with him. Something in Steven's manner was tipping him off.

There was another reason for this visit. A secret Steven had kept to himself for forty years.

* * *

On 24 January 2017, Steven wrote to Denham at Goulburn Correctional Centre:

Hello John,
It's taken me a while to write this, but here I am. I wondered if you would like me to visit you. Depending on how you respond to this note, I will be prepared to drive to Goulburn and visit you. Maybe you get a lot of visitors and don't need another one. I have retired from work and am enjoying myself. Mark and I prepared ourselves well for our post-work life, we travel a lot, here and overseas, mainly to look at art and listen to music.
I will await your response and visit if that suits you.
Forgiveness may take a bit longer.
Steven

On 21 February 2017, Denham wrote back:

Dear Steven,
I must say that surprise greeted my opening of your recent letter. I hasten to stress that it was an agreeable and delightful experience and nudged my memory to recall many delightful times. I say this as I sit in a cell where my cellmate has just turned on the egregious Andrew O'Keefe chattering through his role in *The Chase* – nothing! can spoil the pleasure I received from hearing from you.
Looking at the above I seem to be having trouble with my prepositions, just like Andrew! TV does seem to throw up interesting characters.
A visit would be fantastic. They occur on Saturdays and Sundays and generally last over an hour. Those of us who

are on protection, unfortunately, have to run a gauntlet pass the Remand and Koori prisoners and we attract high levels of abuse (mainly verbal or sometimes apples are used to hurry us along). Visits are more important than these inconveniences and I really would like to see you again. Should you decide to visit, please let me know beforehand so that I can be ready.

Regards to you and Mark,

John

* * *

Sometime before the jail visit, Steven had contacted his friend and former colleague Professor Julianne Schultz about writing an article for the *Griffith Review*, a prestigious literary journal of which she was the editor. He had a title: 'The Betrayal'.

When Steven briefly explained the situation with Denham, Schultz was keen to publish this personal view of a paedophile priest. In February 2017, she met up with Steven to discuss the story in greater depth. They spoke about Steven's perspective on why he hadn't been targeted by Denham along with other boys at his school. He told her it was because he had a strong family. He told her that Denham had taken him away for the weekend but that nothing had happened to him, and he added that because he'd known he was gay from a young age, Denham's actions hadn't affected him. Schultz understood that Denham seemed to have played the role of an older brother figure who had basked in the reflected glory of Steven's career success. The psychological control was there, in a devious way; Denham had used Steven to cover up his actions.

The article was going to be framed by Steven meeting the former priest in jail. Schultz told Steven he could still write it without visiting Denham, but Steven was insistent. He felt deeply aggrieved and sad about the whole thing. He understood the courage required for victims to take their cases to court; some had breakdowns mid-trial and others couldn't finish their testimony, so their trials were aborted.

Steven told Schultz the betrayal was of his status, his standing, his prestige – it was duplicity of the highest order. He said he also felt terribly guilty that by writing that reference he had hurt the victims' cases, and he felt he had damaged their chances of success.

* * *

Around this time, a book came out called *The Priests*, written by an ex-student of St Pius X, James Miller. In it, he accused Father Tom Brennan of sexually assaulting him soon after he'd come to the school in 1978 when he was in Year 10.

One day Brennan had asked him to come to a classroom at the second half of lunch. The principal unlocked the door and asked James to sit at a work desk and to read his religious instruction workbook. Brennan then moved his chair to sit very close to James, too close, and his mood changed. His face took on an intense expression. He put his hand on James's leg and proceeded to undo his trousers. When the boy protested, Brennan said, 'It's very normal, James, don't be alarmed.' He masturbated the boy, and when James complained, Brennan noted the boy's erection and said, 'Now, James, if it was wrong would you be like this.' Brennan then forced James to hold his penis and masturbate him until he ejaculated into James's hand.[2] The principal then spoke in a clipped voice: 'Tidy yourself up. This must stay between us, James. Everyone has their private moments. Alright?'[3]

Brennan would prey on the boy for the rest of the year; he acted as if they were in a relationship. The abuse only stopped when James approached Father Helferty, the deputy principal, and told him he wanted help. Helferty replied, 'Be careful, Master Miller. We won't put up with boys telling lies about Father Brennan, or anyone else.' Helferty then told him to 'keep his stories to himself'.[4]

James had been two years below Steven at the school, and the book caused the diocese to acknowledge Brennan had been a child sex offender.

Another of Steven's mentors was a paedophile.

* * *

By March 2017, Steven had hatched a plan to visit Denham in the supermax prison at Goulburn about two hours south-west of Sydney.

It was a Saturday, when he and Peter drove down the monotonous Hume Highway. The cityscape made way for the rolling green fields and farms of the Southern Highlands, before the sprawling regional city of Goulburn came into view.

The conversation in the car turned to Denham, and Steven dropped a bombshell. He told his brother that Denham had sexually interfered with him when he was in high school.

They drove on for a few minutes in silence while this news sank in.

Peter realised Steven was preparing him for the meeting that was about to take place: Steven would confront the former priest about his own abuse.

Steven played down the severity of what had happened. He said he'd been groped and touched up.

But Peter remembered that Steven had gone away for weekends with Denham to Taree and Wingham, and he had told his family another priest was there. On one occasion, Steven had been in a swimming pool when Denham had taken a young teenage boy from the pool into the house. Steven had also told his family Denham would give him and the other boys alcohol. Peter wondered if there was a lot more to the story, and he hoped his brother would tell him everything.

Other victims who had gone away with Denham on similar trips, at the same time and a few years later, had reported being sexually abused after being plied with alcohol. These victims said another priest was there, Father Ron Picken.[5] In 2015, Justice Syme, while sentencing Denham, had referred to this practice of other men being involved in the abuse as an 'organised criminal activity'.

Picken had told the court he had offered alcohol to boys at the Wingham presbytery during overnight trips with Denham. One boy had consumed nearly the whole contents of a bottle of Scotch, which the priest claimed had required him to then bathe the boy. Syme wrote, '[Father Picken] did not ask about the sleeping arrangements when Denham and several boys were required to sleep in the presbytery's second bedroom.' She added, 'The combined set of facts lead to an inescapable conclusion of the active or tacit collusion by at least two other Church officers.' Syme then named Picken and the former principal of St Pius X, Brennan.[6] Picken died in April 2015.

Peter had always suspected that something had happened to Steven, but it had never been spoken aloud. Now it was clear to Peter: Steven had been sexually abused. Steven insisted, '*not as bad as the other boys*'. In previous conversations, years before, Steven had denied emphatically that any abuse had taken place. There were a lot of unanswered questions. Had he been suffering in silence all these years?

Steven asked Peter a funny question, 'Are people evil?'

Peter replied, 'I don't think people are evil, but they do evil acts.' This question from his younger brother troubled him at the time and would haunt him in later years.

* * *

Steven and Peter pulled into the open-air carpark at the front of the Goulburn Correctional Centre, its brick and sandstone exterior covered in razor wire. Built in the nineteenth century to house only the most hardened criminals, it was now home to Denham. In front of the jail an abandoned railway line led to a dead end. Above the watchtower, a large black crow rode the thermals rising from the hot ground.

Before Steven and Peter began the short walk from the carpark to the reception area, Steven turned to his brother and said, 'I can do this on my own. I will meet Denham by myself.'

Peter later recalled that Steven wasn't tense; he was very calm. He was ready for this confrontation, and he wanted to do it on his own, something he'd thought about since writing that blighted reference.

When the brothers checked in at reception, they had to give the corrective services officer their mobile phones and have their identities checked. They waited patiently before the corrective services officer behind the front desk waved Steven to approach him. He told Steven the prisoner had changed his mind – Denham had withdrawn permission for the visit.

Steven was shocked, hurt and angry. His former mentor had committed another heinous act, as Denham must have known that he was wounding Steven deeply. He still had power over his victim; he would torment him one last time. He would not let Steven have closure and relief.

* * *

Soon after this thwarted visit, Steven told Julianne Schultz he could no longer write 'The Betrayal'. She said he seemed distracted and unhappy.

Around the same time, Steven learned that Denham had been charged with still more child sex offences. This victim had been younger than twelve when the abuse had occurred at the Taree parish from 1979 to 1980 – the same area where the former priest had taken Steven on one of their overnight trips.

A year later, in October 2018, Denham would be convicted of all the charges, bringing his number of known victims to 58 boys between 1968 and 1986, including many students at St Pius X. They ranged in age from five to seventeen years old.

A number of these men have since taken their lives, and the police believe he had many more victims.

The 77-year-old priest wouldn't be eligible for parole until 2028.

* * *

When Denham had been based in Newcastle in the late 1970s, he'd sometimes travelled to Sydney to attend so-called 'priest parties'. One day he called up his mate Picken in Taree and invited him to come along, and Picken agreed, deciding to take a sixteen-year-old local boy with him – Picken had been sexually abusing the teenager for some time. The man and the boy drove to Newcastle to pick up Denham, then the three of them drove to Sydney. They entered a large red brick building where another priest lived. It belonged to the Church.

The three of them went to dinner nearby. The boy had never been to Sydney before so didn't know where he was. Later, as an adult, he remembered a red brick building on a main road. The boy was given a bedroom there to spend the night.

The next day more priests arrived. Inside the main room were at least twenty priests of all different ages. They were smoking cigars and drinking alcohol, and many were in various states of undress. Some were only in their underwear. To get away, the boy asked Picken if he could go to the toilet. He was frightened.

The boy was made to walk through a large group of half-naked priests who asked him if he'd like to join in.

He recognised one man at the party because this cleric had officiated at several masses he had attended. It was Bishop Leo Clarke, the most senior cleric of the Maitland-Newcastle Diocese.[7]

The victim has made an official report to police.

* * *

On 26 March 2017, Denham wrote to Steven, ostensibly to explain his behaviour at the jail.

Dear Steven,
Please accept my apologies for the long journey you undertook with your brother, to no avail. The authorities informed me you left no contact number, and thus, I was unable to personally inform you of my change of mind.

When I first received your letter, I was overjoyed but then I began to think (there's plenty of time to do this here) and a number of issues surfaced: –
   a. It's been almost 10 years since our last contact

b. You were employed by the Newcastle Herald, a tabloid concerned with following a journalistic 'angle' rather than addressing the greys of any topic. The virago who won journalism's highest distinctions has plagued me on a number of occasions in her proposed award-winning pieces (award-winning inventions)

c. Until you retired, you worked for the ABC – an organisation seemingly intent on destruction of the Church and any of its leaders who disagreed with it.

Therefore, you can see how the above, plus advice from my barrister to be careful what I said to you in the visit, helped urge the cancellation. Keep in mind also that most prisoners live on a healthy serving of paranoia.

I still believe however, that the friendships forged so long ago in the fleshpots of Newcastle remains but I fear the risk of exposing myself to, albeit, imagined possibilities. They say age advances one's personal wisdom, but often it's seasoned with doubts in no way allayed by prison life.

I'm still very much in favour of a visit and all the joys flowing from it but from my angle there is an additional problem. When protected prisoners receive visits their names are called out over the speaker system just before the event takes place. This alerts the other yards, giving them time to assail and assault (verbally) those taken from the protection yards for visits. The feral humans in these yards sometimes throw missiles at you as you progress to the Reception Area. I'm now 74 and find my 'dodging' powers somewhat mitigated. I have cancelled other visits on account of this situation so don't feel too singled out.

We are allowed to make telephone calls, and should you feel able you could give me a contact number so that I might speak with you on and off. I speak with most of my friends and relatives on a regular basis using this facility. Please don't give up on me, and please reply to this disjointed epistle, as soon as you are able.

Still thinking of the good times.
Love
John.
P.S Please keep in contact
P.P.S The authorities are working on the problems found by
protected inmates re: visits but as yet nothing has eventuated

A week later, on 2 April, Steven penned a response.

John,
Thanks for getting back to me. Nothing you said surprised me,
sadly. You spent most of our encounters over three decades
arguing the abuse in the Catholic Church was a beat-up. That
the people responsible were journalists and editors who made
up all these stories. But of course, it was not the journalists and
editors who raped the little boys. The boys who grew up to be
the men who killed themselves, in agony and in shame.

John, I hoped that you would by now stop blaming other
people. But your letter to me talks about the ABC, about
the Newcastle Herald. I thought you would stop blaming
others, finally. Your comments about Joanne McCarthy were
particularly gruesome.

I don't suggest you did to me what you did to so many
others. But what I wanted to talk to you about when I saw
you was the extraordinary betrayal of sitting across a table or
a bar for decades, and you would pretend you were good, to
abuse me about the media, to pretend, most horribly, that we
were friends.

I met you, as kids often do, thinking what a good teacher,
how much I could learn ... what an utter betrayal.

I went to you when I realised I was gay at 19 to seek some
sort of guidance – not knowing you – a priest would be gay,
but just thinking you might be able to guide me in some way.
And we stayed in ways connected over more than 30 years. Of
denial by you, of extraordinary accusations about the media,
which I was naïve to not understand. And then, of course,

the charges, the convictions, and the overwhelming sense of stupidity. I could not believe that I had missed what you had done, how I had not realised who I had been sitting across from at the bars and the tables.

This is what betrayal looks like. And I am what collateral damage looks like.

Steven left this handwritten draft letter sitting on top of a small, neatly stacked parcel of earlier correspondence between him and his former teacher.

CHAPTER 29

The Trial

DURING 2017, GLEN'S HEALTH DETERIORATED EVEN FURTHER. He'd had so many operations on his stomach that he was finding it hard to eat solid food.

Still to come, in November 2017, was the trial of Archbishop Wilson, in which he would be one of the prosecution witnesses. He'd told friends he was scared stiff about being cross-examined again, and the authorities already had his extensive statements to the police and to the NSW Special Commission of Inquiry.

On a Tuesday in late August, Glen received a call from a Marist Brothers representative: Norm Maroney, a former assistant police commissioner, now the professional standards officer for the Marist Brothers Province of Australia. He was responsible for dealing with claims of child abuse for the Brothers.

Glen then received an email from Maroney on 31 August 2017, less than three months before the priest was scheduled to testify at the Wilson trial.

Just a short note regarding our telephone call on Tuesday. As the Provincial, Brother Peter Carroll is overseas and the acting Provincial Brother Ken McDonald will also be away from tomorrow both not returning for two months (Marist Chapter)

I would just like to briefly confirm Tuesday's conversation. I want to do this so you at least have something in writing and being able to feel more comfortable that something positive has occurred regarding your complaint. I am sorry that you have endured your suffering for so long.

Father Glen, I am sorry for the delay in finalising this part of my review, however, there were the normal commitments and other issues that interfered with the review and of course endeavouring to seek as much available information as possible. I basically carried out the review examining many documents and clarifying what I considered to be relevant, it was most important that I didn't miss any information which was available that could assist me in making my determination regarding your complaints made against Brother Coman Sykes. The original assessment finding of 'NOT SUSTAINED' was made on the balance of probabilities that the abuse occurred or did not occur.

I found as a result of my review, that your complaints against the Brother were 'SUBSTANTIATED' and the Independent Assessor's Finding of 1998 is rescinded. This was the finding and recommendation to the Acting Provincial, Brother Ken McDonald.

I have discussed the result of my Review with Brother Ken and he accepted the 'SUBSTANTIATED' FINDING', and from my conversation with him, it is obvious to me that he is also saddened by your experience with the Brothers. Brother Ken would like to meet with you on his return from overseas. I will make contact with you then. In the meantime, feel free to ring at any time.

Glen's complaint against Coman Sykes was now believed. It was 'substantiated'. The injustice of the past nineteen years welled up inside him.

* * *

In the following days, Glen studied the email from the Marist Brothers. Why now?

He would soon be testifying at the trial of Australia's highest cleric to be charged with concealment. The pressure on Glen was growing daily. There was speculation in the media. There was no escape.

What Glen didn't know was that the Marist Brothers had compensated a man in 2015 who had complained to them of being sexually abused by Sykes. The crime had occurred in 1972, when the victim was twelve years old and attending Marist Brothers Kogarah.

So why had the Brothers waited two years to contact Glen about his complaint? Why hadn't they got in touch once they'd paid out compensation to the other victim in 2015?

One of Glen's closest confidants thought it might have been a deliberate move to destabilise the priest before the trial. But Glen couldn't know this for sure. Whatever the case, it was yet another move from the Catholic Church that caused him immense distress.

The timing was certainly curious. If the Crown won the Wilson trial, this would establish a legal precedent affecting all clergy and religious – many of them would then be under threat of prosecution. And the Marist Brothers might have guessed that Glen was terrified his own sexual abuse would be made public.

When recently asked to comment on this, the Marist Brothers said they had been reviewing all cases following the Royal Commission's harsh criticisms. But Glen's friends have said the unexpected news was the last straw for Glen. He had been repeatedly abused by his teacher and superior, as an eighteen-year-old, for more than a year. Then he had been repeatedly betrayed by his Church.

Although the re-emergence of his claim at this time could have been a coincidence, it didn't feel like it – it felt like a deliberate attempt to destabilise him.

* * *

John Walsh contacted his brother about six weeks before the Wilson trial and became very worried about Glen's health, both mental and physical.

The stress of having to testify again was taking its toll. Glen talked to his brother about what had happened to him during his cross-examination by the Special Commission of Inquiry. He was anticipating further isolation in the diocese; he would again be ostracised. He worried his own abuse would be brought up.

Glen now had a good idea of the full scale of the cover-up in the Maitland-Newcastle Diocese. He was in the middle of something that he could not control. On top of all that, he told John he couldn't face another barrage of questions from an aggressive barrister.

A little more than two weeks out from the trial, the Marist Brothers got in contact with him again to make an appointment about Maroney's email. Glen would be required to attend a legal meeting at Marist Brothers HQ in Drummoyne, a Sydney suburb, on Tuesday, 7 November 2017.

Around the same time, on 24 October 2017, Bishop Bill Wright had a meeting with Glen, who was keen to hear what roles he might play in the diocese. Wright's response was devastating to him.

At three-thirty the next morning, Glen emailed a friend. 'Bishop visited me,' he wrote. 'Pleasant enough meeting. The following is STRICTLY CONFIDENTIAL. The Bishop admitted there is no future for me in any form of ministry in this diocese. He will look overseas (third world) where I can live out my days in the service to Christ and his poor, preferably as a contemplative to a leper colony. He told me to feel free to seek out a position as well. I fear I will never see him again.' Glen then revealed: 'He advised me that the presbyterate will never forgive me for exposing them for what they are in relation to the recent scandals and so my place here is untenable. Anyone would think that I am the scandal not them ... at least I will get a supportive letter of recommendation from the bishop.' Glen told his friend, 'Please pray for me ... I am begging you to say nothing about the Bishop's plan for me – for if it gets out before it is arranged, the savagery of the presbyterate will devour and destroy what just might be my way to God and a final chance at holiness for which I do dearly long for.'

Glen's health wouldn't survive a 'third world' posting. He knew he was being dumped again, and his anguish grew as the trial date approached.

* * *

On the Friday before the Tuesday meeting with the Marist Brothers, Glen sent all the documents pertaining to his complaint to a friend and told that person to keep them safe. That person would bring those documents to the meeting with the Brothers.

After receiving the documents, the friend was worried and tried to contact the priest. He didn't return the calls.

Glen called one close friend over the weekend and told her, 'I have nothing more to give.'

* * *

This Depression-era street in Newcastle was like many others. Rows of Federation-style dark-brick bungalows, prewar architecture with mature lemon trees in the front yards, kids' toys strewn across the freshly mown grass, and cars in various states of repair. But there was something striking that couldn't be avoided from any vantage point: at the beginning of the street, a large white cross marked the boundary of the Marist Brothers Hamilton School.

In one of those houses, a priest was preparing for his death. The night air was cool on Monday, 6 November 2017. Darkness was enveloping his home. The only light was from an aromatic candle, wafting a scent through the dimly lit rooms.

In the dancing shadows, illuminated by the flickering candlelight, stood the priest's private altar. Among the statues of Jesus and several sets of coloured rosary beads was a prayer card.

This priest was Glen.

He had suffered from ill health for many years. His surgery some months earlier had left him in considerable pain and discomfort.

That night, he was fully dressed in his black robes. His priest's uniform.

He went to the bathroom cabinet, took out the pain medication he'd been hoarding for months, and swallowed it in one dose. He then lay on his bed.

On the following day, Glen didn't show up to the important meeting with the Marist Brothers. Frantic calls were made to his mobile phone. There was no answer.

* * *

When the police broke into the house, and the family followed, they found all the wastepaper baskets full of shredded documents. The jagged strips of white paper were even overflowing from the backyard bins.

The police established a crime scene and wouldn't let the family take too many effects. The house felt dark and eerie.

John Walsh had been told the news on the morning of Tuesday, 7 November.

'I was at work as the payroll officer at St Joseph's College, Hunters Hill. It was Melbourne Cup day. I put Glen in the sweep and Glen ultimately won the $5 sweep at Joeys and I still have the money in the envelope. That envelope will never be opened. I had a missed call from my mother, she left a voice mail message and said; John! it's Glen! I've got some news to tell you about Glen. I thought he had died. I thought he had died from all his physical ailments, I thought he had had a heart attack. I really did. When I finally found out he was dead, I screamed out NO NO! in the office at Joeys, and everyone looked at me and said what's wrong and I said Glen is dead.'[1]

John headed up to Newcastle the next day to meet with his family. They sat in silence, engulfed by grief.

John said, 'It ripped the guts straight out of me; no one should have suffered like he did.'

The news of Father Glen Walsh's passing shocked many of his family members and friends – including Steven, who had maintained a friendship over the years with his former neighbour. Steven had always admired Glen.

CHAPTER 30

A Tragic Death

IN DECEMBER 2017, NSW POLICE CHARGED BROTHER JOHN O'Brien, a former footy coach and Marist Brothers Hamilton teacher, with child sex offences alleged to have been committed at St Joseph's College, Hunters Hill, between 1966 and 1970. St Joseph's College was the place Glen had been the chaplain. He had loved his time there despite his health problems.

O'Brien was one of the men who visited Audrey Nash the night of Andrew's death. He was charged by Strike Force Gallagher with nine counts of inciting an act of indecency and four counts of indecent assault, involving four students. (He has since pleaded not guilty to the charges, with his trial due to commence in late 2020.)

Audrey did the sums. Of the priests and Brothers who had come to her house that night, only one hadn't been charged or investigated over child sex offences: Father Bill Burston. Even Father Helferty had received complaints against him many decades earlier.

Several years later, Burston would tell a television documentary he 'was sick of Andrew Nash'.[1] He would also dispute the police claim that Andrew had suicided because of sexual abuse at Marist Brothers Hamilton. This was despite Burston's own apologies to Audrey.

* * *

On 7 December 2017 a law legalising same–sex marriage throughout Australia was passed by Parliament. Steven was thrilled and excited about marriage equality. By late 2017, he was preparing to marry Mark, who had proposed back on 2 June 2015. Now it was legal, Steven and Mark chose the date: 3 March 2018.

A week later, the Royal Commission into Institutional Responses to Child Sexual Abuse delivered its findings to the prime minister of Australia. The report describes the sexual abuse of so many Australian kids as being a 'national tragedy'.

In a blow to the denialists in the Catholic Church, the report says, 'The largest proportion of these survivors spoke to us about child sexual abuse in Catholic institutions. We heard from 2,489 survivors about child sexual abuse in Catholic institutions, representing almost two-thirds (61.8 per cent) of survivors who told us about child sexual abuse in religious institutions and more than one-third (36.2 per cent) of all survivors we heard from in private sessions. In private sessions we heard about child sexual abuse occurring in 964 different Catholic institutions.'[2] It concluded that there were catastrophic failures of leadership in the Catholic Church.

According to the report, claims of abuse against the Marist Brothers accounted for a quarter of all claims received by religious institutions with only Brother members, and 10 per cent of all child abuse claims. Between 1980 and 2015, 486 people made a claim of abuse against the Marist Brothers. Eighty-nine per cent of these claims identified one or more Brothers as a perpetrator. The average age of the claimants at the time of the abuse was twelve.

On 6 September 2016, a list of 154 Marist Brothers was tendered as evidence to the Royal Commission: Exhibit #43–021. It was lodged by the Marist Brothers Provincial Brother Turton as part of Case Study C43 at the Newcastle Court House. These 154 Marist Brothers had been the subject of an allegation of child abuse in the form of an official claim to the order, or had claims that were found to be substantiated.

Volume Four of the Royal Commission report focused on identifying child sexual abuse and understanding disclosure. It found that disclosure is rarely a one-off event – instead, it's a process. Disclosure may be partial, as the survivor may not tell the whole story in one sitting. The report said that many victims don't disclose their abuse until many years after it has occurred. Analysis from all the private sessions held with survivors found that it took, on average, 25.6 years for men and 20.6 years for women to disclose their child sexual abuse.

Two key recommendations refer to the Catholic Church: that parish priests should no longer be the employers of principals and teachers in Catholic schools, and that the Holy See (Vatican) should amend Church laws relating to child sexual abuse, including removing the requirement to destroy documents under certain circumstances and to consider introducing voluntary celibacy: 'we recommend that canon law be amended so that the pontifical secret does not apply to any aspect of allegations or canonical disciplinary processes relating to child sexual abuse'.[3]

Another key recommendation that raised the ire of the Church was that priests should be legally required to report child abuse disclosed during the confessional.

Survivors and their families were relieved by the report and responded positively to it. Their claims had largely been vindicated by this judicial inquiry.

Glen wasn't alive to see the positive response from so many victims nor the Catholic Church's dismissal of some of the key findings. This was another blow to the people who loved and cared about him.

Each night, Steven would stay up into the wee small hours poring over the Royal Commission reports. Sometimes he wouldn't sleep until 2 a.m. Mark worried that his partner seemed a bit obsessed and that he was immersing himself in such darkness.

* * *

In early January, Steven texted a good friend of his, Matin Safi, wishing him well and saying they would catch up soon. He had met Matin in Afghanistan, as he was the correspondent's producer on the ground. Matin had noticed Steven had lost weight at their last meeting, but Steven brushed it off saying he wanted to look good in his wedding suit. Nothing appeared amiss.

On Sunday, 14 January 2018, Steven was at home and received the news from Mark that Glen's brother, John, had dropped by to see him.

Steven called John back and learned he was on a mission from his mother. She had asked John to visit Steven to thank him for the card and flowers he and his sister had sent their family, but there was another message she wanted to impart. She asked John to tell Steven that her son Glen had not suicided. It seemed an odd message, but Steven assumed she was referring to the Catholic teaching that suicide was a mortal sin, and therefore had to believe her son had not killed himself.

John dutifully passed this message to Steven in a phone call on the Sunday night. Disregarding this blunt message from Glen's mother, both men spoke about Glen for some time. During the phone call, Steven asked John, 'How did Glen kill himself?' John answered, 'He saved up his medication.'

After this phone call, Steven seemed to be suffering from a heightened state of anxiety and moments of depression, amid what was a normal day of wedding planning. The next day Mark and Steven went to choose their wedding shirts. At times it seemed like any other day, but there were more moments of anxiety. Mark suggested that Steven call his sister, Libby, for a chat. They had a close relationship, and they had always lifted each other's spirits in times of stress.

Libby spoke to Steven on 16 January, the Tuesday night after the Sunday phone call with John Walsh. As the conversation went on, Steven's mood shifted and he was laughing with her about what sort of dresses she and her girls would wear to his upcoming marriage. He quipped, 'Are you wearing pink taffeta?'

At some stage between late evening 16 January and the early hours of 17 January, Steven, quietly and in an organised manner, took a fatal combination of well-researched pharmaceutical drugs.

Next to the empty vials, Steven left a note. A poignant, articulate letter of love and apology to Mark. The heartbreaking words gave no hint whatsoever as to why Steven had taken this action at what was objectively perhaps the happiest stage of his life, just weeks before his wedding to his partner of thirty-eight years.

David Alward called his brother Peter early that Wednesday morning; he could hardly say the words. 'It's Steven.' Those words pierced Peter's heart. The brothers sobbed together on the phone, unable to speak to each other for what seemed an eternity.

Slowly, in the weeks and months that followed, the shocking bewilderment felt by Steven's bereft partner and siblings slowly gave way to some understanding, as they had a compassionate policeman working on the case who had pieced together the circumstances of this mysterious death.

Steven's disclosure to Peter about his sexual abuse by Denham was in the police report attached to the coroner's findings.

Mark was shocked, as were the rest of the family. Steven had not told Mark, or two of his other siblings. He had told Peter on the way to the jail to confront Denham.

The Royal Commission report confirms that it isn't unusual for victims to keep their abuse from their closest loved ones. It takes an average 23.9 years for survivors to disclose their abuse to family and friends, and some never disclose: 'Survivors disclosed because they could no longer carry the burden of the secrecy of sexual abuse … underlying these factors is the vulnerability of a child and the inherent power imbalances and complex institutional environments that they are required to understand and overcome in order to disclose abuse … research shows individuals assess their personal situation and may disclose, or partially disclose, depending on their reading of anticipated risks and benefits… one of the most common barriers to disclosure … is shame and embarrassment.'[4]

When asked for her thoughts on this, Libby said, 'I know, he must have been in so much pain to end his life … he loved everyone at the ABC, and all of his family. His nieces, his nephews. Everyone.'

He was surrounded by love, and yet he couldn't deal with what had been done to him.

With wry sadness, Libby said, 'Something had eaten at him that night and he thought, *I can't do this anymore.* He is at peace, but we're not … and he's a little bugger for doing this to us.'

* * *

A few days after Steven's death, Libby called John Walsh to tell him the news. She recorded the conversation, and John gave permission for some of it to be repeated here.

After they exchanged some pleasantries, Libby broke the news. 'Steven isn't with us any longer.'

John was taken aback. 'Steven?'

'Steven passed away on Wednesday morning.'

'Steven Alward?' John says, sounding incredulous.

'Yep.'

'You're joking!'

'No, he took his life on Wednesday, through Tuesday night.'

John exhaled. 'That's terrible.'

'Yeah, it is. Devastating.'

'That's unbelievable. I was only there, Libby, this time last Saturday.'

'Yeah?' asked Libby, her voice cracking slightly.

John described how he'd popped by and chatted with Mark, then spoken to Steven on the phone that Sunday for 'a good thirty or forty minutes'. They'd talked about Glen, and John implied that he thought Steven had kept track of Glen over the years through their mutual connection with Aunty Mary.

Steven had told John that now he had his phone number, they'd have to catch up sometime for dinner. John had let him know that he'd retired on 7 September 2017 after resigning from his job at

St Joseph's College; he'd given the Marist Brothers four months notice. 'One of the reasons,' John said to Libby, 'was to go back to sort of look after Glen, you know. Just being in his presence. I knew all his physical illnesses. I knew he had depression, but I didn't know how deep his depression was … Unfortunately, I was two months too late.'

John again expressed surprise at Steven's death, adding 'he's a very successful person'. Libby said she couldn't believe it either, and she told John about Steven and Mark's wedding plans. John said, 'Yeah. We talked about old times, and I said, "Look, Steven, I haven't probably seen you since we were twelve years old when we left Our Lady of Victories. But I … remember your family very well. Your dad was a man of very few words, but I always had good, fond memories of your parents and all you—"'

'All the kids,' Libby interrupted.

'Yeah. I can even recall being there … the first time I had Coco Pops and played Mouse Trap was at your place.' John was sounding whimsical as he remembered their childhood, but there was an edge to his voice.

'Oh, really?' Libby asked, a slight edge to hers too.

'Yeah. See, my mum, we just had the bare Rice Bubbles or something … Mum kept all the photos – I said [to Steven], I've still got the photo of Steven and myself when we … made our first …'

'Holy Communion?' Libby asked.

'Yes.' John moved the conversation back to Steven's death, checking if it had happened on Tuesday night.

Libby confirmed this, adding, 'Then I rang at ten past eight on Wednesday morning, and the police answered the phone. So he took medication between going to bed and the next morning.'

The old neighbourhood mates now saw the similarities in how their beloved brothers had died.

'That's how Glen did it too,' said John. He told Libby that despite this, his family had found 'a whole lot of prescription tablets' remaining in Glen's bathroom cabinet. John went on to say, 'I just hope me going down there last Saturday didn't flash

[Steven] back to childhood or something – not me directly, but you know when you have a flashback in his life and put him in sort of a bad frame of mind. I just don't think I'd do that.'

'So he didn't give you any clue or anything that he had concerns or anything like that, John?'

'No, not at all. I apologised to him – we hadn't been in contact for forty-five years, but basically what I said to him is, one thing is, Steven, whether I haven't seen you for five minutes or forty-five years, you and your family will always be held in high esteem by both myself – even Glen. Even Mum and Dad, because Mum made a point of saying – she's eighty-one, but she sent me a little handwritten note and said, "Would you make the point of going to see Steven?" I said … "I'll definitely make a point." Not because Mum told me to, but because also I went to school with Steven. And I also thought very well of your whole family.'

'Yeah, all of us kids mucking around together. And Glen used to come on holidays. We thought a lot of all of you kids too.'

'You could knock me over with a feather, what you just told me. But he gave me no indication. It was like Glen, too. Glen spoke to me. I hadn't spoken to Glen for about three weeks prior to him taking his own life. All I can say is, Glen obviously prepared me for … uh, he himself taking his own life. It took eighteen months to two years beforehand. But Glen had that many physical illnesses, stress-related, brought on by the Church … I spoke quite a lot about that to Steven. I just said I never suspected that Glen would take his own life. I just thought that he was preparing me for the next operation that he wouldn't pull through. Because you could talk to Glen, like Steven – and Steven more so was very educated, very learned – and Glen probably never gave us even an inkling or a sign.'

'Yes.'

'And that's what he kept saying – "Look, I love Glen as a friend."'

'So you and Steven never spoke about the … Catholic Church with the priests?'

'No. I sort of touched on it, but Steven said, "Yeah, I knew about this and I knew about that." I was like "fair enough" and we moved on to the next subject. In view of the fact that he said that when his aunty was dying that he asked Glen to offer the prayers et cetera, I said, "That's great that you spoke to Glen then." There was nothing …'

'No, because we just can't work it out, why he's done that. They're wealthy, they live at Double Bay. They've been all around the world millions of times, and getting married. It was very out of the blue. We're just trying to find some answers.'

'Yeah. See, I really feel for you and your family and Mark because at least I had answers. I can't say that "S" word. I didn't need to see an "S" note, you know what I mean? I knew everything about it. And maybe there was some unanswered things, but in my mind I pretty much knew what Glen was going through. And it was chronic pain, both physiological and psychological that he was going through.'

* * *

ABSENCE

The booming silence of you,
here though you are not.
This roar of nothing,
that whisper of thunder,
fading to where it begins.

Rewind to the end,
swim back to where you drowned.
Or walk surefooted across our desolate sea.
Return to me like Jesus,
three days have come and gone.

It happened, make it unhappen.
Because mad is the new normal,
here, where nothing makes sense,
or there, where the unimaginable is real;
anywhere in this world awash with your absence.

– Mark Wakely

* * *

Denham, aged seventy-six, was again convicted in 2019 on more charges of child sexual assault also committed in Taree. This brought his victim tally to 59. The victim had been an altar boy, and Denham had asked that boy to stay back for an 'initiation ceremony', which was code for rape. The victim told the Royal Commission into Institutional Responses to Child Sexual Abuse that he was abused by two Catholic priests and a youth worker in the late 1970s and early 1980s in Taree. The same man accused Father Barry Tunks of sexually assaulting him when he was a child. Father Tunks was charged, but the charges against him were soon dropped due to a lack of evidence.

Father Denham was sentenced to a maximum of thirteen years in jail. He has been in jail since 2008, and his earliest possible release date is July 2029.

In the aftermath of Steven's death, Peter Alward decided to do something quite bold. He decided to write Denham a letter.

Hi John,

You don't know me personally, but you would know of me, I am Steven Alward's elder brother, Peter Alward.

As you would be aware, Steven and I travelled to Goulburn in March 2017 to visit you after you had agreed to meet with him. Unfortunately, you withdrew that opportunity, so on our arrival at the Goulburn Correctional Centre, we were turned away at the reception.

While the trip was a great disappointment to Steven, it was a real opportunity for us 2 brothers to converse for around 6 hours on that long trip from Sydney. Steven looked forward to that visit, albeit with a little trepidation.

We had discussed the trip for months, and I had convinced him that a meeting with you would be good for him, and maybe even good for you. He agreed to go, on the condition that I would go with him, an assignment I gladly accepted to support my little brother in his time of real need.

I am not sure if you are aware John, but Steven passed away under very tragic circumstances on 17 January 2018. Obviously, this was devastating to Steven's family and friends and particularly to his life partner, Mark.

John, Steven really wanted to see you, and to talk to you about his feelings towards you following your trial. Understandably, he did feel deceived and betrayed by you who he saw as he grew up in Newcastle as a good teacher and someone he could learn from, a person of integrity and significance. He really wanted to see you face to face, man to man.

Steven's opportunity to see you has passed, but what I would ask is if you would agree to meet with me in Goulburn. I see this as unfinished business for Steven, and I would like to close that chapter of his life for him and our family.

John, I don't want to meet you out of anger or a feeling of seeking justice, but really to satisfy Steven's interest in meeting with you face to face, and maybe pose some of those unanswered questions he had for you and shared with me.

I look forward to your positive response.

Regards

Peter Alward

At the time of writing this book, Peter had heard from Denham's lawyers but not the man himself. The answer was no.

Epilogue

It's November 2018, around one year after Father Glen Walsh died. I'm driving to a small country town, surrounded by towering gums and forested hills, where Glen is buried. As I near the cemetery, I wind down my window to get some fresh air, and I'm immediately serenaded by a loud chorus of bellbirds. This is a beautiful, peaceful place. I understand why he wanted to be buried here.

I park my car and walk up to the little chapel at the beginning of the graveyard. There is a plaque on the church that reads, '10 Sisters of St Joseph taught here from 1880 to 1896. Memorial Place of Sister Mary MacKillop.' How fitting, I think, given she also stood up to a paedophile priest and was tossed out of her parish.

As I walk towards Glen's grave, I notice I am the only one here. Most of the headstones are old and covered in moss. The chapel is from the 1800s. I am transported back to the beginning of the colony when all these clergy and religious ventured here from Ireland and England, to spread the word.

In front of Glen's tombstone is one daisy. He was born on 14 November 1961, so it could be for his birthday or for the anniversary of his death on 6 November 2017.

It's a poignant scene, his headstone and the limp daisy.

Around him in this graveyard are some of his relatives, from years gone by. Maybe that's why he wanted to be here – the Martin and Sylvester clans are all around his burial plot. It's a tradition for family members to be buried here.

He was so young when he died.

What he didn't know was that Archbishop Philip Wilson's trial proceeded, and he was convicted of the concealment charges in May 2018. Magistrate Roger Stone quoted Glen's police statements and other testimony. He confirmed Glen's evidence.

Wilson would have his conviction overturned on appeal in December 2018. Survivors of Father Fletcher's abuse, especially Peter Gogarty, Daniel Feenan and Peter Creigh, were devastated when Wilson won his appeal. The District Court Judge Roy Ellis said it was within the bounds of possibility that Wilson couldn't remember two reports of sexual abuse by two children in 1976 against Fletcher. Worse still for Creigh and the other man, the judge questioned whether they had made the reports in the first place.

Wilson has never returned to his position as Adelaide's archbishop.

* * *

A little over two months after my visit to Glen's graveside, it's the first anniversary of my friend Steven Alward's death. As survivors and their loved ones will tell you, every anniversary is hard. Everyone marks it in their own way.

David Alward has been preparing a beautiful memorial garden in Steven's honour.

Before the anniversary I travel to his home to meet him, Libby, and David's wife, Theresa. They live in the countryside about forty minutes from Newcastle.

The memorial garden is built on a grassy hillside. David explains the meaning embedded in it: 'It's got the rainbow that Steven was so passionate about, everyone voting for the gay rights and what have you. The little stone is from Libby ... and we've actually ordered a glass cube that will have Steven's 3-D image in it, that goes inside the stone.'

David tells me the garden is also in Mark Wakely's honour. 'This was Mark and Steven's garden originally. When we renovated Steven and Mark's laundry, we wouldn't take any money, so Steven finished up getting money into Theresa's account, which is the way he operated. He wouldn't take it back, so what we did was establish this garden – bought all the plants and stuff with that money. We did that for Steven and Mark. We set up a garden for them that they could visit on their way to holiday places they liked to visit.'

As the four of us, David, Libby, Theresa and me, stand there in silence, Libby says, 'I miss him so much. I know he must have been in so much pain to end his life. He was loved by so many people.'

They wrote this poem for their brother and uncle:

A Message to Steven
Although you can't be here with us
We're truly not apart
Until the final breath we take
You will be living in our hearts.
David, Peter, Libby

Libby, David and Steven's childhood friend Narelle invite me to the Shortland Church and then to the columbarium, which adjoins the red-brick chapel. The columbarium amounts to a series of red-brick walls, which include rows of little receptacles that can hold a deceased person's ashes and a flower. There is a plaque as well. Steven's mum's and dad's ashes are here, as are Father Roland Smythe's, the beloved priest they grew up with as children. We walk up and down the rows, and Libby, David and Narelle remark on the people they know.

There are rows and rows of plaques and flowers, members of that bustling Catholic community that is no more. This community is now full of renters, students from the local university, and only a few of the original families remain in Malta Street.

We pass Brian and Joan Alward, Steven's mum and dad. Brian died at the age of sixty-nine from a heart attack; Joan at seventy-four from ovarian cancer, in 2003.

We eventually come to Steven's plaque in the crowded columbarium. Libby puts a posy of kangaroo paw, azalea and cherry blossom, all pink, in her brother's vase. Half of Steven's ashes are in this wall next to his parents'.

I ask the obvious question: 'Why did you want half of Steven's ashes to be here? In a Catholic columbarium?'

'Because our parents are here and we want Steven to be close to Mum and Dad, and his favourite aunty is here, so …' She quickly adds, 'Steven wanted nothing to do with the Catholic Church.'

'So this wasn't Steven's choice?' I ask.

David responds, 'It's not Steven's choice. But by the same token, this was home. As you've seen, this is where we grew up; it's where we were. That's where Mum and Dad are, and they were there before we knew all this. None of us had any desire to hold a Catholic service in the church, to say a prayer over Steven when we interred him, or to even enter that church. We didn't want to go in. It just doesn't have that place for us anymore. And our priests here were good, old Rowley Smythe was a saint and we all loved him.'

He adds, 'But now what we know about the Catholic Church, if we never saw another Catholic Church we wouldn't care, honestly.'

On Steven's plaque are the words:

In loving memory of Steven James Alward
3-3-1961 – 17-01-2018, aged 56
Dearly loved son of Joan and Brian,
treasured brother of David, Peter, Libby and their families,
life partner of Mark Wakely.
Rest in Peace

* * *

Bob and Beverley O'Toole live in the newish suburb of Raworth, on the outskirts of Maitland. Back in 2009, Bob set up the hugely successful survivors' group in the Hunter Region known as the Clergy Abused Network (CAN), which has more than 140 members, including academics from the University of Newcastle. It started as five people meeting in a park in Maitland. As the group grew, survivors and their families would exchange information, and Bob would introduce them to the police and Joanne McCarthy. He also had a good relationship with Helen Keevers.

Bob was sexually abused by a Marist Brother at the Hamilton school in the 1950s. The offender, Brother 'Leon' Mackey, had been through four schools in five years before he came to Newcastle, where he stayed for seven years.

A staffer at Zimmerman House encouraged Bob to meet with the Marist Brothers' head of professional standards, Brother Alexis Turton, a former principal of Marist Brothers Hamilton. Bob remembers the meeting with some distaste. Turton told Bob that Mackey had been his football coach and that he 'was a good bloke'. Turton added, 'You're the only person who's ever made a complaint against this Brother.' Bob thought, *That can't possibly be right, because I knew other kids in the class were copping it too.*

At the end of the meeting, Turton made a strange comment. He said there had been another complainant, but he was a bit scattered and it was a minor issue, just some touching.

Bob decided to take matters into his own hands. In 2009, he put an advert in the *Newcastle Herald* asking any man who had attended Marist Brothers Hamilton between 1948 and 1955 to please contact his email address. The first time Bob did this, he was contacted by six men; four said they'd been abused by Mackey. One said he couldn't talk about it because he was shaking so much.

Bob waited another six months for news, then put another advert in the local paper on 5 June 2010. He got calls from nineteen more people about Mackey. Some didn't want to do anything about it at all, some did, and some joined Bob in a complaint to the Marist Brothers.

As part of his research into this matter, Bob found out that a report had been made to the Marist Brothers principal two years before Bob had started high school in 1955. Bob and all the others could have been saved this terrible trauma.

At seventy-five, Bob looks like anyone's cuddly grandpa with his big smile and shock of white hair. His warm demeanour hides a tough centre and a penchant for taking on challenging battles. He's not only the conduit between the Church and survivors, but he has also played various roles in his efforts to expose clerical abuse – including being a damn fine investigator and super sleuth.

At the beginning of their marriage, Bob made light of what had happened to him at Marist Brothers Hamilton. Bev says that with hindsight there were red flags, signs of his childhood trauma.

Bob works closely with Detective Sergeant Kristi Faber and Joanne McCarthy, along with Audrey and Geoffrey Nash, and many other family members and loved ones of clerical abuse survivors within the diocese. He's always got his ear to the ground trying to help locals find information about their abusers.

It was soon after he set up CAN that he and others noticed the high number of suicides among graduates of three schools in the diocese: Marist Brothers Hamilton, Marist Brothers Maitland and St Pius X. At the request of Audrey Nash, Bob began a register of names of men who had suicided and others who had died in a risky manner. Most were aged between forty and sixty, but there were others like Andrew Nash, the youngest of them to suicide.

Sixty men. A generation of men. All born between 1959 and 1980.

Each name on the list had a traumatic backstory. One man lived during his final school year with the priests in their accommodation at St Pius X, even though it wasn't a boarding school. He suicided without any warning in his forties, and his family are still looking for answers.

Bob tendered this register with the Royal Commission in 2016. He's also provided it to the NSW Police Force.

Marist Brothers Hamilton is now St Francis Xavier's College.

Marist Brothers Maitland is now All Saints College, St Peter's campus.

The names on the register include three brothers who were abused by Denham when he was a priest.

Detective Sergeant Faber has seen this list. She said to Bob, 'You haven't got them all.'

* * *

The collateral damage of a cluster of paedophiles with some in leadership positions at Marist Brothers Hamilton was revealed during the Royal Commission. But what about the other sixty-plus schools in the diocese under the control of the director of Catholic Education, who also had control of hiring and firing the priests and teachers?

Between 1974 to 1990, Monsignor Frank Coolahan was in charge of fifty primary schools and close to ten high schools. The diocese, known as Maitland then, extended across a huge area, from Taree and the Manning in the north, to Morisset in the south, and up to Merriwa, Denman and Murrurundi in the Upper Hunter Valley. The director had the ultimate responsibility for thousands of students and controlled the movement of priests, Brothers and lay teachers. In those days, you didn't apply for a job and get it, you were told where to go. The director was answerable to the bishop.

Justice Syme, in her summing-up in one of John Denham's trials, said, 'There was sufficient evidence to support a finding of "an organised criminal activity".'[1]

Who at the top might have had inside knowledge and protected these priests despite the complaints? Monsignor Frank Coolahan, the director of Catholic Education from 1974 to 1990, was also a child sex offender. He was a mate of Father Fletcher and Bishop Clarke.

His victim has come forward with the support of John Wakely. They went to school together at Marist Brothers Hamilton in the 1960s and early 1970s, just before Andrew Nash was there.

Paul Hughes was born in 1954 to a devout Catholic family from the working classes. They went to mass every Sunday, like most of the community. Their parish priest was Father Coolahan, a former student of Marist Brothers Hamilton; he was the curate, or the assistant priest. Paul went to St Joseph's Merewether. Like lots of boys at his school, he was made an altar boy from the third grade, and as part of that role he was required to assist the priests one weekday in the morning and at one or two masses every Sunday.

When I speak to Paul in the winter of 2018, he tells me he remembers Coolahan being quite aloof. 'Priests thought themselves pretty special, and he thought himself especially special. He was always quite impeccably dressed and well-groomed. He had an overpowering aftershave.' Coolahan was renowned for his Brut aftershave.

As an altar boy, Paul also had to do 'messages' for the nuns on a Saturday morning. This actually meant he went and did their shopping. He would go to the convent and get their lists and bring back their purchases every Saturday morning.

Paul would also accompany Coolahan and other priests to the St Joseph's Nursing home at Sandgate. He would go with them in the car, and often wait outside while they administered last rites to an elderly person in the home. Paul never questioned why they needed an altar boy to accompany a priest to the nursing home. You did as the priests said – pronto. 'I just sat in the car. The priest would go off, then I'd be bored. And I hated that trip. I hated it! It was slow – it took about an hour to get to Sandgate in those days.'

On this day Coolahan had driven Paul to the nursing home on his own. When Coolahan returned to the car, he was accompanied by 'another man who was probably about his age ... These are people in their late twenties, I guess. Both Father Coolahan and this other man were the same age. Maybe even thirty, but no more than that.' Without saying anything to Paul, Coolahan got in the driver's seat, and the man got in the back seat – 'they just conversed over me,' Paul says. 'I had no idea what it was about.'

He didn't dare turn around from the front seat and stare at the man because that would have been rude. Paul adds that at that time it wouldn't have been unusual for an adult to ignore a child and not introduce themselves, but he remembers thinking the man was a doctor, maybe from Newcastle hospital. Paul can't remember why he thought this; it was just a vague notion.

'So,' he continues, 'something really odd happened on the way back … along Maitland Road, still in Sandgate, probably around the cemetery … I suddenly lost consciousness. It was not like going to sleep … almost as suddenly I woke up, and we were almost home. We were in Stewart Avenue … just near Hamilton South Public School, just about to turn into Kenrick Street. My first thought was, *Gosh, this is fantastic! The trip's over!* I was really happy. But I was puzzled.'

Paul distinctly remembers not feeling groggy. 'It was immediate loss of consciousness and immediate regaining of consciousness. I was completely back in full consciousness when I woke up. There was no sense of time associated with it. When you fall asleep, you know that you've been asleep. You had that sense of falling asleep, you had that sense of waking up. And there's time in between. There was no sense of time in between.'

He remembers the rest of the drive like it was yesterday. 'So we turned into Kenrick Street, which is the street that the church and the presbytery are, and we turned into the double garage. We went out the back door, which was very close to the front door of the presbytery. We went into the presbytery, which I'd hardly ever been in. I think if anything, I would have only been into the receiving room, the sort of sitting room where people would be taken when they went to visit the priest.'

It was the first time Paul had ever been in the garage. Its back door was about three metres from the front door of the presbytery. 'I had been in that front room, I had been in the hallway. But there was another room on the right that I had never been to. I think that might have been the dining room. And there was a single stairway leading upstairs.' The eleven-year-old was led out of the car, and the first thing he saw was the door out of the garage. Then over to the left, Paul saw the main door to the presbytery. One of the men with him opened it, and he was ushered in. The three of them walked up the stairs, 'which was really strange. And, again, I thought, *This is something special. No one gets invited upstairs!*'

At the top of the stairs they reached a landing. Paul was then led to turn left and left again, and on the right was a bedroom. He remembers walking into that room. 'Then this immediate loss of consciousness happened again.' There's a long pause. 'I woke up, but again there was no sense of time passing. I woke up back down in the receiving room, and I was in a comfy chair, and Father Coolahan was sitting in a chair opposite me, near the window. I was closer to the fire, I'm not sure there was an actual fire, there might have been a heater on. Father Coolahan smiled and said, "Oh well, it's time for you to go home." And I did. But I felt uneasy. I felt not well. You know, I felt something. Yeah. This was different from the waking up in the car. I don't know what it was, but I felt miserable.'

Paul went home, a walk of about ten to fifteen minutes. As soon as he arrived, he rushed to the outdoor toilet, and when he pulled down his underpants there was blood on them. 'The toilet was … just next door to the kitchen where Mum was getting tea ready. I called out to her and said, "Mum, Mum! I've got blood on my underpants!" But nothing really happened about that. I was puzzled by the whole thing, by the whole experience of that day.' Paul had received injuries that day that would haunt him later in life. 'I knew something funny had happened.'

He goes on to say, 'It did seem to me that I was still something special to Father Coolahan. But the next time I served mass for him, he was really aloof. He was even more aloof than he had ever been. Quite disdainful to me, in some ways. So that puzzled me.'

Paul has a theory about what actually happened in the car. 'Well, I suspect that what I think was a doctor was in the back of the car, and he just used a handkerchief with ether or something like that. I don't recall any smell, because it was immediate. I don't know. The only thing that I can compare it to is when I've been under anaesthetic, which was just as immediate. Both the going to sleep and the waking up.' He remembers the immediate feeling of being knocked out. And, he tells me, 'I remember when I was in the bedroom, they were both behind me. I'd been ushered in first, and I think I was facing the bed. It was just a single bed. I think it might have been a metal-framed bed. I'm not sure.'

This eleven-year-old boy never felt the same again – he felt a feeling of malaise and melancholy had descended on him, which rarely lifted. 'It was weird, because I had this nausea … It had something to do with aftershave. I said, "I feel sick, but I think if I drank aftershave I would vomit and I would feel a lot better. You know, I'd get it out of me." I couldn't explain that.' To this day, Paul can't stand aftershave. Once, he wore it, and the next morning he scrubbed himself in the shower to rid himself of the smell.

Paul doesn't think anyone would have believed him back in the 1960s. At the time, he tried to convey some details to his sister, but when he raised it with her recently she said she doesn't remember any of it. He sees nothing sinister in that – she was a few years older, and he thinks back then she believed he was just telling stories.

There were injuries that had to be dealt with when he was nineteen, about eight years after the incident, that Paul puts down to that terrible day. He noticed bleeding from his anus and skin growths that eventually needed surgery.

Father Frank Coolahan was a teacher at St Pius X when he drugged and raped eleven-year-old Paul. Steven Alward attended the school ten years later.

Paul asked John Wakely to inform the diocese, which he did. They recommended John go public with the story to see if there were any more victims, as this has worked with other perpetrators.

In 1972, Bishop Toohey appointed Coolahan as assistant director to Monsignor Dilley, and two years later Coolahan became director in his own right. That year, 1974, Coolahan employed a teacher by the name of Tony Bambach to work as a teacher in the Maitland-Newcastle Diocese. This was despite the fact Coolahan knew that Bambach had been convicted of sexually assaulting five boys at Stroud, NSW, in 1962.

In the 1980s, Bambach was employed at St Michael's Primary School in Nelson Bay. Coolahan promoted Bambach to the position of deputy headmaster, a role that gave him ultimate power and control over the students. One day he removed a young boy from his classroom and raped him in a public toilet; Bambach threatened to 'kill the boy's mother' if he revealed anything of the incident.

Bambach's 2005 affidavit to the NSW Supreme Court says he told Coolahan of his convictions when he was interviewed for the job. Bambach claimed Coolahan had dismissed his concerns and said he would fit in very well.[2]

In 2012, three of Bambach's victims sued the Catholic Church and the case revealed Bambach had received a formal warning from the Catholic Education Office 'regarding similar matters' in the fourteen years before his arrest.[3]

One parent, a solicitor, bypassed the diocese and went to the police. Bambach was eventually charged and convicted of multiple offences, mostly with boys aged nine to twelve.

In 2015, Joanne McCarthy wrote an article for the *Newcastle Herald* that revealed the former principal of Marist Brothers Maitland Brother Nestor had sexually abused a boy at the school in 1976 when he was eleven years old. He had just started there and was in Year Seven. By 1993, Nestor had already been found guilty of child sex offences.

Why were the three main Maitland–Newcastle Catholic boys' high schools contaminated with so many child sex offenders from the 1960s to the 1980s? It's a complex question with a complex answer. But the fact that Coolahan was a child sex offender while the principals in these schools were also child sex offenders clearly made it easier for this type of criminal behaviour to flourish and go unpunished. In the 1970s, Brother 'Christopher' Wade, Brother John 'Nestor' Littler and Father Tom Brennan were paedophile principals at Marist Brothers Hamilton, Marist Brothers Maitland and St Pius X respectively, and there were clusters of child sex offenders among the staff. What hope did the children have?

* * *

The light is fading as people start to take their seats. Plastic chairs have been placed in rows on the grass in front of Marist Brothers Hamilton. The more elderly people in the audience take the front seats; some younger men with tattoos, wearing dark glasses, stand silently at the back. A row of Brothers stand along the back and the side, recognisable by their very short haircuts and nearly uniform pants and shirts; they hardly mix with anybody.

They're all here in late March 2019 for the opening of a special memorial to the victims of clerical child sexual abuse that was rampant from the 1950s to the 2000s at this school and elsewhere. Five decades of unchecked behaviour.[4]

Bob O'Toole had a stressful time negotiating this memorial. He insisted it be at the entrance of the school – not out the back, out of the way, but right at the front so people had to be reminded every day about the carnage that had gone on at this school.

It's Geoffrey and Audrey Nash's turn to speak. Standing next to Audrey is a boy in school uniform holding a large framed picture of Andrew in his Marist Brothers Hamilton uniform back in 1974. Just before he suicided.

Geoffrey speaks in a clear and direct voice. 'The parishes around these schools were awash with paedophile priests … Being a young Catholic boy in this town was a dangerous occupation – many of these boys, like my little brother, lost their lives.'

Audrey says the Brothers lied to her. They destroyed her beloved son.

It's a moment when the Nash family take back their power.

Each person then picks up a little white stone and places it on the memorial, representing all the victims who couldn't make it and died before this day.

Mark Wakely and the Alward family are there too. They walk up and lay a white stone on the memorial for Steven.

Endnotes

Preface

1   I have used the term 'clerical abuse' to cover sexual abuse by clergy and religious orders. This term was adopted by the Australian Broadcasting Corporation to cover both. I accept clergy and religious are separate and distinct entities but for comprehension I have just used 'clerical abuse' to cover both.

2   On 26 May 2008, I did a report for *Lateline* on ABC TV about why Bishop Malone was the only bishop in Australia to call on the Pope to apologise to survivors. This was my first meeting with Helen Keevers: http://www.abc.net.au/lateline/content/2007/s2256146.htm

Prologue

1   https://www.newcastle.edu.au/__data/assets/pdf_file/0009/41868/Research-document_John-Maynard_whose-land.pdf

2   Kieran Tapsell, *Potiphar's Wife: The Vatican's Secret and Child Sexual Abuse*, ATF Press, Adelaide, 2014, page 16.

Chapter 1: The Night That Never Ends

1   An altar boy (young boy or teenager) or altar server (usually an older person) was a lay assistant to the priest of member of the clergy during the Christian mass.

2   Marist Brothers Hamilton, *Year Book 1974*, page 131.

3   Ibid., pages 27–28.

4   Bert Nash died in 1998, at the age of sixty-eight, after a long period of illness.

Chapter 2: Early Beginnings

1   In the BHP plant alone there were 274 deaths from 1926 to 1999. Report by Ian Kirkwood, *Newcastle Herald*, 3 September 2015.

2   Mark Wakely, *Sweet Sorrow: A Beginner's Guide to Death*, Melbourne University Press, 2008.

3   www.maristbr.com/about-us

4   Chris Geraghty, *The Priest Factory*, Spectrum Publications, Melbourne, 2003, page 27.

Chapter 3: *Viriliter Age* – Act Manfully

1   Witness statement of CQT, Royal Commission into Institutional Responses to Child Sexual Abuse, case study 43: Catholic Church authorities in Maitland–Newcastle, 2 September 2016, point 15, page 4. Stat. 1173.001.0002_R

2   Tony Butler FMS, *A Hermitage in the South: A History of Marist Brothers Mittagong 1906–2006*, Marist Brothers, Sydney, 2006, page 213.

3   Brother Coman Sykes, correspondence with Brother Ray Foster, cited in Tony Butler, *A Hermitage in the South*, Notes, chapter 15, note 3, page 276.

4   childabuseroyalcommission.gov.au/sites/default/files/CTJH.053.24002.0363_R.pdf. Point 102, page 20.

5   Tony Butler, Ibid., page 215.

6   Marist Brothers Hamilton, *Jubilee* magazine, 1978, Year 11 report, page 36.

7   Marist Brothers Hamilton, *Year Book*, 1974, pp 27–28. Witness statement of Brother Alexis Turton, Royal Commission into Institutional Responses to Child Sexual Abuse, case study 13: Marist Brothers, 31 May 2014, exhibit CTJH.500.28001.0001_R, page 3.

8   Letter of complaint by Father Glen Walsh to the Marist Brothers.

9   Dermot Browne, former student of St Pius X, interview in 2018.

10   Ibid.

11   Dave Murray, University of Newcastle, interview, 2018. David Murray summed up his school life this way: 'Overall I look back on the Catholicism practised at St Pius X as religion at its cultish worse – where faith and obedience were always preferred to facts or reason. This helped make it nasty in its inward-looking exclusiveness. Living a Catholic life was premised philosophically on an unquestioning belief in the ephemeral dogma the Church scattered as spiritual birdseed. As messengers in this equation, the priests were untouchable. Priests like [John] Denham who exploited this could in their own mind (I think) justify the abuse of minors as a bonus in the necessary maintenance of power. And yet, the Church today still scratches its pig-head, utterly perplexed as to why it is losing so many punters. Seriously, you couldn't make it up.'

12   Dave Murray, University of Newcastle, interview, 2018.

13   Giselle Wakatama, 'Victim of Ted Hall tells of anger after learning Catholic church falsely told him abuser was dead', ABC News Online report, 13 December 2018. https://www.abc.net.au/news/2018-12-13/mans-anger-after-catholic-church-told-him-abuser-was-dead/10616554. Ted Hall has been convicted of child sexual assault offences and is in jail. He has launched an appeal that is due to be heard in late 2020 or early 2021.

14   R v John Sidney Denham in the NSW District Court. Judgment by Justice Megan Latham, 1 September 2000. DC Z1238 BG-D. File number 99/11/1180.

15   The Royal Commission into Institutional Responses to Child Sexual Abuse found 75 child sex offenders attended the Corpus Christi Seminary at Werribee. *The Age* newspaper, 17 September 2019.

16   Confirmation is the sacrament where Catholics receive the Holy Spirit. The bishop anoints the person using oil of Chrism (consecrated oil) to make the Sign of the Cross on the forehead while saying the person's new confirmation name. Children make this sacrament typically in fourth grade. Their confirmation name is usually taken from one of the saints. The Marist Brothers Provincial Council (Sydney) was in charge of Marist schools, but the bishop could veto decisions if necessary.

Chapter 4: The Aftermath

1 A monsignor in the Catholic Church is a senior priest who has distinguished himself and has been given the special title by the Pope.
2 Letter of complaint by Father Glen Walsh to the Marist Brothers.
3 Royal Commission into Institutional Responses to Child Sexual Abuse Report, case study 13: The response of the Marist Brothers to allegations of child sexual abuse against Brothers.
   • Kostka Chute and Gregory Sutton (November 2015) concluded, in relation to Brother John (Kostka) Chute (who pleaded guilty to and was convicted in 2008 of 19 child sex offences against six of his former students during the period 1985 to 1989):
     • that Turton, who was the Provincial at Marist College Canberra from 1989 to 1995, was in 1993 told of unwanted conduct of a sexual nature by a victim of Chute's, failed to adequately understand or address the conduct or the ongoing risk that Chute posed to children; and after receiving a second complaint from another victim, did not tell the Marists Brothers community, or other teachers or parents about his investigation into Chute's conduct, or that Chute was removed because of the complaints; and
     • several Provincials between 1962 and 1993 failed to take adequate steps to prevent Chute having contact with children, failed to keep any written records of accumulated allegations, and failed to report any allegations to police.
   • See https://www.childabuseroyalcommission.gov.au/media-releases/report-marist-brothers-case-study-released, especially pages 5, 7, 8, 9.
   • For a report of Turton's Royal Commission testimony in relation to sending Brother Gregory Sutton overseas (Sutton was extradited from the United States in 1996 to face 67 counts of child sexual abuse) see https://www.abc.net.au/news/2014-06-18/marist-brothers-provincial-denies-shipping-paedophile-overseas/5533226a
4 Witness statement of CQP a survivor, Royal Commission into Institutional Responses to Child Sexual Abuse, case study 43: Marist Brothers, October 2016, point 15, page 4. STAT.1210.001.0001_R
   https://www.childabuseroyalcommission.gov.au/sites/default/files/STAT.1210.001.0001_R.pdf
5 Letter of complaint by Father Glen Walsh to the Marist Brothers.

Chapter 5: The Ties That Bind

1 Father John Denham, chaplain's report, Waverley College, *Year Book 1986*.
2 Letter of introduction written by Father Glen Walsh to the Mother Teresa Missions in India, 2007. In this letter he outlines his life story.
3 Ibid.
4 Ibid.
5 Fletcher had been Clarke's Master of Ceremonies at the Pro-Cathedral. This meant he organised and oversaw all the liturgical functions when the bishop was present. He also had been the administrator, or priest in charge. This was a temporary position before a parish priest was appointed.
6 Foreword by Ted Kennedy, in Chris Geraghty, *The Priest Factory*, Spectrum Publications, Melbourne, 2003, page 9.
7 Ibid., page 361.

8 Tony Abbott, 'Why I left the priesthood: Seminarian's years of disillusion', *The Bulletin*, 18 August 1987.
9 A vice-rector or rector in the Catholic Church is someone who holds the office of presiding over an ecclesiastical institution. The vice-rector is the rector's deputy.
10 Letter from Father Glen Walsh to his 'brother priests' at the Missionaries of Charity Priests in India, page 2, 2007.

Chapter 6: 'The De-sexto Business'
1 NSW Special Commission of Inquiry into matters relating to the police investigation of certain child sexual abuse allegations in the Catholic Diocese of Maitland–Newcastle, report by Margaret Cunneen SC, 2014. Letter from Monsignor Cotter to Bishop Leo Clarke, 17 May 1976, exhibit 2S: FDMCA-VOL1/4.
2 A pectoral cross is a cross worn on the chest. From the Middle Ages, the pectoral cross signified someone was a bishop.
3 Bishop Michael Malone, testimony to the NSW Special Commission of Inquiry, 10 July 2013.

Chapter 7: Operation Sentol
1 Royal Commission into Institutional Responses to Child Sexual Abuse, case study 43: Catholic Church authorities in Maitland–Newcastle, transcript taken on 31 August 2016, page 18.
2 Dr Peter Evans, testimony to Royal Commission, case study 43: Maitland–Newcastle, 2016.
3 Letter from Monsignor Patrick Cotter to Dr Peter Evans, 16 December 1975. Evidence submitted to the Royal Commission, case study 43: Maitland–Newcastle. (CTJH.210.01025.2675_R)
4 (a) In an unsigned statement dated 20 October 1997, Monsignor Cotter said that he told the bishop that Ryan was getting treatment in Melbourne, and that he 'informed the bishop on his appointment on all relevant matters that were going on in the diocese. For example matters to do with education, a whole range of matters, and we also discussed Vince's position in Melbourne' (CCI.0228.00005.0082_R, TB86).
(b) In an interview with solicitors on 7 July 1999, Monsignor Cotter said that he told Bishop Clarke that he was in Melbourne because 'he was homosexual and that there had been some problems with children, and that on his return to the diocese, Monsignor Cotter told Clarke that he believed he was 'cured of it' (CCI.0049.00009.0359_R, TB95).
5 Letter from Monsignor Patrick Cotter to Bishop Leo Clarke, on 2 June 1996, page four. Royal Commission into Institutional Responses to Child Sexual Abuse, exhibit CTJH.210.01193.0001.
6 Police statement of Monsignor Patrick Daniel Cotter, taken at Wangi Wangi on 20 October 1997.
7 Father Bill Burston, testimony to the Royal Commission, case study 43: Maitland–Newcastle, Day 168, September 2016. Q. Did Monsignor Cotter or anyone else tell you why he had been sent to Melbourne? A. There was a complaint about inappropriate behaviour with boys, but that's as much as Monsignor Cotter told me.

8   Ibid., page 6.
9   Statement of Audrey Nash, Royal Commission, case study 43: Maitland–
    Newcastle, 2 September 2019, page 7. (STAT.1172.001.0006_R)
    https://www.childabuseroyalcommission.gov.au/sites/default/files/
    STAT.1172.001.0001_R.pdf
10 Ibid.
11 Police electronic interview of Father Vince Ryan.

Chapter 8: 'He did not want to cause trouble'

1   *The Guardian*, Associated Press Dublin, Tuesday, 18 January 2011.
2   Kieran Tapsell, *Potiphar's Wife: The Vatican's Secret and Child Sexual Abuse*, ATF
    Press, Adelaide, 2014, page 23.
3   Photo of Taree Catholic Church priest board. Supplied by source. Of the eight
    priests who had been the subject of child sexual abuse complaints or cover-up
    allegations, two had been convicted by police by 1999.
        1958–1959 Rev Denis McAlinden (substantiated complaints)
        1973–1974 Rev Lewis Fenton (charged with concealment)
        1973–1982 Rev Barry Tunks (charges dropped)
        1981–1986 Rev John Denham (convicted)
        1982–1987 Rev Patrick Helferty (complaints)
        1985–1990 Rev James Hughes (complaints)
        1988–1990 Rev Peter Quirk (complaints)
        1995–1995 Rev Vincent Ryan (convicted)
4   Memorandum of Understanding on Co-operation between the Catholic Church
    and the NSW Police Service, page 1, point 2, Background. Exhibit 228, Police
    Integrity Commission Inquiry (Operation Protea), 2015.
5   Refer to endnote 4 at Chapter 25. Also, as reported in *The Guardian* at https://
    www.theguardian.com/australia-news/2016/sep/19/catholic-mission-director-
    denies-covering-up-child-sexual-abuse. Lucas disputed claims he covered up
    child sexual abuse, saying none of the cases he dealt with needed to be passed
    on to police.
6   Exhibit 328B.pdf, NSW Police Integrity Commission Inquiry (Operation
    Protea), 2015.
7   Transcript of the Royal Commission into Institutional Responses to Child
    Sexual Abuse, Case Study 43, C166, 1 September 2016, page 5, point 43.

Chapter 9: An Unexpected Call

1   R v John Sidney Denham, NSW District Court, 1 September 2000. File number
    99/11/1180. Judgement by Justice Megan Latham.
2   Interview with John Walker, lawyer, former student from Taree.
3   Following is the list of the Law Society of NSW Presidents: 1989–1990: G.M.
    Robertson; 1990–1991: D.A. de Carvalho; 1991–1992: J.R. Marsden* (John
    Marsden); 1993: J.M. Nelson; 1994: D.G. Fairlie; 1995: D.M. Stack (Maurie
    Stack Taree); 1996: N. Lyall; 1997: P.V. Fair; 1998: R.K. Heinrich; 1999: M.C.
    Hole; 2000: J.F.S. North. (*In 1990 the Council decided to adjust the term
    of President to start in January rather than November. So J.R. Marsden was
    President for 14 months rather than 12 months. Email from Sue Finn, Law
    Society of NSW Media Adviser.)

4   Court records show Denham was arrested on 2 July 1996 and charged with having homosexual sex being a teacher with a student under the age of 18, at Waverley College. He was found not guilty. In 1997, he was charged again over a student at St Pius X and was convicted and sentenced in 2000 when he was found guilty of two offences.

5   Interview with Maurie Stack on 21 October 2019. Text message 21 October 2019 confirming dates of his various roles on the Executive of the Law Society of NSW and Law Society Council.

6   Indictment of Father David O'Hearn, by Detective Sergeant Kristi Faber, 23 July 2014. District Court of NSW.

7   Police statement of psychologist Bryan Michael Gray, 31 October 2010, re Father David O'Hearn.

Chapter 10: The Cover-up

1   Howard Murray, the private investigator for the Catholic Church, was engaged by Cardinal Pell over a case involving a priest in 2008.

2   NSW Ombudsman website.

3   Child Protection in the Workplace, Report by NSW Ombudsman Bruce Barbour, 2004. Royal Commission into Institutional Responses to Child Sexual Abuse, exhibit OMB.0010.001.005.

4   NSW Ombudsman Report, November 2003, page 4.

5   Provincial Council minutes, 19 March 1999, quoted in Tony Butler FMS, *A Hermitage in the South: A History of Marist Brothers Mittagong 1906–2006*, Marist Brothers, Sydney, 2006, page 276.

6   https://www.childabuseroyalcommission.gov.au/sites/default/files/STAT.0079.001.0020_R.pdf

7   https://www.childabuseroyalcommission.gov.au/sites/default/files/STAT.0079.001.0020_R.pdf

8   Nick McKenzie, *The Age*, 2012.

9   Witness statement of Brother Alexis Turton, Royal Commission into Institutional Responses to Child Sexual Abuse, case study 13: Marist Brothers, 31 May 2014, exhibit CTJH.500.28001.0001_R, page 3.

10 Child Protection in the Workplace, Report by NSW Ombudsman Bruce Barbour, 2004, page 19. Royal Commission exhibit OMB.0010.001.0055.

11 Letter From Professor Patrick Parkinson to Police Minister Paul Whelan, released Police Integrity Commission Inquiry (Operation Protea), 6 August 2014.

Chapter 11: The Secret Deal

1   R v John Sidney Denham, NSW District Court. Judgement by Justice Megan Latham, 1 September 2000. File number 99/11/1180.

2   Steven Alward, 'Webs of power', *The Griffith Review*, March 2005.

3   Police Integrity Commission Inquiry (Operation Protea), transcript of proceeding, 6 August 2014, page 69.

4   Ibid., page 75.

5   NSW Police Crime Command Memorandum dated 30 July 2004, exhibit 13, Police Integrity Commission Inquiry (Operation Protea), 2015.

6   Letter from Michael McDonald CCER to Superintendent Kim McKay, dated 18 June 2003. Exhibit 31 Police Integrity Commission Inquiry, 2014.

7   ACBC Plenary Meeting 2–12 May 2005, Bishops' Committee for Professional Standards, report by Most Rev. P. Wilson, chair, Most Rev. J. Foley, secretary, 8 May 2005. Exhibit 56, Police Integrity Commission Inquiry (Operation Protea).

8   Refer to endnote 4 at Chapter 25. Also, as reported in *The Guardian* at https://www.theguardian.com/australia-news/2016/sep/19/catholic-mission-director-denies-covering-up-child-sexual-abuse. Lucas disputed claims he covered up child sexual abuse, saying none of the cases he dealt with needed to be passed on to police.

9   Police Integrity Commission Inquiry (Operation Protea), transcript of proceeding, 6 August 2014, page 53.

Chapter 12: 'This was my beloved son in whom I was well pleased'

1   Patricia Feenan, *Holy Hell: A Catholic Family's Story of Faith, Betrayal, Pain and Courage bringing a Paedophile Priest to Justice*, Fontaine Press, Fremantle, 2012.

2   Father Glen Walsh appeared in the St Joseph's College Hunters Hill yearbook for the years 1999 to 2001.

3   Email dated 23 June 2007 from Father Matthew Muller to Father James Lunn re Father Glen Walsh's health.

4   Provisional report of the NSW Ombudsman, November 2003.

5   Interview of Father James Fletcher by Detective Sergeant Peter Fox at Maitland Police Station, 14 May 2003.

6   Transcript of interview between Detective Sergeant Fox and father Fletcher on 14 May 2003 as reported in the provisional report of the NSW Ombudsman, November, 2003, page 16.

7   Interview by Father James Fletcher with Sergeant Peter Fox at Maitland Police Station, 14 May 2003, page 60.

8   According to the findings of the Special Commission of Inquiry into the Maitland-Newcastle Diocese Report, 30 May 2014, Vol 4, (released 2019), pages 106–111.

9   Ibid, according to its findings.

10 According to the findings of draft NSW Ombudsman's Report, November 2003, page 15, point 2.2.4, referring to Bishop Malone statement to police on 21 May 2003, paragraph 5.

11 According to the findings of the NSW Special Commission of Inquiry into matters relating to the police investigation of certain child sexual abuse allegations in the Catholic Diocese of Maitland-Newcastle, report by Margaret Cunneen SC, 2014, vol.2 (released 2019), Malone Conclusions, vol.2, point 15.22, page 110.

12 Interview with John Feenan by the NSW Ombudsman on 21 August 2003, page 10. NSW Ombudsman Report, November 2003, page 16.

13 According to the findings of draft NSW Ombudsman's Report, November 2003, page 15, point 2.2.4, referring to Bishop Malone statement to police on 21 May 2003, paragraph 5.

14 NSW Special Commission of Inquiry, report by Margaret Cunneen SC, 2014, vol.2, point 15.34, page 112.

15 NSW Ombudsman Report, November 2003, page 18, quoted report by Detective Sergeant Fox dated 29 May 2003.

16 Police statement by Detective Sergeant Fox, dated 28 May 2003, page 4, in NSW Ombudsman provisional report, page 18.

17 Michael Malone: 'I was also conscious that under canon law I could not oblige Fr Fletcher to stand down on the evidence available to me in or around June 2002.' D.F. Jackson QC, *The Jackson Report*, Corrs Chambers Westgarth Lawyers, July 2005, page 23.

18 Provisional report of the NSW Ombudsman, transcript of interview with Bishop Malone, 2 September 2003, by the NSW Ombudsman's office, 2003, page 18.

19 Patricia Feenan, *Holy Hell*, page 74.

20 NSW Special Commission of Inquiry, report by Margaret Cunneen SC, 2014, vol.2, point 15.72, page 119.

Chapter 13: 'Father Jim isn't well at the moment and needed some time away'

1 Pat Feenan, *Holy Hell: A Catholic Family's Story of Faith, Betrayal, Pain and Courage bringing a Paedophile Priest to Justice*, Fontaine Press, Fremantle, 2012.

2 Ibid.

3 Will Callinan, police statement. The NSW Special Commission of Inquiry into matters relating to the police investigation of certain child sexual abuse allegations in the Catholic Diocese of Maitland–Newcastle (report by Margaret Cunneen SC, 2014) found: 'Malone's evidence in this regard was dissembling and constituted an attempt to disperse responsibility (in effect) for his decision not to stand Fletcher down in June 2002 after becoming aware that the police were investigating Fletcher for child sexual abuse. Because it finds there was no meeting between Malone and Callinan on 20 June 2002.'

4 Diary note, Will Callinan, in the NSW Ombudsman Report, order of events, investigation Father Fletcher, 2003.

5 Letter of introduction written by Father Glen Walsh to the Mother Teresa Missions in India, 2007.

6 NSW Special Commission of Inquiry, report by Margaret Cunneen SC, vol.2, page 219. Report of Ray Hanley.

7 Police statement, in the matter of Father James Fletcher, by Colleen Timoshenko, 2 June 2003, page 3.

8 NSW Police statement, in the matter of James Patrick Fletcher, 19 May 2004, at Maitland Police Station. Name redacted.

9 NSW Police statement, in the matter of James Patrick Fletcher, 19 May 2004, at Maitland Police Station. Name redacted.

10 Pastoral letter from Bishop Michael Malone to the community regarding Father Fletcher, 16 May 2003.

11 Police statement, in the matter of Father James Fletcher of 'Elizabeth', 19 May 2004.

Chapter 14: 'Look at everything I have done for you'

1 Interview with Elizabeth Byrne, 2019.

2 Diary entry, Will Callinan, 5 December 2003. Provisional report of the NSW Ombudsman, 2003.

3 Interview with Elizabeth Byrne, 2019.

4 NSW Ombudsman interview with Mr John Daveron [sic], 2 September 2003. Provisional report of the NSW Ombudsman, page 19.

5 Transcript of interview with Bishop Malone by the NSW Ombudsman investigators on 2 September 2003. Provisional report of the NSW Ombudsman, page 20.

6   Record of telephone call to Mr Daveron [sic] on 11 November 2002 and 24 February 2003. Provisional report of the NSW Ombudsman, page 20.

7   Email to Michael McDonald from Mr Daveron [sic], undated (assumed to be after 17 March 2003). Provisional report of the NSW Ombudsman, 2018, page 20, point 2.2.8.2.

8   NSW Ombudsman interview with Mr John Daveron [sic], 2 September 2003, and transcript of email, 22 May 2003. Provisional report of the NSW Ombudsman, page 19.

9   Copy of Bishop Malone's personal diary entry for 20 June 2002. Provisional report of the NSW Ombudsman, 2003.

10 Provisional report of the NSW Ombudsman, November 2003, point 2.2.2.3, page 25.

11 Provisional report of the NSW Ombudsman, November 2003, point 4.2.4, page 27.

12 'Catholic Agencies', NSW Ombudsman's Report, 2004–2005, page 144: 'In November 2004, the NSW Bishops advised us of their willingness to assume head-of-agency responsibilities and asked us to work with their representatives to develop models for diocesan structures. The bishops also invited the Ombudsman to their June 2005 meeting to finalise arrangements and confirm our ongoing support to Catholic agencies. In our recent visits to the dioceses, we noted the commitment and considerable work undertaken to date by the bishops and their staff in developing sound and coordinated diocesan structures and systems. We were also impressed with the quality and expertise of staff involved in child protection. We hope that the new arrangements will allow for more timely completion of investigations and responses to our requests for information, the provision of accurate information to all parties and a more direct cooperative working relationship between diocesan agencies and our office.'

13 Interview with Elizabeth Byrne, 2019.

Chapter 15: 'I am sorry I didn't look after you'

1   'Catholic Agencies', NSW Ombudsman's Report 2004–2005, page 144.

2   Ibid.

3   Ibid.

4   NSW Special Commission of Inquiry into matters relating to the police investigation of certain child sexual abuse allegations in the Catholic Diocese of Maitland–Newcastle, report by Margaret Cunneen SC, 2014, vol.2, point 14.8, page 100.

5   These events were described by Father Glen Walsh in private hearings before the NSW Special Commission of Inquiry. What happened next formed the basis of private and public hearings before the Special Commission of Inquiry in 2013–2014.

6   Respondent's written submissions, Department of Public Prosecutions NSW, 15 May 2017, Supreme Court of NSW case number 2016/336733.

7   Judgement of Magistrate Roger Stone in R v Philip Wilson.

8   Police statement of Father Glen Walsh, clause 14, 10 June 2004.

9   NSW Special Commission of Inquiry, report by Margaret Cunneen SC, vol.2, point 15.120, page 127. Here are the events as described in vol.2 of the report and by other sources.

Chapter 16: 'The old guard rules with an iron fist'
1 Letter from Father Glen Walsh to the principal of St Catherine's College Singleton, Mr Williams, dated 30 April 2004.
2 Letter from Father Glen Walsh to parishioners at Singleton Catholic parish, 17 December 2014.
3 NSW Special Commission of Inquiry into matters relating to the police investigation of certain child sexual abuse allegations in the Catholic Diocese of Maitland–Newcastle, by Margaret Cunneen SC, 2014, vol.2, point 15.115, page 126.
4 Letter from Father Glen Walsh to Missionaries of Charity Priests, India, 2007.

Chapter 17: 'You bastard! You hurt my son'
1 Daniel Feenan's testimony published in Patricia Feenan, *Holy Hell: A Catholic Family's Story of Faith, Betrayal, Pain and Courage bringing a Paedophile Priest to Justice*, Fontaine Press, Fremantle, 2012, page 123.
2 Ibid., pages 127–128.
3 www.brokenrites.com.au
4 D.F. Jackson QC, *The Jackson Report*, Corrs Chambers Westgarth Lawyers, July 2005, point 75, page 25.
5 Ibid.
6 Interview with Peter Cave, 2019.
7 Letter from John Wakely to Shane Wall, 31 July 1998.

Chapter 18: The Whitewash
1 Sentencing remarks of District Court Judge Helen Syme, in R v John Sidney Denham, NSW District Criminal Court, 2010, point 47, page 15.
2 Ibid., point 48, page 16.
3 Royal Commission into Institutional Responses to Child Sex Abuse, exhibit no: CTJH.210.90001.0431.R Document from Bishop Malone to Cardinal Pell in 2010 quote: 'Reported to NSW Ombudsman's Office & NSW Commission for Children & Young People as a Category 1 & as such was not allowed to work in child related employment', dated 2004.
4 Ibid.
5 In 2005, Father Peter Brock's sister, Megan, a nun, was on the Towards Healing staff as part of the National Committee for Professional Standards. This body was charged with dealing with complaints against clergy.
6 Letter from Dr Michael Casey, representing Cardinal Pell, to Ms Sue Phelan, principal investigator, NSW Ombudsman, 21 September 2005.
7 D.F. Jackson QC, *The Jackson Report*, Corrs Chambers Westgarth Lawyers, July 2005, page 2.
8 Ibid., page 3.
9 Ibid., page 3.
10 Ibid., page 23.
11 Ibid., point C8, page 4.
12 Ibid., file note, 7 July 1998, Bishop's Statement, paras 21–22.
13 Encompass Australia is a body established by the Australian Catholic bishops and leaders of religious organisations to 'do assessments and provide treatment for impaired professionals'.

14 D.F. Jackson QC, *The Jackson Report*, Corrs Chambers Westgarth Lawyers, July 2005, page 18.
15 Ibid., page 20.
16 Ibid., point 46, page 17. Interview with Father Peter Brock on 27 June 2005.
17 Ibid., Bishop's Statement, para 27.
18 Ibid., page 14: 'It was not possible to interview Mr Davoren in connection with the preparation of this report.'
19 Ibid., page 22.
20 Ibid.
21 Ibid., pages 27 and 23.
22 Transcript of interview with Bishop Malone for *The Jackson Report*, 30 June 2005, page 28.
23 Royal Commission into Institutional Responses to Child Sexual Abuse, case study 43: Catholic Church authorities in Maitland–Newcastle, Witness Statement CQT, 2 September 2016, point 15, page 4. (Stat. 1173.001.0002_R)
24 *The Jackson Report*, page 25.
25 Transcript of interview with Bishop Malone, 30 June 2005, *The Jackson Report*, July 2005, page 26.
26 *The Jackson Report*, point 134, page 44.
27 Ibid., point 135a, page 44.
28 *The Jackson Report*.
29 Letter from Dr Michael Casey, representing Cardinal Pell, to Ms Sue Phelan, principal investigator, NSW Ombudsman, 21 September 2005.

Chapter 19: Lies and Secrets

1 Neil Keene and Paul Maguire, 'Court rejects priest appeal', *Newcastle Herald*, 11 March 2006.
2 Peter Fox, *Walking Towards Thunder*, Hachette, Sydney, 2019, page 148.
3 Sentencing remarks of Justice Helen Syme, DCJ, The Crown v John Sidney Denham, 2010, page 11, point 33.
4 Letter from John S. Denham to Bishop Michael Malone, dated 13 July 2006, submitted as exhibit in R v Denham, NSW District Court; hearing dates 22 and 25 August 2014, November 2014; decision date January 2015.
5 Royal Commission into Institutional Responses to Child Sexual Abuse, case study 43: Catholic Church authorities in Maitland–Newcastle, exhibit 481, 2016.
6 Obtained via a source.

Chapter 20: Strike Force Georgiana

1 Email from Father Glen Walsh to his solicitor Cliff Fraser, 14 November 2013.
2 Dan Proudman, *Newcastle Herald*, 9 October 2008.
3 Letter from Father James Lunn to Gordon Quinn, 16 October 2007.
4 Interview with close friend of Father Glen Walsh, January 2019.
5 Letter from Father John Usher on behalf of Cardinal Pell, 7 November 2008.
6 Interview with Detective Sergeant Kristi Faber, 2018: 'John Denham's offending was absolutely prolific. Strike Force Georgiana charged him with 38 separate complainants that came forward, with 184 offences'. In 2018, Denham was convicted again, bringing the number of victims to 58.

Chapter 21: 'The fathers don't like that sort of thing'

1   [i] Count 4 – 'Between 1 January 1982 and 31 December 1982 at Taree in the State of New South Wales, did commit an act of buggery with XX. This offence is pursuant to s 79 of the *Crimes Act 1900* and the maximum penalty is 14 years imprisonment.' Judgement of District Court Judge Mahoney, 2019
[ii] 'Ironically he told Dr Nielssen (29/06/2010) that he believed his reputation was "smeared" by sexual allegations when he was in Taree (1981–1985). He was still criminally abusing children up until 1985 and had been doing so for a decade.'
[ii] Judgement of District Court Judge Helen Syme, 22–25 August 2014, page 6.
2   Interview with Detective Sergeant Kristi Faber, November 2018.
3   Interview with Dave Murray, University of Newcastle, 2016.
4   District Court Judge Helen Syme, R v John Sidney Denham, Sydney District Criminal Court, 2010, point 65, page 20.
5   Ibid., point 41, page 14.
6   Ibid., clause 5, page 3.
7   Ibid., clause 12, page 4.
8   Ibid., point 33, page 11.
9   Interview with Derek Devalaar, husband of Helen Keevers, October 2018.
10 District Court Judge Helen Syme, R v John Sidney Denham, Sydney District Criminal Court, 2010, point 41, page 14.
11 Police statement of Helen Keevers, 19 May 2008, page 3.
12 File note, 12 May 2008, conversation with Father Peter Brock, annexure A to Helen Keevers' police statement, 19 May 2008.
13 Police statement of Helen Keevers, May 2008.
14 Joanne McCarthy, *Newcastle Herald*, 12 September 2014.

Chapter 22: A Dream Fulfilled

1   Interview with Mark Wakely, 2019.
2   Letter from Father Glen Walsh to Missionaries of Charity Priests, India, 2007.
3   Letter from Archbishop Philip Wilson to 'Elizabeth' dated 15 December 2009, including a cheque dated 15 December 2009. Letter from 'Elizabeth' to Archbishop Philip Wilson dated 18 December 2009.

Chapter 23: Betrayal of Trust

1   By the time Strike Force Georgiana wrapped up in 2020, Detective Sergeant Kristi Faber and her team had charged 19 priests and brothers with offences relating to 182 victims. Charges against Father Peter Brock did not proceed due to the victim's breakdown but the NSW Ombudsman terminated Brock's right to work with children following an investigation.
2   District Court Judge Helen Syme, R v John Sidney Denham, Sydney District Criminal Court, 2010, point 43, page 15.
3   Ibid., page 15, point 43, District Court Judge Helen Syme, 2010.
4   https://www.abc.net.au/news/2010-06-18/bishop-urges-clarity-on-paedophile-priest/872850
5   The University of Newcastle revoked his honorary degree in 2018. Father Peter Brock died in 2014.
6   Bishop Michael Malone in an interview with Jill Emberson on ABC Newcastle, 5 April 2011.

7   Statement from Bishop William Wright of the Maitland-Newcastle Diocese,
      11 November 2011.
8   https://www.newcastleherald.com.au/story/207615/there-will-be-a-royal-
      commission-because-there-must-be

Chapter 24: The Price for Telling the Truth

1   https://www.mn. Catholic.org.au/people/priests/council-of-priests/
2   NSW Special Commission of Inquiry into matters relating to the police
      investigation of certain child sexual abuse allegations in the Catholic Diocese
      of Maitland–Newcastle, report by Margaret Cunneen SC, 2014, vol.2, point
      12.253, page 72.
3   Ibid., vol.2, point 12.281, page 77.
4   Eliza Harvey, 'Retired Bishop Michael Malone admits he ignored abuse
      allegations', ABC News Online, 13 July 2013: https://www.abc.net.au/
      news/2013-07-13/retired-bishop-admits-he-ignored-abuse-allegations/4818456
5   Email from Glen Walsh to a friend, on 29 June 2013.
6   Email from Father Glen Walsh to a friend, on 1 May 2013. The original email
      was all in capital letters.
7   Email from Father Glen Walsh to Eliane, on 21 July 2013.

Chapter 25: 'I regret opening my mouth. Never again'

1   Booklet from the Requiem Mass for 'Coey' Brother Coman Sykes held on
      25 September 2013.
2   Peter Fitzsimons, *Sydney Morning Herald*, 28 September 2013. https://www.smh.
      com.au/sport/knockout-memories-of-rugby-great-20130927-2ujbd.html
3   NSW Special Commission of Inquiry into matters relating to the police
      investigation of certain child sexual abuse allegations in the Catholic Diocese
      of Maitland–Newcastle, report by Margaret Cunneen SC, 2014, vol.4 (released
      2019), point 52, page 9.
4   The Special Commission of Inquiry into the Maitland-Newcastle Diocese,
      found:
      'adverse findings in relation to the credibility of ... Father William Burston
      and Monsignor Allan Hart. Each was found to be an unimpressive and/or
      unsatisfactory witness in some respects (Vol. 1, point 1.153);
          'The regularity with which Burston replied "I don't recollect" was a feature of
      his testimony. It left an unavoidable impression that, in relation to many matters
      about which he was questioned, he was not prepared to consider the question
      fully or to examine or explore his memory in order to assist the Commission.
      Having regard to the totality of his evidence, the Commission found Burston to
      be an unimpressive witness in certain respects (Vol 2, point 12.281);
          'The Commission also found Father William Burston to be an unimpressive
      witness in certain respects. In oral evidence Burston professed a complete
      absence of recollection in relation to many matters concerning McAlinden –
      in particular, those that might have tended to suggest that he had pre-existing
      knowledge by at least 1993 of allegations that McAlinden had sexually abused
      children. This was in stark contrast with his sharp and specific recollection
      of things that might be perceived as tending to explain his past conduct or
      exculpate him. For example, Burston proffered a clear memory that, in the
      case of AL's complaint, there was a 'very strong refusal [by AL] to take it to the

police'; this evidence was given in the context of a conversation he initially told the Commission he could not be 'terribly precise' about. Regular responses of 'I don't recollect' were a feature of his testimony, such that the Commission formed the view there was a reluctance on his part to fully consider questions put to him or to explore his memory for information that might assist the Commission' (Vol 2, points 20.26, 20.27).

The Special Commission of Inquiry into the Maitland-Newcastle Diocese Volume 4, 30 May 2014 (released 2019), (see especially pp 14–16, points 1.68 and 1.69) found that:

(a) Monsignor Patrick Cotter, Vicar Capitular and interim head of the diocese before Clarke, was from at least 1976 aware of serious complaints made about McAlinden's sexually inappropriate conduct with children while he (McAlinden) was parish priest in Foster– Tuncurry. Cotter retired in 1987 and died in 2007. In a letter dated May 1976 to Clarke (as bishop-elect) Cotter recorded that, among other things, McAlinden had been 'interfering' with young girls and had an 'inclination' towards younger females but not towards the mature female. The 'Cotter–Clarke letter' also demonstrates that the diocese, through Cotter, agreed to execute what Cotter referred to as a 'cover-up' of the 'resignation' of McAlinden as parish priest at Foster–Tuncurry. The device, apparently proposed by McAlinden himself, was a move 'on loan' to Geraldton Diocese in Western Australia.

(b) Monsignor Allan Hart, vicar general of the diocese from 1990 to 1995 and a current priest of the diocese, was aware from at least 1993 that McAlinden had sexually abused AJ when she was a child. Hart had been aware of previous allegations of McAlinden sexually abusing children. He also became aware, through Clarke, that McAlinden had made admissions about sexually abusing children when Father Brian Lucas interviewed him in 1993. While Hart reported AJ's complaint in 1993 to his bishop, Clarke, he took no steps to report McAlinden to police or to counsel and encourage AJ or Clarke to take such steps. He should have done so. AJ would have reported McAlinden to the police had she received the support and encouragement of senior Church officials such as Hart.

(c) Father Brian Lucas, General Secretary of the Australian Catholic bishops Conference and a lawyer, was Secretary to the Archdiocese of Sydney in 1993 and a member of the Special Issues Resource Group, which under a 1992 Church protocol had responsibility for investigating allegations of child sexual abuse by priests. By 1993 Lucas had an established role in persuading priests accused of having sexually abused children to resign from ministry. In 1993 Lucas met with AJ and received details of an instance of sexual abuse McAlinden committed on her when she was a child. This was information Lucas needed in order to confront McAlinden and so persuade him to resign. Lucas met with McAlinden in February 1993. Lucas proffered no recollection of the meeting and took no notes of it. This was consistent with his general practice of deliberately not taking notes of his meetings with priests accused of child sexual abuse. The purpose of this practice was to avoid the creation of documentary records, and a consequence of it was that documents that could later reveal to Church outsiders (including the police or complainants in civil litigation) matters that might bring scandal on the Church – including admissions of child sexual abuse by a priest – did not come into existence. Notwithstanding Lucas's stated non-recollection of the meeting with McAlinden, there is reliable evidence confirming that at the meeting McAlinden made admissions of having sexually abused children. Consistent with his stated practice, Lucas reported these admissions to Clarke. Lucas was also consulted, at least by Hart, about the diocese's plan to relocate McAlinden overseas. From 1993 onwards Lucas possessed information, including admissions of sexually abusing children, that would have been of interest to the police and would have facilitated a police investigation of McAlinden. Lucas failed to report McAlinden to the police. He should have done so in 1993, as should have the diocese.

(d) Bishop Michael Malone, head of the diocese from 1995 to 2011, was aware from 1995 that McAlinden was reported to have sexually abused children and had admitted to such conduct. This was apparent from correspondence Malone read in late 1995 and early 1996, including a letter from McAlinden dated 5 December 1995. Further, in his office Malone had a file on McAlinden that he described in 2002 as 'so big you can't jump over it'. Malone failed to take steps to report McAlinden to police at any time between 1995 and August 1999, even though he must have known the diocese had information that would have facilitated and/or assisted a police investigation of McAlinden. Malone arranged to blind-report McAlinden to the police in August 1999 through the Church's Professional Standards Office. This was the first report by the diocese to the police relating to McAlinden. But Malone provided notice of allegations relating to only two McAlinden victims, AK and AL. There is no good reason why he did not report AK and AL to the police until 1999. (Report by Margaret Cunneen SC, 2014, vol.4 (released 2019).)

Bishop Bill Wright stood Father Bill Burston aside following the findings of the NSW Special Commission of Inquiry:
https://www.abc.net.au/news/2014-06-03/maitland-newcastle-catholic-bishop-apologises-for-child-abuse/5496738

5   Ibid., vol.4, pts E & F, 30 May 2014 (released 2019), point C5.5 and C5.6, pages 242–243.
6   Ibid., vol.4, 30 May 2014 (released 2019), point 18.230, page 225.

Chapter 26: A Meeting with the Pope

1   Royal Commission exhibit NSW 2070 007 0266 _ R
Minutes of Provincial Council Meeting Friday 23 and Saturday 24 June. Brother Coman appointed master of the postulants. Br Coman is the choice of the Provincial council he will be different to Brother Brian in his approach. Rc NSW. 2070.007.0272_R
2   The Police Integrity Commission Report to Parliament, *Protea Report*, Sydney, 2015. https://www.parliament.nsw.gov.au/tp/files/46450/Protea%20Report.pdf
3   Writing on a postcard from Father Glen Walsh to his friend Anne, February 2016.
4   Victoria Police charged Cardinal Pell with a series of sexual assault offences on 29 June 2017. Convicted of child sex offences in Victoria on 11 December 2018. Upheld by the Victorian Court of Criminal Appeal but overturned by the High Court in April 2020. Cardinal Pell was acquitted of the offences.
5   Exhibit CCI 0634 00026 0134 R – CCI Limited Ethical Standards List. Romuald. 1957, Westmead Boys Home.

6   Cross examination, Royal Commission, 8 September 2016. (C171) WHT Wade and Mr Hilbert Chiu.

7   Royal Commission transcript as reported by Christopher Knaus and Ian Kirkwood, *The Canberra Times*, 9 September 2016.

Chapter 27: 'I am starting to think this is what happened to my Andrew'

1   W.J. Burston (Mr Chiu) transcript, Royal Commission into Institutional Responses to Child Sexual Abuse, case study 43: Catholic Church authorities in Maitland–Newcastle, 5 September 2016, page 10.

2   Ibid.

3   Email by Father Glen Walsh, 25 March 2015.

4   http://www.tjhcouncil.org.au/media/122039/160908-2016-RC-Opening-Statement-Peter-Carroll.pdf

5   http://www.tjhcouncil.org.au/media/122039/160908-2016-RC-Opening-Statement-Peter-Carroll.pdf

6   Email from Father Glen Walsh to the Maitland-Newcastle diocese administration, December 2016.

7   *Newcastle Herald*, 23 June 2018.

Chapter 28: The Jail Visit

1   Royal Commission into Institutional Responses to Child Sexual Abuse titled: *Denham 2016 Royal Commission Data report REPT.0010.001.0018*.

2   James M. Miller, *The Priests*, Finch Publishing, Sydney, 2016, page 24.

3   Ibid., page 25.

4   Ibid., page 58. 'I have no doubt Brennan thought there was nothing immoral or wrong about a man imposing himself sexually on a boy. I was only 15 when Brennan began to abuse me. Everything about his attitude said he believed he was entitled to behave as he did. He was not the slightest bit embarrassed or uncomfortable about his conduct.'

5   In 2010, Judge Helen Syme in the District Court of NSW said in her sentencing remarks: 'On several occasions, the offender took small groups of boys on 2-day visits to the Wingham Presbytery. The offender sought written parental permission for such trips. Contrary to all proper expectations, alcohol and cigarettes were freely provided to the boys. The Wingham priest was also in residence. Sexual assaults on some of the boys occurred on these occasions.'

6   Judge Helen Syme, R v Sidney John Denham, 2015, District Criminal Court NSW.

7   Police statement, 2019.

Chapter 29: The Trial

1   Interview with John Walsh, 2019.

Chapter 30: A Tragic Death

1   *Revelation*, episode 2, ABC TV and In Films, March 2020. www.abc.net.au/revelation.

2   Royal Commission into Institutional Responses to Child Sexual Abuse, Final Report, 2017. https://www.childabuseroyalcommission.gov.au/final-report https://www.childabuseroyalcommission.gov.au/religious-institutions

3   Melissa Davey, 'Child sexual abuse royal commission delivers final report',
    The Guardian, 14 December 2017.
4   Royal Commission into Institutional Responses to Child Sexual Abuse, Final
    Report, vol.4, Identifying and disclosing child sexual abuse, 2017, page 10.
    https://www.childabuseroyalcommission.gov.au/identifying-and-disclosing-
    child-sexual-abuse

Epilogue

1   District Court Judge Helen Syme, R v Sidney John Denham, 2015, District
    Criminal Court, NSW. Also reported by Joanne McCarthy, *Newcastle Herald*,
    25 January 2015.
2   NSW Supreme Court case: Gerard Gregory Lloyd v Anthony Gerard Bambach
    and the Trustees of the Roman Catholic Church for the Diocese of Newcastle-
    Maitland, 2005. Also reported by Joanne McCarthy, 'Catholic church denies
    negligence over Hunter paedophiles', *Newcastle Herald*, 16 January 2012.
3   Reported by Joanne McCarthy, 'Catholic church denies negligence over Hunter
    paedophiles', *Newcastle Herald*, 16 January 2012.
4   On 15 September 2017, the Maitland-Newcastle Diocese launched
    'Lina's Project', which they describe as a 'victim-led community event of
    acknowledgement and repentance'. It can be accessed via this website:
    www.linasproject.com.au

Acknowledgements

I AM HONOURED TO HAVE THE TRUST OF SO MANY PEOPLE IN this book, in particular the families and friends of the survivors and the ones who did not survive.

Mark Wakely, Steven's partner of thirty-eight years, has been a constant support and guide throughout this challenging journey. The Alward family – Libby, David and Peter – and John Walsh, Glen's brother, have given me access to their personal stories despite their own grief and suffering. For this, I am truly grateful. Also thank you to many of Glen's closest friends.

Helen Keevers died suddenly on 13 May 2018. We had planned to meet at the trial of Archbishop Philip Wilson the following week. She suffered a torn aorta and was rushed to hospital. Many of her insights can be found in this book. I owe her a debt of gratitude.

Many people have opened their lives and personal stories to me without any caveats. Many have suffered deep trauma, others supported family or friends who were survivors. This book would not have happened without them. I want to thank Lisa Sweeney, Jane Wilson, Nicola Ellis, Peter Gogarty, Pat Feenan, Geoffrey Nash, Peter Fox, Dermot Browne, Dave Murray, Paul Sutherland, Ian Andrews, Narelle Beveridge, Damian Demarco and Bob O'Toole for briefing me so I could fully understand the collateral damage of this epidemic of clerical abuse. There was a priest and some other people as well who cannot be named.

I have had the honour of working alongside Joanne McCarthy for many years. I've had the benefit of her wisdom (and humour!) on many occasions, and my reports have been all the better for it. Thank you, Jo. And my thanks to Chad Watson, at the *Newcastle Herald*, for his assistance.

Thank you to my publisher, Jude McGee, and my editors, Kate Goldsworthy and Barbara McClenahan. I could not have wished for a better team. Jude was there from the beginning and guided the first drafts with sensitivity.

I want to make special mention of my researcher, Anne Worthington. I asked her to look into one cleric, but her forensic skills and indefatigable nature led us to uncover a network of offenders across the state, and beyond.

To former NSW District Court judge and former priest Chris Geraghty, thank you for explaining the complexities of the Catholic Church, which at times I found unfathomable (despite growing up Catholic!), and the other brains trust: Stephen Crittenden and Noel Debien. These three were available day and night, always politely answering my many questions. Senator David Shoebridge, Detective Sergeant Kristi Faber and Troy Grant also lent me their expertise on many occasions.

Thank you to the media staff at the NSW District Court in Sydney for answering my many requests for court files, often historical ones from many years ago.

Thank you to Lucy Palmer, journalist and writer, for setting me straight on several occasions when I was overwhelmed with the traumatic nature of the stories. To Sue Prosser, one of my oldest friends, who took me to Ireland to walk the wild hills of the Connemara after I had written the first draft. To Marianne Leitch, Rebecca Latham, Joanne Shepherd, Cathy Scott, Anne Davies and Bronwen Reed, for their boundless enthusiasm and encouragement. For all the female friends who have kept me going with their love and support, especially Sarah Macdonald, Amanda Collinge and Susie Daniel.

I want to thank all my ABC colleagues during my time at *Lateline*, arguably one of the best current affairs shows on television in its day. Alan Sunderland, John Bruce, Peter Charley, Jo Puccini, Leigh Sales, Emma Alberici, Steve Cannane, Alison McClymont, Tony Jones, Michael Doyle, Sashka Koloff, Bronwen Reed, John Stewart, Chris Schembri, Margot O'Neill, Brett Evans and Cathy Beale all contributed to the many stories I did on clerical abuse for that television program. The legal advice and support from ABC lawyers Michael Martin, Grant McAvaney and Hugh Bennett was invaluable. Thanks to Peter Cave for contributing his personal story to this book and to Ian Walker for his brilliant insights into human behaviour and storytelling.

Stories like this one take their toll on the writer, especially because one of the key figures, Steven Alward, was my friend. I couldn't have finished this book without my family. To Barbara Fitzgerald and Mark O'Flynn, who kept me sane during the hard times, thank you. Also to Aunty Tess Fitzgerald, for telling me to keep going despite the challenges

There were times when I thought that the subject matter was so dark that I would not finish the manuscript. These three people held me up with their love, and I am forever grateful. To my daughters, Isabella and Gabrielle, thank you for your support. And to my husband, James Fitzgerald, who has always been my rock. Thank you from the bottom of my heart.

For confidential 24-hour support, call:
Lifeline – 13 11 14
Kid's Help Line – 1800 551 800